THE FORGOTTEN GIRLS

HAUNTING TRUE CRIME STORIES OF WOMEN AND THEIR COLD CASES

ALYCE CLARK, PH.D.

WILDBLUE
PRESS

WildBluePress.com

The Forgotten Girls published by:
WILDBLUE PRESS
P.O. Box 102440
Denver, Colorado 80250

WILDBLUE PRESS is registered at the U.S. Patent and Trademark Offices.

ISBN 978-1-964730-90-5 Hardcover
ISBN 978-1-964730-91-2 Trade Paperback
ISBN 978-1-964730-89-9 eBook

THE FORGOTTEN GIRLS

DEDICATION

To my beloved wife, whose unwavering support and love have been the guiding light in my darkest moments. Your strength inspires me daily to seek justice for those who can no longer speak for themselves. To the Norfolk Police Department and all the dedicated agencies involved in the pursuit of truth and justice, your relentless commitment to serving the community and uncovering the stories behind these cold cases is unparalleled. This book stands as a testament to your tireless efforts and the bonds we have forged in the service of justice. To my esteemed colleagues at the university, whose intellectual rigor and shared passion for understanding human behavior and societal structures have enriched my journey. Your insights have shaped my perspective and galvanized my resolve. Together, let us honor the memories of the women whose lives were tragically cut short and strive toward a future where justice prevails for all.

CONTENTS

ALYCE CLARK, PH.D.

PREFACE

In the realm of true crime, few topics are more haunting than the cold case. These are the cases that have gone unsolved for years, even decades, leaving families with unanswered questions and a sense of injustice. And yet, among these cases, there is a particular subset that holds a unique fascination: those that involve women as victims. Why do we find ourselves drawn to these stories, to the lives of these women, and to the sense of injustice that surrounds their deaths? I am drawn to the ways in which these cases speak to deeper questions about human nature, morality, and the social and cultural contexts in which we live.

The fascination with true crime stories has been a staple of human curiosity for centuries. There's something about the darker corners of human nature that draws us in, making us question what drives individuals to commit heinous crimes. And yet, despite the widespread attention and scrutiny, many cases remain unsolved, leaving families and investigators with a sense of perpetual grief and frustration. But what happens when the cold case suddenly gets hot? When the investigative team finally cracks the code, and the perpetrator is brought to justice? The satisfaction is palpable, and the relief is immense. One of the most striking aspects of some of these cases is the way they've been resolved. Through advances in forensic technology, innovative investigative techniques, and good old-fashioned detective work, these cases have been cracked wide open.

What does it reveal about our society when we find ourselves drawn to the stories of women who have been brutally silenced? What do their stories say about our own values and priorities? In this book, we will explore the world of cold cases involving women, delving into the complexities and nuances of these crimes. We will examine the ways in which societal attitudes towards women have shaped the way we respond to these crimes, and how these attitudes have been perpetuated by cultural and historical factors. We will also consider the ways in which these cases have been treated by law enforcement and the justice system, and how this has impacted our understanding of justice and fairness.

Throughout this book, we will pose questions about the nature of justice, morality, and responsibility. We will consider the ways in which our assumptions about gender and power shape our understanding of these crimes, and how these assumptions have been challenged by recent events and developments in our society. We will also explore the ways in which these cases can be used as a tool for social commentary and critique, shedding light on the darker aspects of our society.

Ultimately, this book is not just about cold cases involving women and children; it is about the human condition itself. It is about our capacity for good and evil, our struggles with morality and ethics, and our ongoing quest for justice and fairness. By examining these cases through a citizen's lens, we hope to gain a deeper understanding of ourselves and our place in the world.

INTRODUCTION

I wrote this book to share my experiences and hopefully find justice for those still waiting. My inspiration came from the Sigrid Stevenson case because traveling to New Jersey and talking to some of the people involved was inspiring. I never thought a single trip would inspire me to spread the word about cold cases involving women. Although this is my first book publication, I hope it inspires current cold case detectives and the victims' families to keep their hope in finding justice for their loved ones.

This book was written for the victims and the victims' families, but it was also written to give the reader insights into how these investigations are conducted. There is also a learning aspect for students or true crime fans interested in these cold cases. Each case was picked for specific reasons. Talking to the detectives and reporters in this book gave me hope because each person cared deeply about the case they worked on. They are not doing it for the money but because they care deeply about their cases. Some are still actively working, while others are now retired, including myself. I've learned that being retired from the badge doesn't mean you forget about the cases you've worked on or had some insight into the case. Each chapter was written with the support that one day, there will be answers and closure for the family. The word closure is a big word, but sometimes, we as humans need answers. For those cases that were finally closed, this shows that there is hope and someone was still out there willing to find the answers needed for the victims' families.

These cases are not just about solving crimes; they're also about telling the stories of women who were taken from their loved ones too soon. These cases are about honoring their memories and giving them justice. And they're about demonstrating that even in the darkest corners of human nature, there is always hope for justice and redemption. In this book, we'll take a closer look at some of these solved cold cases involving women. We'll examine the investigative techniques used to crack each case, or get close to solving, as well as the personal toll these crimes have taken on their victims' families. We'll also explore the emotional highs and lows that come with solving a case that has been decades in the making.

Join me as we embark on this journey into the world of true crime and explore some of the most remarkable unsolved and solved cold cases involving women. Part 1 is about women that have been murdered, and their cases are still unsolved. In Part 2 we will dive into cold cases where the women have been missing and presumed murdered. Part 3 is about closure to cold cases, allowing hope for the families still seeking answers. Some chapters may be shorter than others, but that doesn't mean they're not as important.

PART I

GONE BUT NEVER FORGOTTEN

CHAPTER 1

MUSIC LEFT AFLOAT

Who is Sigrid Stevenson? Or rather, who was she? At just 25 years old, Sigrid was a vibrant spirit from Livermore, California, drawn to the melodic hum of life and learning at Trenton State College, now known as The College of New Jersey (TCNJ). A gifted musician, she saw music as the essence of her being, infusing every note with her passion and dreams. However, all that potential came crashing down on September 4, 1977, when Sigrid's life was brutally cut short on the auditorium stage beside the piano that once served as her sanctuary.

Now, over four decades later, her case remains cold, shrouded in mystery and unanswered questions. Was this a meticulously crafted murder, or was it a chaotic act of desperation? The truth eludes us, and as time drags on, this unsolved case hangs like a shadow, patiently awaiting the next investigator bold enough to challenge its chilling silence. In the unforgiving realm of justice, sometimes those wheels spin slowly, but for Sigrid, the clock is still ticking.

The auditorium stood silent, its once-vibrant energy drained, leaving an icy void where melodies once danced. The ghostly echo of piano notes lingered in the air, swirling like fragile bubbles from a child's plastic wand, ghostly reminders of Sigrid Stevenson's passion. Just days after her arrival at the college, on that fateful September 4, 1977, Sigrid's light was snuffed out, leaving her dreams entwined with the haunting chords she played. The stark contrast between joyous music and her untimely demise raised an unsettling question: what really transpired in those final hours?

To understand the tragedy that befell Sigrid, we must first peel back the layers of her life, who she was, what she dreamed of, and the intricate web of relationships that surrounded her. Each clue, each detail brings us closer to the truth of that chilling day, as we embark on a relentless search for answers in a case gone cold.

Sigrid Stevenson was a free spirit drawn to the academic halls of New Jersey, where her father held a position as a professor at Princeton University. At just 25, she was surrounded by acquaintances, yet the nature of these friendships hinted at a deeper solitude. The 1970s were a time of exploration and rebellion, and Sigrid epitomized that era as she embarked on a summer of hitchhiking across the vast landscapes of the United States and Canada. Questions linger in the air like the perfume of a fading memory: Did her travels expose her to fleeting romances, or was she merely a solitary wanderer? The investigation suggests that Sigrid had no ongoing relationships at the time of her tragic murder, raising alarming possibilities. Could one of the strangers who picked her up be the key to unlocking this case? As the pages turn, the mystery deepens, and the shadows of her journey beckon us to delve deeper into the untold stories of those she encountered along the way.

Interestingly, rumors exist that she lived with an Ewing Township volunteer firefighter, who was among those interviewed by police alongside over 100 other people. How is this case still unsolved? Someone had to have seen or heard something. Since this case is still unresolved, students who attend The College of New Jersey now share ghost stories, believing her spirit is still floating around in Kendall Hall. Whether or not you believe in ghosts, there's still a murderer lingering nearby, either dead or refusing to speak.

On the night before her murder, Sigrid attended a play in Kendall Hall, traveling on her green bike to get from place to place. Being early and without a place to stay, she utilized a faulty door lock to sneak into Kendall Hall, where she slept on stage in a sleeping bag. Perhaps, well-versed in another unusual place's lodging due to her hitchhiking adventures, she was accustomed to these unconventional lodgings of her free spirit.

On the tragic night of Sigrid's murder, the play showcased was Archibald MacLeish's "J.B." This acclaimed work, penned in 1958, garnered significant popularity for its contemporary reinterpretation of the biblical tale of Job, following a pious millionaire whose blissful domestic life is shattered. Notably, the play features two intermissions, allowing the audience time to reflect on its profound themes.

Gathering initial statements from witnesses that attended the play is essential. This includes attendees who were present in the auditorium during the play, as their observations might provide valuable information. Plus, it was said that Sigrid may have attended. I'd ask them about the moments leading up to the incident, any unusual behavior they noticed, and their locations at the time of the murder. A review of the records of attendees should be completed, both from the play and those who might have been in the vicinity after the performance. Understanding the context and relationships between potential witnesses or suspects could reveal motives or connections that we need to explore further. Detectives should also keep an open mind and consider any connections to previous cold cases, as there might be patterns or unresolved issues that tie back to this event.

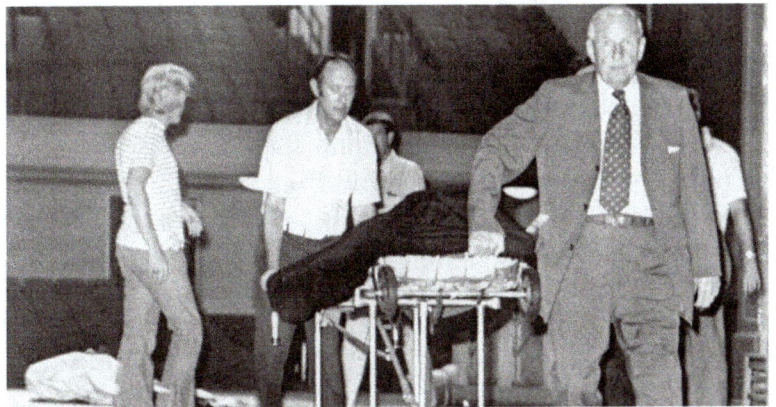

On September 16, 1977, a nationwide broadcast was requested by the Ewing Police Department. The requested teletype stated the following:

> This Dept is investigating the murder of one Sigrid Stevenson, W F 25 Yrs. Victim was found on stage of theater building at Trenton State College by Campus Police approxx (sic) 2330 hrs 090477. Victim was nude, face and head severely beaten with a blunt instrument, believed to have been sexually assaulted. Her blouse was around her neck appearing that it had slipped from her mouth as used for a gag. Victim's hands were restrained from behind. Murder weapon and restraints not found at scene.

Any Dept with similar case or any info, contact PD Ewing TWP 609-882-1313 or Mercer CTY Prosecutors Office Homicide Unit 609-989-6402.

As one gazes upon the diagram, the three prominent entrance doors of Kendall Hall stand invitingly at the front, welcoming guests into its vibrant space. Directly through these doors lies the expansive main auditorium, the heart of the venue. To the rear right of Kendall Hall, nestled gracefully, is the Small Auditorium, where the enchanting "J.B." play was staged.

At the back of the building, an overhead door facilitates the seamless unloading and loading of equipment and props, ensuring that each performance is equipped for success. A closer look at the main auditorium stage reveals that most of the gripping action occurred in front of the orchestra pit, where the final moments of life collided with the stark reality of death, leaving an indelible mark on the theater's history.

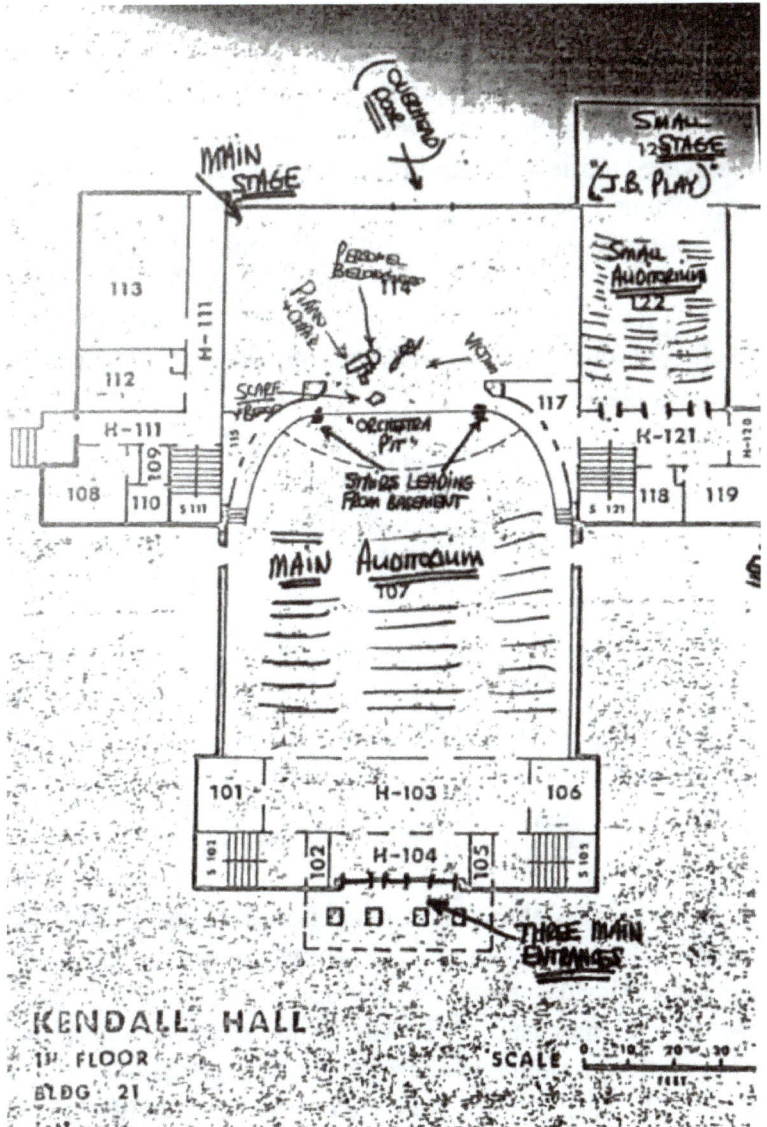

The diagram, marked "Not to Scale," provided measurements. A pool of blood lay near the front of the stage, about 3 feet from its edge, with the further part of the pool dried. Blood normally dries at the edge and moves toward the middle as it dries. The width of the stage was almost 44 feet, measuring at 43 feet and 10 inches. To the right of the pool of blood was an earring.

The piano stood at a height of 4 feet 10 inches, creating a striking backdrop to the scene. Beneath it, police discovered a dried pool of blood, raising questions about the circumstances leading up to this tragic moment. Was Sigrid attempting to seek refuge under the piano? Additionally, police found a third pool of blood located near where Sigrid's head lay, adding weight to the investigation. Each detail beckons us to explore the complexity of the narrative behind this horrific tragedy.

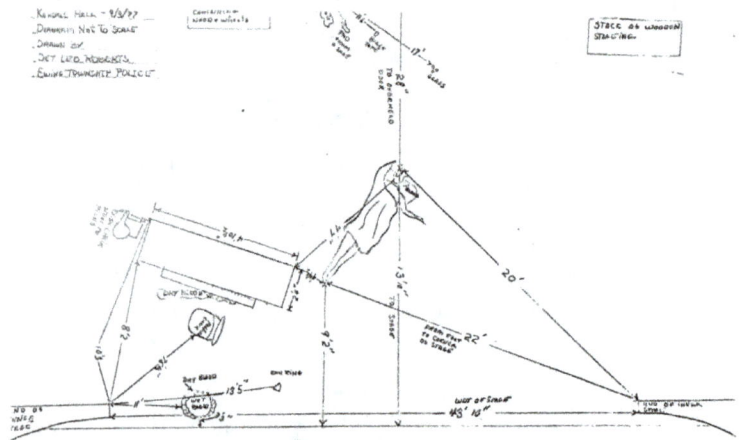

Many theories about what happened the night Sigrid was murdered have emerged. The show *Unsolved Mysteries* recounts Sigrid's story in Volume 4, Episode 4, titled "Murder, Center Stage." It was accurately re-enacted, and I hope that someone comes forward. According to Pulak Kumar (2024), "She was discovered handcuffed and gagged with her own blouse" (para. 10). The initial analysis conducted by detectives pointed to a potential involvement from law enforcement personnel, given that the individual in question was found handcuffed, possibly someone connected to the play. This raised questions about the surrounding circumstances and the possibility of official misconduct.

Sigrid often frequented various campus locations, seeking refuge in secluded spots where she would crouch in contemplation. Unfortunately, her presence did not go unnoticed, as campus security frequently intervened and asked her to relocate. Additionally, her bicycle became a familiar sight to security personnel, further establishing her connection to the campus environment.

Additionally, her bicycle became a familiar sight to security personnel, further establishing her connection to the campus environment.

Jack Knarr (2006), a staff writer for the *Trentonian*, reported the following:

She suffered fractures of the skull and face. Her nose was broken. Two ribs were broken. She suffered more than a dozen deep lacerations of the scalp. She was found naked; her hands had been tied behind her back. She had bruises on the chest, side, elbow, thigh, sources said. (para. 12)

Blood was spattered and pooled all about the stage – starting at the piano at which she loved to practice – and her body was found face down, wrapped in the canvass (sic) cover of the piano, by security guard Thomas Kokotajlo. (para. 13)

Her shirt, drenched in blood, had been pulled off and tied around her face to keep her quiet, investigators said. (para. 14)

This brutal and violent act remains a cold case, with detectives from Ewing and NJ State Police still working tirelessly, hoping someone will come forward. Here's what happens on a cold case detective's desk. The first step involves gathering all existing documentation related to the case, such as police reports, autopsy reports, evidence logs, and witness statements. The detective meticulously reviews this information, noting critical details like the victim's injuries and the crime scene.

Detectives visualize the crime scene based on these details, such as the victim being found naked with her hands tied or handcuffed, suggesting possible abduction and assault. Aside from older photographs, they rely heavily on crime scene photographs as Kendall has undergone upgrades since 1977. The specified injuries, including fractures and lacerations, are scrutinized, and consultations with forensic experts may occur to comprehend how the injuries were inflicted. The detectives also consider whether the broken ribs indicate a struggle or if they were inflicted post-mortem.

Detective work isn't done in isolation. Cold cases may benefit from fresh eyes, leading detectives to turn to the public for tips. They often release information to the media or social platforms in hopes that new witnesses come forward or individuals disclose previously undisclosed information. Shedding light on the victim's last known activities is crucial, involving interviews with friends, family, and associates to establish a timeline of her last day. Knowing when and where the victim was last seen can help identify potential suspects. Although interviews occurred after the murder, some witnesses still alive may be ready to talk, waiting for the phone to ring or a knock on their door.

Based on this evidence and the timeline, detectives generate a list of potential suspects, scrutinizing anyone with motive, opportunity, and means to commit the crime. Past or ongoing disputes may provide leads. A detective might employ a murder board or line items and photographs on a table to visualize connections. Cold case detectives often have access to modern forensic techniques unavailable at the time of the initial investigation, like DNA testing if biological samples or clothing exist that could yield new results. I'm confident that there was some suspect DNA left at the scene; if that's the case, then it may have been collected.

Detectives may collaborate with other law enforcement agencies, particularly if there's an opportunity to connect the suspect to additional crimes. I know in this case, Ewing Police is working with the New Jersey State Police.

Sometimes, seemingly insignificant evidence at the time can take on new meaning later. The detective must revisit all leads previously investigated, considering any that could be re-explored using modern understanding or technology.

This tragic case exemplifies the horrifying brutality that can occur in our communities. Cold case detectives from Ewing and the New Jersey State Police continue pursuing justice for Sigrid by meticulously reviewing all documentation and revisiting the crime scene with fresh perspectives. They utilize forensic expertise to analyze injuries and rely on the community's collaboration to uncover new leads that may have surfaced over time. As they work to establish a clearer timeline of events leading to the crime, the voices of witnesses who may still be hesitant to come forward might hold the key to unlocking this case. With advancements in forensic technology and law enforcement's determination, there remains hope for clarity and closure regarding this unresolved violence. Each step taken and every piece of evidence revisited brings them closer to the truth, reminding us all of the importance of perseverance in the face of unanswered questions.

In the spring of 2023, I had the intriguing opportunity to journey to Ewing, New Jersey, with hopes of engaging with a detective involved in this captivating cold case. Though the detective was somewhat reticent, they graciously provided me with a copy of the publicly accessible documents related to the case. Having served as a forensic investigator for the Norfolk Police Department in Norfolk, Virginia from 2012 to 2016, I've witnessed how advancements in forensic science have transformed criminal investigations. Examining the case's diagram was enlightening; while sparsely populated with information, it was enough to ignite my curiosity.

What continues to puzzle me is the persistence of this unsolved case, especially given the wealth of modern forensic technology, such as DNA analysis and genealogical research methods. One must wonder: What are the odds that family members of the suspect might have uploaded their DNA to genealogical databases seeking their ancestry?

I had the chance to visit Kendall Hall alongside several colleagues, and it was a fascinating experience. As we explored the building, we ventured inside and found ourselves in the lobby, where we had the pleasure of chatting with Scott Napolitano. Scott, a high school video production teacher and adjunct professor at Rider University, is also an accomplished filmmaker. Meeting him was a highlight of our visit.

Our conversation delved into the intriguing history of Kendall Hall, particularly because Scott is a graduate of TCNJ and has firsthand knowledge of its captivating tales. He recounted his freshman year in 2002, sharing stories from fellow students about a tragic murder associated with the hall. This sparked his curiosity, and by his senior year, Scott became eager to uncover the truth behind the mysterious events surrounding Sigrid Stevenson's case. Ultimately, he channeled his fascination into his thesis, creating a compelling 20-minute film that explores the ghostly lore of Kendall Hall. It was inspiring to hear his insights and the experiences that shaped his creative journey.

Scott's curiosity deepened as he sought to uncover the truth behind Sigrid's identity and the circumstances surrounding her tragic murder. After graduating in 2006, he proactively reached out to the Ewing Police Department, fueling his determination to resolve the mysteries of that fateful night on September 4, 1977. Through conversations with various individuals who had known Sigrid, Scott pieced together her story, learning about her individuality and how much joy she derived from playing the piano.

Following our captivating discussion about "Who was she, and who did it?" we ventured to the very stage where the murder unfolded. Though the setting had been transformed since 1977, a palpable stillness lingered in the air. I found myself saying, "Talk to me, tell me your story." Deep down,

I felt she was listening; perhaps this was my way of giving voice to her narrative. It has been 46 years since she drew her last breath.

The haunting tale of Sigrid Stevenson continues to resonate more than four decades after her tragic and abrupt death. A young woman with dreams and a passion for music, Sigrid embodies not just a victim but also a symbol of unresolved tragedy, intertwining the fragile threads of memory, mystery, and the pursuit of justice. The various layers of her life, from spirited hitchhiking adventures to quiet solitude amid the vibrancy of campus life, paint a portrait of a complex individual whose potential was unjustly extinguished. Today, as we reflect on her story, it becomes clear that the auditorium that once embraced her musical aspirations now serves as a stark reminder of the darkness that can seep into our lives. The investigative efforts that persistently seek to uncover the truth underscored both the limits of justice and the potential for new technologies and insights to illuminate forgotten cases. As we honor Sigrid's memory and those who seek answers, her narrative implores us to listen closely to the echoes of the past, to uncover the truth hidden in the shadows, and to ensure that these chilling stories do not fade away into silence.

"But the cowardly, the unbelieving, the vile, the murderers, the sexually immoral, those who practice magic arts, the idolaters, and all liars–they will be consigned to the fiery lake of burning sulfur. This is the second death."
~ Revelation 21:8

CHAPTER 2

BIG MESS IN TEXAS

The mysterious case of Caitlyn Rose Case, born on January 25, 1989, remains an unsettling enigma. Vanishing at the age of 33, she left a trail of unanswered questions that haunt all who learn her story. As we delve into her physical description, we are drawn deeper into the mystery of her disappearance. With shoulder-length brown hair and warm brown eyes, Caitlyn's radiant smile could light up any room, hinting at a vibrant life abruptly interrupted (NamUs, 2022). Her radiant smile, capable of illuminating a room, whispers hints of a life cut short. At five feet five inches tall and weighing around 130-140 pounds, Caitlyn's physical appearance belies a complex inner world.

A closer look reveals intricate tattoos: a dragonfly on her left foot, a dragon on her rib cage, and a triangle symbol between her shoulder blades, each representing fragments of her thoughts and emotions. A small mole above her lip serves as a unique marker of her identity. On that fateful day, Caitlyn was last seen wearing a black spaghetti strap top, blue jeans, and red tennis shoes, an outfit suggesting both casualness and an adventurous spirit. Behind the wheel of her black 2006 GMC Envoy, bearing Louisiana tag 957FDO, Caitlyn's disappearance has sparked reflection on profound questions: where did she go and what secrets did she carry into the unknown?

Caitlyn's story is not isolated; every year, thousands of individuals mysteriously vanish in the United States, leaving families in turmoil. While many are ultimately found, around 4,400 bodies remain unidentified, with roughly 1,000 of those cases still unsolved after a year. As of 2018, medical examiners and coroner offices reported an astonishing 11,380 unidentified remains on record. This is where the National Missing and Unidentified Persons System (NamUs) plays a crucial role, serving as a comprehensive database that unites law enforcement agencies with forensic science and technology to confront missing and unidentified person cases across the nation. Funded by the National Institute of Justice, NamUs represents a vital, free resource that enhances authorities' abilities to identify missing individuals and reunite them with their families.

Caitlyn Rose went missing on August 5, 2022. So, what is law enforcement doing about it? Caitlyn's family finds themselves working harder than the police to locate her. Her mother, Peg Melancon, established a website, findcaitlyn. com, dedicated to finding Caitlyn and documenting the timeline of her disappearance. Although the website has since been taken down, the family's determination has characterized this grueling journey, as they seek to unravel the mystery of what truly happened to Caitlyn. Their story is drawn from the accounts of Caitlyn's parents, Gordon and Peggy Melancon Case.

The existence of missing persons and unidentified bodies invites us to ponder the nature of evil. Are some individuals simply lost or forgotten, or is there a more profound moral or existential explanation for such disappearances? The concept of identity is central to this issue. Who are these individuals and what fundamentally defines them? The integration of forensic science and technology in systems like NamUs is an invaluable asset to cold case investigations.

Caitlyn had recently relocated to Blackhawk, Colorado in 2022, started a new job at the Lodge Casino, working in their engineering department as a technical mechanic. Caitlyn was happy with her new job, and during the summer, she chose to return to her hometown by plane, buy a new-to-her car there, spend time with her family, and afterward, drive back to Colorado by herself. Caitlyn arrived in Louisiana by plane on July 31st, 2022. She then purchased a black 2006 GMC Envoy, stayed in Louisiana for several days, and departed for Colorado on August 4th, 2022, ready to reclaim control over her life. However, as she navigated rural Texas roads, an unexpected navigation failure ensued. Amid this uncertainty, Caitlyn clung to her phone connection with her father, Gordon Case, who provided her reassurance amidst spotty cell service.

During Caitlyn's drive, she became lost or disoriented; Gordon tried to guide her to the interstate. He recalls their conversation vividly:

I was asking her what her location was, and she was telling me that she was passing some dairy farm or some type of farm, which in that area, is a lot of cattle in that area. And she was telling me that she was, you know, that she was just going by, and she didn't sound, you know, too worried. She sounded very quiet, which I kind of felt, you know, I don't know, she was very quiet. But anyway, we did speak. She was telling me that she was on some road with, you know, passing up some cattle and we're on the phone for about seven minutes. And I could barely hear her because she was on a gravel road.

Apparently, her windows were down because she didn't have any air condition (sic) in that vehicle. And anyways, we talked and that's basically all we were saying. And I could barely hear her through all the noise from the gravel road. And then our phone was disconnected. And I tried calling her back and I never was able to reach her again. (Grace, 2023, 5:35-6:28)

One of the worst things happened, the connection between Caitlyn and her father was lost on August 5, 2022, around 5 p.m. The sudden silence on the phone line serves as a poignant reminder that even our most intimate relationships can be fragile. Like the fleeting nature of a phone signal, our connections with others can drop out at any moment, leaving us feeling lost and disconnected. Imagine the anxiety of being on the phone when you have no clue where you are, and the phone goes dead silent and the call drops. The last known area where her family could see where she was by the Wi-Fi signal was about five miles southwest of Bogota, Texas. It's a scary thought.

According to Gordon Case, Caitlyn may have been driving seven to eight hours that day she went missing (Grace, 2023). During that drive, she did have to eventually stop for gas. According to Caitlyn' s father, she was in Gilmer, Texas when he finally spoke to her around 1 p.m. (Grace, 2023). Gordan Case said the following about Caitlyn's drive while in Gilmer:

And that's when I started to navigate her up to 271 to get her up through (sic) you know, to get her on the route, to get her out of that area. But we were on the phone at in (sic) Gilmour (sic), and then we were also on the phone a couple hours later when she got to Mount Pleasant, and then when she got to Mount Pleasant, she you know, she ended up.

We got her back on the road again, and then you know, of course in Bogota, we were on the phone again when she was in those solar field areas where we lost connection. (Grace, 2023, 8:38-9:06)

Caitlyn's circumstances present a classic problem of being a female driving alone in a spotty cell phone coverage area, which could indeed make her more vulnerable to potential threats like human trafficking. Her parents' concerns are understandable given the risks associated with these circumstances. However, this also highlights the tension between individual agencies and external circumstances. Can we, as a society, blame these external factors like poor cell phone coverage for putting someone in a vulnerable position versus taking personal responsibility for one's own safety?

Not only did Caitlyn struggle with technology, but societal perceptions complicate the vulnerabilities women face while traveling alone. Women are often socialized to appear vulnerable and dependent, which can lead to exploitation. This dynamic creates a landscape in which women traveling alone, such as Caitlyn, may be perceived as easy targets. The dangers escalate as technology becomes a tool wielded by traffickers who operate in the shadows, using social media and online platforms to reach vulnerable individuals.

Caitlyn's situation raised concerns related to the dangers faced by women traveling alone, especially in remote areas with unreliable cell service. Brian Fitzgibbons, Vice President of Operations at USPA Nationwide Security, highlighted the dire implications of this:

> I want to add one piece to that cell coverage in those hours that Gordon was just describing. To paint this picture a little bit more, you'd have to imagine she's using maps on her phone that as she loses data connection, she may have no maps for hours at a time. Where Gordon was communicating

with her to send screenshots of where to go. So, it's a particularly harrowing scenario for a woman, a beautiful young woman, alone in that remote of an area. (Grace, 10:42-11:17)

The shift from physical maps to digital navigation systems has dramatically altered the way we comprehend and interact with our surroundings. Prior to the advent of GPS, we relied on tangible maps, which required a more active engagement with the physical environment. We had to physically touch, manipulate, and study the map to commit its information to memory. Sometimes we highlighted the route we were taking. In contrast, modern navigation systems provide an instant and effortless solution, often supplanting our own cognitive abilities.

Caitlyn's travels, like many others, exemplify this reliance on technology, as she likely relied on her phone's map app or in-car navigation system to guide her through unfamiliar territories. I remember before GPS we bought local maps and used that to navigate travels. I remember the police department printing maps of the city for the academy recruits. Many people depend on their map app on their phone or their navigation app in their vehicle. This most definitely played a role in Caitlyn's travels.

When Caitlyn traveled alone, she may have been more susceptible to human trafficking due to several factors. One key consideration is the notion of power dynamics. In many societies, women are often socialized to be vulnerable and dependent on men, which can lead to a lack of agency and confidence in their ability to navigate unfamiliar environments. When a woman travels alone, she may be more likely to be perceived as an easy target by traffickers who prey on this vulnerability. Another factor is the absence of a support network, like Caitlyn's cell phone service. When traveling alone, a woman may not have access to the same level of social support and protection that she would have with friends or family by her side; however, Caitlyn had her father for her lifeline while traveling. Being alone can make her more susceptible to manipulation and exploitation.

Furthermore, societal attitudes towards women can also play a significant role in perpetuating human trafficking. In many cultures, women are viewed as commodities rather than individuals with autonomy and agency. This attitude can be internalized by women themselves, making them more likely to accept exploitative situations or feel guilty for asserting their boundaries. Caitlyn was in an area with gravel roads and farmland. It was once told to me that if you go down the wrong dirt road, be prepared.

Additionally, the rise of modern technology has created new opportunities for traffickers to target victims. Social media platforms, dating apps, and online marketplaces can provide a veil of anonymity for traffickers to operate undetected. Women traveling alone may be more likely to engage with strangers online or in public spaces, increasing their risk of being targeted. Maybe she was being followed, and someone somehow came in contact with Caitlyn at a gas station or on the side of the road.

A woman traveling alone, much like Caitlyn is not inherently more susceptible to human trafficking than anyone else. However, a combination of societal factors, power dynamics, and individual circumstances can increase her vulnerability. By recognizing these complexities and taking proactive steps to educate ourselves and the police can work towards creating a safer world for all individuals, regardless of gender or travel status. Traffickers have these situations down so they get the trafficked out and away as fast as they can without being detected.

Crime Online discussed Caitlyn's travels and here is what they said:

> After the call with her father, Caitlyn Case continues driving. Cell tower tracking indicates that Caitlyn

Case continues northward Paris, Texas. Shortly after seven p.m. (sic), her cell phone pings to cell towers in Pattonville, Texas and south of Paris. At 9:17 p.m. (sic), a license plate reader captures her car leaving Paris on the south loop of Highway 286 and traveling northwest Fm 79. Her cell phone last pings to cell towers in Choctaw County, Oklahoma. Her vehicle is believed to have been traveling on Highway 271. According to Caitlin Case's mother on findcaitlin. com website, a cell phone tower ping is recorded in Hugo, Oklahoma. The Oklahoma Missing Persons Department immediately deploys a search team to that area. (Grace, 2023, 13:59-14:39)

Hugo, Oklahoma is a small city near the southeastern part of Oklahoma and the center of Choctaw County, nine miles north of the Texas line. Hugo's population is a little over 5,000 people and it is known as Choctaw Country. Almost half of the population are white and only less than a quarter are Native American. Caitlyn isn't the only missing woman in Choctaw County.

Human trafficking is a very serious topic right now, especially with the United States border open. There are three types of human trafficking: sex trafficking, labor trafficking, and domestic service trafficking. Human trafficking is the second largest criminal activity in the world and makes about $150 billion a year (Mahaffey, 2020). In the 2019 statistics for Oklahoma, there were a total of 109 cases reported that involved a total of 207 victims. Out of the 109 cases, 77 involved sex trafficking, 15 involved labor trafficking, 5 involved labor and sex trafficking, and there were 12 cases that were not specified.

In cases where there are many missing women, it can be challenging to determine the exact cause of their disappearance. Is it due to human trafficking, natural causes, or other factors? The lack of concrete evidence and eyewitness accounts can lead to uncertainty, making it difficult to pinpoint the root cause. When dealing with a high volume of missing persons, particularly women and children, there is a strong moral imperative to act quickly and decisively to ensure their safety and well-being. However, this can sometimes lead to a rush to judgment, which may result in misidentification, false accusations, or wrongful conclusions. At an early age, I learned that when I jumped to conclusions, I was wrong in most cases. Following the facts is how to accurately solve a case. It appears in Caitlyn's case this wasn't done, and witnesses were overlooked or not taken seriously.

Since Choctaw County, mainly Hugo, Oklahoma, has a small population, this means fewer people, fewer witnesses. The witnesses that Caitlyn did have were not taken seriously. We know that Caitlyn had never been to this area before, so this was truly a journey for her. When Gordon Case was asked if Caitlyn had ever been in Choctaw County, here is what he said:

> No, she'd never been in that area, ever. And I might want to add, there's no proof my daughter ever made it out, out of uh Paris, Texas. She never was in control of that vehicle. There's no there's no way, the way the way that the traveling that we have on record. My daughter was not in control of that vehicle going into Paris, Texas. Whatever happened to my daughter happened in the in the in the Bogota between the Bogota and Jennings area. This I can guarantee. (Grace, 2023, 16:25-16:55)

As Gordon's phone call with Caitlyn suddenly dropped, he felt a growing sense of unease. Their connection, once a lifeline to her father's guidance, was severed. This disruption sparked a cascade of unsettling questions in Gordon's mind. Perhaps he wondered if there was someone else present in the car with Caitlyn, or was she being watched? Had she unknowingly stumbled into a precarious situation? The uncertainty gripped him like a vice. Caitlyn's uncharacteristic behavior only added to his anxiety. Was she hiding something, or was her demeanor a result of external circumstances beyond her control? The police's subsequent search of the abandoned vehicle yielded nothing but unanswered questions. The locked car doors and Caitlyn's belongings lay in silence, leaving Gordon to ponder the mystery and the fragility of the human connection with his daughter.

Gordon described the abandoned vehicle that left questions in his own mind. Here is what he said about finding the vehicle:

> No, I found her vehicle. Both her phones were in the vehicle. The vehicle never made it into the river. It got caught between two trees. Her phones were in the vehicle. Her vehicle was locked up, the windows were locked up, it was in neutral, the key was on. She was not in the vehicle. We know nobody was in that vehicle. The airbags didn't deploy, and you could tell the vehicle had been manually pushed down that hill to go into that river on that property. There's a lot of information that I don't know what you do or don't have. (Grace, 2023, 17:10-17:42)

I'm deeply disturbed by the discovery of Caitlyn's vehicle, which had been intentionally pushed down a hill, coming to a stop between two trees. Caitlyn's phones were still inside, and despite being locked up with the windows rolled up, the vehicle was in neutral, and the key was still present. The most unsettling aspect, however, is that there is no indication of anyone being in the vehicle. It's as if Caitlyn had simply left it there, unaware of what had transpired or something more serious, abducted. The lack of airbag deployment and the telltale signs of manual manipulation suggest that this was no accident. I can only imagine Caitlyn's distress and confusion as she tried to make sense of this inexplicable and frightening event.

Here is how Gordon Case found Caitlyn's vehicle:

> We got a ping on the location where her vehicle was, and it was on the (sic) George Harrington's property up there at Fort Towson, Oklahoma, behind a locked gate, and I was told by the local Hugo department that we were going to get in, that he was going there immediately. I was still in Paris, Texas. I asked him, I said well, can I meet you up there? He goes, well, why don't you just sit still, and we'll let you know if you need to come up here if we find anything. Well, I didn't sit still. I drove up there. He said he was on his way. He said he was on his way. He was a mile away. I was thirty miles away.

> I got there before him by ten minutes. We finally got onto the property and during our search in that afternoon, I was able to locate her vehicle, just walked right into it. It was on its side and it was ready to go down the embankment. All the windows were locked up, everything was shut tight. We didn't know if she was in it or not. We finally got the door open, we realized she wasn't in it. And anyways, all her stuff, every one of her, everything she owned was in it, including the shoes she was wearing. The pants she was wearing were inside out across the center console. The people that live there are Will Harrington and his wife, Haley Harrington. They are the son and daughter in law of George and Elizabeth Harrington that owned the property. That the wife told us repeatedly that at eleven o'clock on that night,

on the fifth, that two vehicles entered her property at a high rate of speed. (Grace, 2023, 17:55-19:22)

As an investigator, I have a few questions. First, we know that Caitlyn's vehicle may have arrived on the Harrington's property about 11:00 p.m. When the vehicle was found, Caitlyn's clothing was still in the locked car. Why were all her belongings still inside her vehicle, including the shoes she was wearing? Was there a medical issue that caused her to remove her clothing because she was hot, or was someone there that told her to remove her clothing so there wasn't any evidence? After all, Haley Harrington stated that she saw two vehicles driving at a high rate of speed on the property.

More importantly, can Haley Harrington provide a more detailed description of the two vehicles she saw entering the property or did she see anyone get out of these vehicles or notice any suspicious behavior? I'm curious as to why the police weren't called when she saw two vehicles on their property. Can she explain why she didn't report this incident to the authorities immediately? Just throwing it out there, but what was their alibi for the time when Caitlyn's vehicle arrived on their property? Was there any motive to be involved in Caitlyn's disappearance besides being the property owners? I have other questions involving the property and the vehicle. Were there any signs of forced entry or struggle around Caitlyn's vehicle? Were there any shoe or tire impressions? Did the lights on Caitlyn's vehicle work?

As if things weren't complicated enough, Apple has this wonderful thing called, "Find My," to help find your iPhone or other Apple products. Due to the swift thinking of Caitlyn's brother, he was able to determine an area where the phone may be located. When an iPhone is pinged, it usually shows a map of the area. Although it may not be exact, it will definitely place you in the right area. On August 12, 2022, the Hugo Police Department was notified of this location finding and had to get on private property, which was gated, to where the phone was showing to be located. Sadly, Gordon Case was the one that found Caitlyn's vehicle on that gated property around 3 to 4 p.m. that same day.

Here is Gordon's continued recollection of the day he found Caitlyn's car after Haley Harrington stated that she saw two vehicles driving at a high rate of speed on the property:

> And then she heard the dogs bark, and she looked out the window and saw these cars come on to her property, dust flying, whatever, and then she said, a little while later the dogs barked again, only one car was exiting their property at a high rate of speed. The detective asked her directly, "Are you sure of the time?" She said, absolutely, it was eleven o'clock. Told us how she went to dinner, her and her husband. They left the gate wide open. They came home, and oh, they forgot to leave the gate. They forgot to shut the gate.

> So anyways, the vehicle left out of there at a high rate of speed. He asked her, did you get a license plate? She said no, it was moving so fast, and the dust was flying all I could see was the taillights. That was the event of that evening.

> It went on to about eleven o'clock at night before we excavated the vehicle from where it was lodged between the trees, and there was a lot of forensic people there, the crash guide, the pathologists and they were going through the entire vehicle, and I took pictures as well. And anyway, the next day we were supposed to show up there with the owner's consent, with a set of dogs that Peggy had found, Caitlyn's mom, had set up a dog search team. When we got there, the gate was locked. We were not going to be

able to get in. The wife said that she that he never got up to look to see who came onto that property that night, or (sic) did he investigate the next day to see why only one car left.

And that's when that's when that's when OSBI, Oklahoma Bureau of Investigations detective got involved. And then he took that story from Will's wife, Haley Harrington, and say he talked to the husband. The husband got up and he said he only saw one car enter. Well, then when I said, well, why wouldn't you get up to see who was entering your property at eleven o'clock, then he said, I'm not going to argue with Gordon, there was only one car that came in there. And then it went from the one car to there was no car. No, he didn't see any car. It was real quiet that night. There was nothing going on, no car, no nothing.

He didn't see anything at the end of his story, and he already got done telling Peggy that you know, he was kind enough to take him back there and show him the set of second set of vehicle tires that had left the property. Right, so then it went from all that to absolutely seeing nothing. And that's when I knew things were not going to go right. So, I mean, I could go on and on and on for a long time about what's going on up there. (Grace, 2023, 19:22-21:54)

There's a lot going on here. This is not only interesting, but it's also very concerning. The first thing that stands out is the role of perception and observation in this case. The woman, Haley Harrington, claims to have seen two cars enter her property at 11 p.m., but then later, her husband changes the story to say that he didn't actually see a car at all. The husband, Will, initially claims to have seen only one car enter the property, but then contradicts himself by saying he didn't see anything at all. This raises questions about the reliability of their perceptions and the possibility of misinformation or maybe even lying about what they saw. Possibly scared of repercussions. It is interesting how Haley and Will's stories contradict each other and even change over time.

Can we trust what people tell us? Are the Harringtons accurately reporting what they saw or experienced? In this case, it seems that Haley and Will may have been influenced by their own biases or motivations when recounting their stories. Another interesting aspect is the role of evidence in this case. The OSBI detective mentions that there were forensic experts present at the scene, collecting evidence and taking pictures. This highlights the importance of evidence in verifying or disproving claims. However, even with physical evidence, there is always a possibility of misinterpretation or contamination of it.

Here is Gordon discussing the appearance of Caitlyn's vehicle when it was found:

> We actually got in through the back door, but the windows were completely rolled up tight and there was no air conditioning in that vehicle. So, it was eighty something degrees in Texas that evening all that day. She did not drive around in Texas where her windows rolled up in the middle of that heat with no air conditioning. And if she crashed the car, which she did not, she was not in that vehicle. She would have never rolled the vehicle the windows up when she left. She wasn't parking at Walmart. She just crashed the car. She would not be concerned about that, but they never found any fingerprints. Not only like two fingerprints are hers in the entire vehicle. (Grace, 2023, 22:57-23:28)

Let's talk about evidence for a minute so you can understand and break down what Gordon is talking about. So far, we have physical evidence versus circumstantial evidence. Gordon is drawing attention to the condition of Caitlyn's vehicle as circumstantial evidence. Circumstantial evidence refers to indirect evidence that suggests something happened, rather than directly proving an event. It leads the investigators in a certain direction, but it's not completely factual. In this case, the rolled-up windows and the temperature conditions imply Caitlyn would not have willingly left her vehicle in that state if she could still use it.

Now, let's break down Caitlyn's behavior as her father sees it. Gordon highlights a behavioral expectation regarding his daughter's actions. He argues that someone in a hot environment would typically keep windows open or use air conditioning. This creates a narrative about Caitlyn's intentions and actions, suggesting that something unusual happened if the windows were rolled up when the vehicle was found. Gordon also suggests that if Caitlyn had crashed her vehicle, it does not align with how people generally act in those moments. This statement infers that Caitlyn's actions did not match the assumptions made about her behavior in a crisis.

The mention of not finding any fingerprints except for a couple raises questions about Caitlyn's presence in the vehicle. Fingerprints, also physical evidence, are often crucial in determining who occupied a space; the few found might imply she had very limited interaction with the car after the incident. Perhaps it may have been wiped down clean. Sometimes physical evidence in establishing a narrative or understanding an event can be extremely important, but it doesn't always end up that way.

Here is more of Gordon describing Caitlyn's vehicle hung up in trees:

Well, what happened was it went down the only hill on their property, the only place that you could launch a vehicle on its own that would go down to that bar was that right where the vehicle was. And that vehicle, what happened was it was put (sic) neutral, and the key was on, so the steering wasn't locked. It went down the hill and it went over a little knoll and it hit a tree root and it spun that front tire sideways, and it spun the whole vehicle sideways, and it caught between two little tiny trees no more than eight inches or something... (sic), real small sapling trees, and these it caught her back bumper, her back tail hitch in the front of the vehicle, and it kept it from going over into the river. They wanted it to go in the river. But the thing is that there was no water at the bottom of that embankment for another twenty feet. It was a fallen tree, so it probably never would have made it into the river to begin with. (Grace, 2023, 23:39-24:34)

The central question I find myself grappling with is what circumstances led to the vehicle being left in neutral, with the key still in the ignition. Personally, I find it hard to believe that someone who made the effort to travel a distance, specifically for a car, would then proceed to push it off a cliff, hill, or any other precipice. It seems imperative that investigators thoroughly examine potential physical evidence—such as tire tracks, footprints, or any signs of disturbance—that may have been overlooked during the initial investigation, especially since the car was discovered in the cover of darkness. If the vehicle was placed in neutral intentionally, it could indicate a deliberate attempt to cause harm, either to oneself or to someone else; however, I genuinely doubt that Caitlyn intended to inflict harm upon herself in any way.

There is a significant expanse of private roads and farmland in the area where Caitlyn's car was discovered. Many of these private lanes are seldom traveled, adding an air of mystery to the situation. Caitlyn's car was precariously wedged between two trees at the edge of a 75-foot cliff, suggesting that someone may have attempted to dispose of the vehicle by pushing it toward the Kiamichi River, though their plans seemed to have gone awry.

Gordon Case was there, and this was his recollection of what he saw when the vehicle was stuck between the trees:

> Yeah, it wasn't like a straight down cliff, but it was on an embankment. From about the point where the vehicle was on its side, caught in those trees, it would have been about seventy feet actually to the river. Yeah, that's how I found it. (Grace, 2023, 28:31-28:46)

Maybe the individual that pushed the car didn't know they were not successful at that time since it was in the dark of night, their first mistake. Here is what Gordon believes happened:

> Well, it's my theory that they probably did, and that's why they got out of there fast, you know. They came in (sic) they, absolutely knew the property. There's no way they would have found that hill behind that barn if they didn't. And also, when you travel on to that property, there's a lot of machinery that was there, the farm equipment that was in tall grass, and if there was somebody who didn't know their way around that property, they would have probably crashed in that if they were coming in at a high right rate of speed. They knew exactly where to turn behind the hay barn to find that hill to launch that vehicle.

And when Ms. Haley Harrington said that that vehicle, she said it was there a little a little while a little while later I heard the dog's bark. We don't know, because nobody's ever asked this woman how long that vehicle was there. Matter of fact, the Bureau of Investigations detective has tried to make that out like it never happened. The Bureau of Investigations detective theory was that, well, we think she got out of the vehicle and she got eaten by wild hogs and in the end, the tracking dogs would not be able to get her scent if she was torn to pieces. That's what he told my daughter's mother.

And then the second theory was that she made it out of there and she walked down to the main road, which is two miles in the pitch black by a bunch of wild dogs in the street, and got down there and hitchhiked out of there what with no shoes, no pants, no clothes. That never happened. And I tell you what Paris Police Department, detective over there, he absolutely will do nothing to help us. He was originally contacted by the Attorney General's Office in Louisiana. At first, he was super nice and all of a sudden, he quit texting. He no, no contact with him at all. Another one, Lamar Sheriff's Department, absolutely nothing would not return my calls. I finally told him I'm going national with this. He called me within two days to find out what was going on, said he was going to call the FBI, knew somebody. He never did nothing. He just wanted to see what I knew and how mad I was. And believe me, I'm furious.

I've contacted the governor's office in both states, the (sic) Texas and Oklahoma. I've contacted the attorney generals in both those states. I have gotten no response from anybody. And Hugo Police

Department, the detective that was there the night that we found the vehicle, blocked my phone and told me to call the Lamar Sheriff's department. Why would I call the Lamar Sheriff's department, it's her car found in Fort Towson, Oklahoma. So, this is what I'm dealing with over there. And also, I wanted footage from Bogata where she was. We actually got a witness that talked to my daughter in Bogata, Texas the day she went missing. Police never investigated. Told that police department she didn't spend any money in your town, so there's no need to look for her. And when I (sic). Because I spoke to a police officer there, and that's exactly what he told me. (Grace, 2023, 28:54-31:47)

Gordon Case feels that law enforcement officials are not seeking the truth and are instead dismissing evidence. I don't blame him. He thinks that there might be a cover-up regarding the circumstances of his daughter's disappearance, citing inconsistencies in police theories, lack of communication, and the dismissal of crucial evidence and witness accounts. Society expects public officials to act in the best interests of their communities, and when this trust is violated, it raises moral questions about their obligations to uphold justice and support those they serve. So what's happening in Oklahoma?

Gordon mentioned that they found a witness that spoke to Caitlyn when she was in Bogata. Here is Gordon talking about the witness:

She works, a it's a female, she works at the Dollar General, I guess. This is all we know at this point. They're still trying to locate her because they talked to another girl that you know, said that that's what you know, she spoke to my daughter that day and she actually said she was coming back to the store, and she left and never came back. But I asked from day one, I said, you know, will you go back and check the footage and those stores and at Bogata there's only a couple of stores there. He got furious with me. He said, no way am I going back there. We got her in Paris, Texas, there's no need to go do that.

Well, guess what, she was in that town and if they looked at the footage, they would have seen her there and maybe somebody with her or followed her out or something. But he didn't want to do that. (Grace, 2023, 31:53-32:38)

This was at the Dollar General in Bogata, Texas. Gordon has also mentioned that Caitlyn would have been in Bogata around the same time since they had spoken on the phone around 5:30 p.m. My curiosity has significantly deepened as I've delved into researching this case. Rather than criticizing law enforcement, I prefer to focus on constructive dialogue about how the police can improve their practices and effectiveness. Cases like this end up as television shows or documentaries on the ID channel.

If we are to trust the witness who reported seeing two vehicles enter the premises while only one vehicle left; it raises an important question: why didn't the property owners initiate an investigation? Furthermore, it's noteworthy that Gordon and the Case family have not reached any resolution with the police regarding the investigation. The Case family has persevered in their quest for justice, often taking the initiative to pursue leads independently. Given the complexities of this case, compounded by conflicting witness testimonies, one might wonder if there are underlying issues or information being concealed.

I had a thought that maybe there were drugs in the car and maybe the owner of the drugs started to follow Caitlyn to recover their drugs, farfetched I know. Dave Mack from Crime Online stated the following:

According to Caitlyn's mother, Caitlyn Rose Cases's vehicle landed at the final destination according to GPS hit-Gmail at 11:46 p.m. August 5th. Once the vehicle was found, according to Caitlyn's mother, the Hugo Police Department detectives and the OSBI failed to secure the property or treat the area as a crime scene when that vehicle was located on August 12th. Officially, Caitlyn Case's vehicle, a 2006 black GMC Envoy with the Louisiana license plate, was found abandoned behind a private gated property along a steep embankment on the Kiamichi River near Frogville, Oklahoma. But where is Caitlyn Rose Case? (Grace, 2023, 35:02-35:40)

In recent years, the issue of sex trafficking has increasingly captured public attention in the United States, raising significant concerns about the exploitation of vulnerable individuals. This alarming trend reflects broader societal issues, including poverty, lack of education, and systemic inequalities, which often leave people, particularly women and children, at risk. As awareness of sex trafficking grows, many communities and organizations are mobilizing to address this crisis, advocating for stronger laws, better victim support systems, and educational programs aimed at prevention. By confronting the root causes and supporting survivors, society can take meaningful steps toward eradicating this grave violation of human rights. According to the National Human Trafficking Hotline (NHTH):

Human trafficking is a form of modern slavery that occurs in every state, including Oklahoma. The NHTH works closely with service providers, law enforcement, and other professionals in Oklahoma to serve victims and survivors of trafficking, respond to human trafficking cases, and share information and resources. (National Human Trafficking Hotline, 2021, para. 1)

As the police began to investigate, more leads came to surface. Crime Online reported the following:

> Two eyewitnesses come forward. They tell police they believe they saw Case on August seventeenth; this is five days after Case's car was found. She was crying in the backseat of a disabled white suv. It had been pushed from the road by two women into a gas station in Paris, Texas. The witnesses said there was a dark colored SUV that came to assist the disabled SUV. (Grace, 2023, 35:50-36:13)

During this time, Caitlyn's family has been contacting any and every police agency in the area where Caitlyn went missing, including the FBI. To Peggy Case, it seemed like none of the police agencies were willing to assist them in her missing daughter's case. Peggy stated the following:

> We provided them with the bank statements like critical, you know, I went into the bank, we filed the missing person's report on Saturday on the on the (sic) August the sixth, Gordon and I. We got the first cell tower ping on August the seventh, that Sunday. We were at the police station around 10 p.m. when they got the first ping and it was in Hero (sic), Oklahoma. They immediately contacted missing persons in Oklahoma and Jim Parrish is the person that manned that search around the cell towers. Like it was a six-mile perimeter on the on the (sic) western side I think they did first and in the eastern side they did later. Six miles in the opposite direction, and that was a core joint effort whoever, whatever was, whatever agencies work with Oklahoma missing persons. But too, there was supposedly dogs and drones and foot

traffic and they found nothing. (Grace, 2023, 36:49-37:51)

The case of Caitlyn's disappearance has left a void in the lives of her parents, who are now burdened by the weight of uncertainty. Despite her adulthood, their love and concern for her well-being remain unwavering, and the lack of answers is a constant source of worry. The investigation's incomplete puzzle has sparked a flurry of questions which have yet to be addressed. The fact that Caitlyn's parents have taken on a more active role in searching for her raises questions about the effectiveness of the official inquiry. This intriguing mystery has piqued public interest, as people are left wondering what measures the authorities are taking to uncover the truth.

Since it was unlike Caitlyn to not have contact with her parents, on August 6, 2022, her family decided to file a missing person report with the Houma, Louisiana Police Department. During that time, license plate readers (LPRs) were issued in surrounding states. LPRs are those little black cameras on police cars, usually on the trunk area of the car. The police cars can have four cameras for LPRs. While the police officer drives the car, the cameras are taking pictures of license plates and storing it with the location. The police officer will later download the data into the database so it can be read. This is a great tool for police to use. Homicide investigators use LPRs quite frequently in their cases. It helps with finding leads and last known areas of the victim or suspect.

Along with filing a missing person report and LPR use, Caitlyn's information was placed into the National Crime Information Center (NCIC) database. This is used nationwide and allows police to pull up any information on a subject. This database holds a lot of information, and police get certified to use it about every two years. If police came across Caitlyn, they would run her information, and it would come up that she was considered "missing." This database is very important in police work. It allows the police to know vehicle information, driver information, and wanted information, along with other details to assist the police in their investigation.

On August 7, 2022, the Oklahoma Missing Persons Department had deployed a team to search for Caitlyn after they discovered her cell phone pinged in Hugo, Oklahoma. Unfortunately, there were negative results. This wasn't like Caitlyn, so as a parent, her father decided to go to Hugo, Oklahoma the next morning. This is where Gordon Case started to make Hugo his part-time home. As parents, they were smart to have Caitlyn's credit card and banking information. This was imperative because there was finally a place to start the investigation. This information was given to law enforcement to assist in their investigation to see the purchases and locations where transactions were made. Most importantly, they could see where Caitlyn had stopped to get gas for her vehicle and check the cameras at those locations. Fortunately, the police were able to gather videos from these locations.

When Caitlyn's vehicle was finally located, this case became very real to Caitlyn's parents. I'm sure, as a father seeing his daughter's car overhanging a cliff was surreal. It appeared that the vehicle was pushed off a cliff where it got stuck between two small trees. The vacant vehicle was hanging about 75 feet over the Kiamichi River, cradled between the trees. Since the vehicle was hanging over a cliff and stuck in two trees, it took around four hours to bring the vehicle to a flat surface. The question was, Where's Caitlyn? Her belongings were left in her vehicle, including her two cell phones and red tennis shoes. The fact that Caitlyn's belongings, including her phones and shoes, were left behind in the vehicle, adds another layer of complexity to the situation.

When encountering such a situation, a person may experience a variety of emotions and reactions. Let's explore these from a philosophical perspective. For everyone on scene, the police, tow truck driver, any witnesses, and Caitlyn's father, empathy comes to mind. Seeing a vehicle stuck in an unusual and precarious position can evoke a sense of empathy. You might imagine yourself in the driver's shoes, contemplating the fear and uncertainty they must have been feeling. This can serve as a reminder of our shared vulnerability as humans.

The awe and wonder would take my breath away. The sight of the car alone, suspended between two trees, hanging over a cliff with a river below, might inspire awe or wonder. This peculiar scene challenges our expectations of how objects and situations should typically appear. It can provoke questions about the laws of physics, the limits of human ingenuity, or the unpredictability of life. We can become thankful that it wasn't us in that car.

The unusual sight of a vehicle stuck in such a precarious position might lead to epistemological doubt. It challenges our understanding of reality and our ability to accurately perceive it. One might question whether what they are seeing is real or an illusion. This raises broader philosophical questions about perception, knowledge, and the nature of reality. How could this have happened? Observing the car in such a dilemma could prompt existential reflection. The vulnerability and fragility of life may come to the forefront, reminding us of our mortality and the inherent uncertainty of our existence. It may lead us to ponder the meaning and purpose of life or even the concept of free will. Encountering a car stuck between two trees, hanging over a cliff with a river, can spark a range of emotions and provoke philosophical contemplation about empathy, awe, epistemology, and existentialism.

During the 3 to 4 hours the vehicle was being raised to flat ground, the police were interviewing witnesses from the private property the vehicle was located on. During this interview, Gordon Case and other neighbors were present. The police were told by the property owner's daughter-in-law that she and her husband currently live on that property. The police were also told that there were two vehicles that entered the property, but only one had left. This is interesting to me because that would have made me curious. The Hugo Police Detective asked the daughter-in-law if she could identify any part of the vehicle that had left the property, like a license plate. The daughter-in-law told the detective that the vehicle was moving at a high rate of speed and could only see the taillights as it sped off.

The police agencies involved did not treat this scene as a crime scene according to Caitlyn's mother. They did not secure the scene or the property area where Caitlyn's vehicle was ultimately found. On August 5, 2022, at 11:46 p.m., according to Caitlyn's GPS – through her Gmail, this was the last date, time, and location of Caitlyn's existence. Caitlyn was still missing. When a vehicle is found, whether it's abandoned or involved in a crime, it becomes a potential piece of evidence. It could be located by law enforcement officials, a concerned citizen, or even by the owner themselves. The initial discovery is crucial for starting the investigation. Later, the case was turned over to the Oklahoma State Bureau of Investigation (OSBI). This case started to become complicated due to the multiple states that were now involved: Oklahoma, Texas, and Louisiana.

Now we lead into the preservation of evidence. Once located, the vehicle needs to be secured and preserved to ensure that no evidence is tampered with or destroyed. This involves creating a barrier around the vehicle, documenting its location, and possibly taking photographs or videos. The primary aim is to maintain the integrity of any potential evidence. The question is, was this even done by the police? After securing the scene, investigators begin their investigation and analyze the vehicle. They will thoroughly search for any physical evidence, such as fingerprints, DNA, or other trace materials, inside and outside the vehicle. This may also include documenting any visible damage or signs of forced entry. Additionally, the vehicle's registration and ownership details are examined to establish its legal status and identify potential suspects or witnesses connected to it.

The investigators would find a resolution and then piece together all the collected evidence and information to form a coherent narrative. This can involve cross-referencing the vehicle's location with other crime scenes or incidents, identifying potential motives, or correlating any fingerprints or DNA found with existing databases. The aim is to uncover the truth about what happened with the vehicle and, if applicable, connect it to any broader criminal activities. To understand this more clearly, think about this example: Imagine a stolen vehicle is found abandoned after a robbery. The police secure the scene, document the vehicle's position, and collect any evidence left behind. They may find fingerprints or DNA on the steering wheel or a discarded mask in the backseat used in the robbery. By examining the registration, they may discover that the vehicle was reported to be stolen by its owner. Using this information, investigators can trace the registered owner to potentially identify the thief or gather more evidence related to the crime.

In Caitlyn's case, what are the ethical responsibilities of the police in such a situation? In society today, was understand that there are limited personnel and resources. Did the police decide to focus on other pressing cases and not investigate Caitlyn's abandoned car thoroughly? Yes, the car was abandoned, with Caitlyn nowhere to be found. As an investigator, that vehicle that sped away is now on my mind. As I mentioned before, I still have questions!

The next day on August 13, 2022, a non-profit search and rescue team searched the area where Caitlyn's vehicle was located with canines. The police were not involved in this search, as the search was coordinated by Peg Case, Caitlyn's mother. This search, however, was never finished because the property owner's son wanted the search to stop. He had requested the search team leave his property.

On August 19, 2022, OBSI released additional information on the missing person case of Caitlyn Case attempting to find her whereabouts. OBSI reported that Caitlyn was traveling northbound along Highway 271 heading towards Paris, Texas. Soon after 7 p.m. on August 5, Caitlyn's cellphone transmitted on cell towers at Pattonville, Texas and a tower located south of Paris (McCandless, 2022). At approximately 9 p.m. on August 5, 2022, Caitlyn's vehicle had traveled around the south loop of Highway 286 in Paris to FM (Farm to Market Roads) 79 where it proceeded in a northwest direction from Paris. The vehicle is believed to have traveled north in an unknown path headed toward Oklahoma. After Caitlyn entered Oklahoma on Highway 271, the vehicle turned east on Highway 109, south of Grant, Oklahoma.

According to McCandless (2022), the OSBI report on Caitlyn Case stated:

At this point in the investigation there is concern that someone other than Case was in control of the vehicle. It is believed that an attempt was made to deposit the vehicle in the Kiamichi River to hide its location during the late-night hours of August 5. It is not believed at this time that Case physically entered Oklahoma. (para 5)

It was reported that:

Case was driving a black 2006 GMC Envoy with Louisiana plates 957FDO. She is described as 5'5", 140 pounds with brown hair and brown eyes. She was wearing a black spaghetti strap style top, light blue jeans, and red tennis shoes. (McCandless, 2022, para 7)

The OSBI is the lead investigating agency for this case.

Caitlyn's family is hoping to find someone that knows what happened. There was a 911 call made on August 5, 2022; however, it was never dispatched. According to Peg Case, this 911 call would have been crucial in this case. There may have been answers into who was in control of the vehicle and why it ended up hanging between trees. The family believes there are gaps in the last known location of Caitlyn since she was talking to her father on the phone when the communication had abruptly stopped.

According to Caitlyn's family, there was no GPS signal or Gmail data available from 5:16 p.m. to 6:59 p.m. on August 5, 2022. There was, however, a Wi-Fi hit at approximately 6:10 p.m. in Cunningham, Texas. This was where an eyewitness supposedly spoke to Caitlyn in his driveway. Caitlyn had told this witness that she had made a wrong turn. The OBSI had mapped her GPS locations and had Caitlyn leaving Cunningham at approximately 6:59 p.m. The family is still seeking information about this encounter.

Peggy Case (2022), stated on her website, findcaitlyn. com (which no longer exists):

Deceased or alive. Our family will be providing a reward to the person/persons once the information is verified. We believe our daughter was abducted and are desperate to find answers that will finally piece together what happened to her. Our family will never give up looking for our daughter and never give up fighting for the justice she deserves. Our daughter is one of the kindest, most trusting human beings on this planet (para. 22).

As if this wasn't enough for this family to wonder about Caitlyn and her whereabouts, not knowing always takes a toll. It was over a year before there were any kind of real answers. According to Lisa Monahan (2023), skeletal remains had been discovered by a Choctaw County landowner in October 2023. The unidentified remains that were discovered had been located on the other side of the river where Caitlyn's vehicle was found by her father and police authorities.. Finally, the OBSI had reported that the vehicle appeared to have been hidden or someone tried to hide the vehicle. What is interesting is that there have been conflicting stories between these police agencies regarding if the area where the remains were located was searched thoroughly.

Caitlyn's parents, after nearly a year of searching for closure, learned about the discovery of skeletal remains in October 2023, believed to belong to their daughter. As they grapple with emotions ranging from hope to despair, they are encouraged by the possibility of closure but also face the reality of grief. This tragic narrative exemplifies the complexity of human experiences in the face of loss.

> "We've been in limbo forever, (sic) was she trafficked? Or is she still out there? We don't know where she is – it is a horrible balance to live through every day," Peggy explained. "Each day, it is where could she be. (Monahan, 2023, para. 14)

Caitlyn's parents were shocked. "To get that phone call out of nowhere from the lead investigator who has not spoken to us for nearly a year, we thought he must have a reason to believe it is her," said Peggy (Monahan, 2023, para. 16).

Caitlyn's family waited to see if the remains were in fact Caitlyn's. They provided their daughter's dental records to be used in the identification of the remains to see if they were in fact Caitlyn's. Lisa Monahan (2023) reported that

Gordon and Peggy Case advised her, "That the Oklahoma state medical examiner made the identification using Caitlyn's dental records. Those records were compared to the skull, found along with incomplete and scattered skeletal remains in October" (para. 2). Forensic odontology uses dental records, such as radiographs, treatment records, and X-rays for personal identification.

Think for a minute about being a parent, a parent who just found out that the remains they were told about are their daughter's. So many things go through your mind. When we learn that the remains that were found were a loved one's, we are confronted with the reality of their existence coming to an end. This can raise questions about the irrelevant aspects of their existence, such as memories, legacies, and the impact they had on us and others. Reflecting on the essence of existence and what remains beyond the physical can help in finding solace.

Our personal identity is indirectly tied to our memories and experiences. When someone is missing and there's the "not knowing," finding their remains might reaffirm their identity and bring an unfortunate closure to their absence. This discovery can solidify memories and contribute to the narrative of their life. Contemplating the relationship between identity, memory, and the physical remains can aid in understanding how we remember and honor those we have lost.

The Case family learned that the medical examiner had ruled Caitlyn's cause of death as undetermined. Her remains were weathered and there was obvious animal activity. Let's examine a theory surrounding the discovery of Caitlyn's vehicle, which was found with her clothing still inside and her remains located nearby, but only after some time had passed. This peculiar situation raises questions about the timeline of events and the circumstances leading to her death. Why might Caitlyn have left her clothing in the vehicle? Did she encounter a situation that forced her to leave in haste? The proximity of her remains to the vehicle suggests a narrative of struggle or a significant event that transpired shortly after her departure from the car. Analyzing this theory allows us to explore the implications of the evidence found at the scene, guiding our understanding of the potential scenarios that may have unfolded and highlighting the complexities involved in determining what truly happened to Caitlyn.

Everyone has their assumptions about this case, but we need to find the truth about what actually happened to Caitlyn. The ethical responsibilities of law enforcement come into question, alongside societal perceptions of vulnerability, identity, and the implications of technology in personal safety. The depths of anguish experienced by families navigating the uncertain terrain of missing persons resonate universally, prompting us to imagine the fragility of human connections and the urgency of seeking truth in the realm of injustice. Her family is still actively investigating, and I don't blame them. They want answers, they want some type of closure. I will end this chapter with a quote from Gordon Case, "We will not let those involved get away with this. I promised my daughter that they all will be brought out into the light and justice will be served" (Wildmoon, 2023, para. 9).

Anyone with information is encouraged to call the OSBI at 800-522-8017.

"Now hope does not disappoint because the love of God has been poured out in our hearts by the Holy Spirit who was given to us." ~ Romans 5:5

CHAPTER 3

THE LIFEGUARD THAT DISAPPEARED

On June 27, 2000, the small town of Warren, Massachusetts, was poised for an ordinary summer day filled with sunshine and laughter. Instead, it became the backdrop for a heart-wrenching story that would grip and haunt the community for years to come. Sixteen-year-old Molly Bish, a bright and enthusiastic lifeguard, was reported missing after failing to return home from her job at a local pond. Her disappearance unraveled a tapestry of hope, fear, and the relentless pursuit of justice that extended far beyond the borders of Massachusetts.

Molly was a typical teenager, brimming with aspirations and dreams. On the day of her disappearance, she left home early, eager to perform her duties as a lifeguard—a job she loved and approached with youthful enthusiasm. The day unfolded like any other until sunset arrived, and her family grew concerned when she did not come home. As time passed and the clock ticked past the expected hour, what began as a routine day morphed into a frantic search.

Molly's story began on June 26, 2000, when the sun cast an orange glow over the pond where she had spent countless afternoons safeguarding swimmers. That day, her mother, Magdalen (known as Magi), caught a fleeting glimpse of an unsettling figure: a mustached man behind the wheel of a white car parked inconspicuously in the lot. At the time, she thought little of it, considering it an inconsequential detail in the tapestry of a typical summer day. Yet, as tragedy unfolded, this moment would haunt her.

The following morning, at precisely 9:45 a.m., Magi dropped Molly off at Comins Pond, near the lifeguard area, unaware that it would be the last time she would see her daughter. Just eight minutes after Molly arrived, other parents and children arrived for swim lessons. Noticing there wasn't a lifeguard on duty, another swimmer's mother reported Molly missing using a police radio. Shortly afterward, the lifeguard whistle in that mother's hands echoed through the stillness, summoning the attention of responders who initially thought there was a drowning. However, Magi would not be contacted until three hours later. As the mystery of Molly's disappearance loomed larger, memories of that tranquil summer night began to fade.

Reflecting on the initial events, Magi Bish stated:

> When this first took place, they called me after three hours. They thought that Molly had left and gone off with friends. Molly never had any history of being truant from school or from work. She had worked two jobs, jobs that weren't as important as this job. She was so excited about making $9 an hour. She

prepared all winter for this job. (Grace, 2006, para. 13)

As a detective, here are my first thoughts. (1) The victim, Molly, was known for her reliability and excitement about a new job paying $9 an hour. (2) The timeline starting with the initial call came in three hours after her disappearance. (3) Initial assumptions of Molly's friends believed that Molly had left voluntarily, thinking she might be off with other friends. (4) The key details of these first moments showed Molly had no prior history of skipping school or work. She was dedicated and had prepared all winter for this opportunity. The assumption that Molly simply left is questionable given her commitment. We've got a potential case of something more serious at play here.

Magi Bish was understandably confused; this behavior was uncharacteristic of Molly. Like any concerned parent, she rushed to the beach after receiving the call at 1:30 p.m.(Grace, 2006). Her older daughter met her there, along with her baby, in search of Molly. Magi felt an increasing sense of dread as she stated:

> Molly's shoes were left. This was a sign to me. Molly never went to the beach without her shoes. We were pool people. She was the best swimmer in her class. She wouldn't go in the pond without her shoes because she didn't like the way the icky bottom felt. (Grace, 2006, para. 15)

> We knew this was a sign there was something very wrong. People started saying, Go to the police. Go to the police. So, I went to the police. My daughter met me on the way. The police just thought she'd gone off with friends, and they didn't know what to do with us. They just had us standing on the side. So, my daughter and I, we stood, we were too nervous to stand still and just wait, so my daughter decided

to go see her boyfriend and another friend, and then I went to another friend. And then I went to get my son. And all the friends were accounted for. And then my son, who was a lifeguard for three years prior at this local pond, this was a town job that Molly had. She was responsible. She was going to work at 10:00 o'clock in the morning. This was her eighth day of work. (Grace, 2006, para. 16)

We should know that Magi's knowledge comes from her direct experiences as a parent, which lends her perspective a certain weight. The police, however, operate based on protocols and policies based on experiences with similar cases.

The investigation took a grave turn when authorities speculated that Molly's disappearance might be linked to a possible drowning. In the mounting chaos, Magi's son plunged into the murky water, desperately searching every nook and cranny for traces of Molly. Search teams, equipped with boats and aided by cadaver dogs, scoured the area, but it felt like Magi and her family were trapped in a haunting nightmare, each moment etched with crushing uncertainty. The crime scene tape appeared, marking the reality that the situation was dire.

As Magi was getting more shaken about Molly missing, she expressed the following:

We knew she was the best swimmer. I kept saying, "Go, go to the highway. Someone took her." There had been a car, a vehicle in the parking lot the day before. There was a man in a white car who had been there at 10:00 o'clock, approximately the same time I dropped her off. I was very concerned about this individual. The police know. It was on record as we followed back in the case. I told them, this is who we have, a possibly, you know, a picture of him. In fact, we had Jeanne Boylan come out and do a second drawing because we were so concerned about this person who might have been there at the same time, to give us a better perspective, to give us a better look because when we did the first diagram, it came from the police, where you take eyes and nose composite. (Grace, 2006, para. 20)

Jeanne Boylan is a renowned American forensic composite artist with extensive experience collaborating with the FBI on numerous high-profile criminal cases. Notably, she has created composite sketches of the infamous Unabomber and Oklahoma City Bomber, as well as the suspect involved in the tragic murder of Polly Klaas..

Community members, law enforcement, and volunteers poured into the area, searching for any sign of Molly. They canvassed woods, beaches, and surrounding neighborhoods, their hopes intertwined with the anxiety and uncertainty hovering over them. The heart of the community beat in rhythm with their relentless efforts, reflecting a deep sense of loss and an unyielding determination for the truth.

In total, 8,000 leads were pursued in Molly's case, with over 250 individuals testifying before a grand jury and 70 exhibits presented as evidence (Grace, 2006). Despite this extensive investigation and the revelation that 11 individuals failed lie detector tests, authorities failed to identify any suspects. The sheer number of leads and witnesses reveals considerable momentum in the early stages of the investigation, emphasizing the need for persistence, as even cold cases can gain renewed life through fresh perspectives.

As detectives sifted through the wealth of gathered information, they faced the monumental task of determining the relevance and credibility of each piece of evidence. The context of the failed lie detector tests could provide valuable insight or lead to new avenues of inquiry. The detectives might consider revisiting witness testimonies, evaluating the potential for contradictions or consistencies that could reveal further lines of investigation. Advances in forensic technology could also play a role in revitalizing the case, pushing the detectives to explore methods unavailable during the original investigation, such as DNA analysis or digital forensics.

Advances in forensic technology and investigative methods could play a pivotal role in revitalizing the case. The detective might investigate new techniques that weren't available during the original investigation, such as DNA analysis or digital forensics. With thousands of leads but no clear suspect, the detective might consider engaging the public or using media outreach to gather new information or witness accounts that could have been overlooked previously, which the police department has done exhaustively.

Such a lack of progress can be frustrating for the detective. It underscores the challenges involved in solving cases, especially cold ones where memories fade, evidence deteriorates and leads to grow stale. However, it also serves as motivation to dig deeper and explore unconventional methods to uncover the truth. The cold case detective inherits a substantial amount of work.

Molly's father, John Bish, recalled the heartbreaking day when they discovered her bathing suit. Ironically, it was also the commemoration of Missing Children's Day, a cruel twist of fate. As he stood there staring into the depths of the woods, an instinctual feeling tugged at him. He felt certain it was Molly's bathing suit, invoking dread. "I mean, what would a bathing suit even be doing out there in the middle of nowhere?" he reflected. The finding was shocking, especially given its proximity to their home, a distance they had traversed countless times (Grace, 2006).

The police and district attorney delivered the devastating news that Molly's bathing suit had been found, not to provide closure but to deepen the sense of loss. Magi wept upon seeing the photograph. "I ran to my room. I fell on the floor, and I wailed. There are those primal feelings that you can feel in the depths of sadness," she said (Grace, 2006, para. 50). For three long years, their lives had been a tableau of uncertainty, shared through the murmur of the media, had ignited a flicker of hope to find Molly.

For nearly three years, their lives were immersed in uncertainty, and the media's murmuring occasionally ignited a flicker of hope for Molly's return. Ultimately, the grim reality set in when, in 2003, her remains were discovered in a wooded area of Worcester County, approximately 30 miles from where she had vanished. The tragic revelation shattered both her family and the community that had clung to hope for so long. What was once a vibrant young life had been extinguished, leaving behind a legacy of unanswered questions. Molly's remains had been uncovered over several weeks. On June 9, 2003, Molly's skull was found, it appeared that it had rolled down a hill and rested in foliage (Chan, 2025). Out of Molly's 209 bones, only 26 were recovered (Chan, 2025). Later in the day, District Attorney John Conte made the following statement, "We have identified Molly's remains. We just came back from notifying the Bishes" (Pombo, 2003, para. 2).

"We believe that it was a shallow burial because all of the bones were found on the surface," Conte advised the citizens (Pombo, 2003, para. 6). The chilling echoes of the past still linger in the air as detectives piece together the tragic events surrounding Molly's disappearance and murder. Evidence suggests that animal activity may have disturbed her final resting place, a grim reminder of the recklessness of her killer. Marginally aware of their surroundings, most murderers opt for the expedient solution of a shallow grave, driven by a desperate sense of urgency. No one wants the uncomfortable spotlight of detection cast upon them, and digging a six-foot grave is far more time-consuming than a three-foot one. Each moment spent in the act of burying a victim only heightens the risk of exposure. In Molly's case, the abduction, the swift transportation to the chosen site, and the brutal act that followed all unfolded within a window of perhaps three hours before anyone was aware she was gone. A fleeting grace period before those who cared for her became aware of her absence, compounding the complexity of the investigation. Time was both ally and adversary for the killer, each second ticking away the chance of being discovered.

The typical adult human body is comprised of about 206 bones (Helmenstine, 2024); however, variations, such as accessory bones or differing vertebrae counts, can lead to slight differences. Infants are born with approximately 270 bones, which fuse together as they mature, resulting in 206 in adults (Helmenstine, 2024). To break it down further, the human skeleton is divided into two main parts: the axial skeleton, which includes the skull, spine, ribs, and sternum (comprising 80 bones), and the appendicular skeleton, which consists of the limbs and the pelvic and shoulder girdles (comprising 126 bones) (Helmenstine, 2024).

As investigators worked tirelessly to piece together the puzzle, they turned to the unyielding science of DNA testing. The bones, along with a solitary tooth unearthed alongside them, became pivotal in a race against time. Forensic experts meticulously compared this dental evidence with existing records, ultimately leading them to a heartbreaking conclusion—the identification of the 16-year-old who vanished without a trace.

District Attorney John Conte stated during a press conference, "We have recovered other remains, and they are now in the hands of our state police detectives. All of the remains were found within a circumference of 1,000 feet" (Pombo, 2003, para. 4). The unthinking expedience of a shallow grave is alarming, revealing the desperation inherent in the mind of a murderer.

As investigators delved deeper, they revisited previous suspects interviewed after Molly's disappearance (Pombo,

2003), given the location of the bones close to where her bathing suit had been found. As the investigations progressed, various theories and suspects emerged, each adding layers of complexity to the case. Despite advances in technology and law enforcement's tireless efforts, the lack of conclusive evidence transformed this case into an unresolved mystery, leaving Molly's family to grapple with their overwhelming grief.

What should have been a joyful occasion, Molly's 20th birthday, turned into a somber gathering marked not by celebration but by the stark finality of a funeral. Friends and family came together to say tearful goodbyes, their hopes for a life filled with promise overshadowed by profound sorrow. As Molly's remains were laid to rest, questions filled the air: How did a day intended for laughter morph into one steeped in heartache? Who held the responsibility for robbing her of the future that lay ahead? The weight of these unanswered questions fueled a relentless chase for justice, demanding closure for those left behind.

In 2017, the Bish family convened an important event with private investigator Sarah Stein, inviting the community to shed light on Molly's enigmatic disappearance (Sarkar, 2021). This gathering proved vital, unearthing chilling accounts from multiple independent witnesses who recounted sightings of a man at a campground in West Brookfield—merely a stone's throw from the site of Molly's abduction (Sarkar, 2021). Strikingly, each account converged on unsettling details: the man disappeared from town on the very day Molly went missing, sporting blood and deep scratches on his body, suggesting a violent encounter (Sarkar, 2021). Though these unsettling coincidences raised countless questions, the elusive answers remained hidden in the shadow of this unsolved case.

The year 2018 marked a pivotal turn in the cold case investigation when a cryptic tip led investigators to retrieve a concealed vehicle potentially linked to Molly's disappearance (Sarkar, 2021). Utilizing advanced ground-penetrating radar technology, the team meticulously combed the area, uncovering the long-buried white sedan that Molly's mother reported nearly two decades before in 2000 (Sarkar, 2021). Despite the hope that this find could yield critical information, the identity of the car's owner remained frustratingly elusive. With the case languishing in uncertainty, no arrests have emerged, leaving a lingering silence where answers are desperately needed.

In this case, I can picture detectives staring at the wall covered with photographs and notes, a tangled web of over a hundred interviews swirling in their mind like a storm. On a murder board, each face of the witnesses, to the elusive friend of the victim, telling fragments of stories that never quite fit together. Yet there are still no leads. Despite the relentless pursuit of the truth, every lead seemed to dissipate into the ether, leaving the cold case enduringly frozen in time.

In the detectives' minds, hundreds of interviews and pieces of evidence swirled like a storm as they pored over photographs and notes on their murder board. Yet, despite their diligence, no solid leads seemed to emerge. The more they investigated, the more frustrating the task became. One particular lead brought a glimmer of hope but also a chilling reminder of the darkness surrounding the case. A woman recalled the trauma inflicted on her by a man she had loved, revealing that he had forced her into unspeakable actions, leaving behind a long shadow of suspicion begging to be unraveled in the pursuit of justice (Ring, 2011).

As she gazed at the images of Gerald B. Battistoni and the sketch of the man sought in connection with Molly Anne Bish's tragic murder, an overwhelming wave of emotion washed over her (Ring, 2011). The woman, his second wife, instinctively shielded her face with trembling hands, the weight of recognition etched across her features (Ring, 2011). Slowly, she shook her head, the gesture a silent denial that seemed to echo through the room (Ring, 2011). Tears began to gather and spill, each droplet a testament to the turmoil within, as the haunting possibility settled like a heavy fog in her heart. In that moment, the cold case of Molly Anne Bish seemed to intertwine with her own turbulent past, intertwining their fates in a chilling narrative that demanded to be unraveled.

Gerald Battistoni, a 49-year-old man serving a prison sentence for raping a young girl in the early 1990s, emerged as a complex figure amidst these chilling memories (Ring, 2011). Private investigator Daniel E. Malley's comprehensive investigation uncovered unsettling details about Battistoni's violent history against children, casting a shadow over a case that had long lain dormant. Questions emerged regarding the depths of his crimes and whether he was connected to other unsolved cases in the area.

As Malley reviewed the case files, the chilling account of Battistoni's past siphoned dread into the present. His victim, now an adult, had once lived near Comins Pond in Warren, the same place where Molly took on the role of a lifeguard (Ring, 2011). The haunting proximity of past crimes and present lives mingled together, weaving intricate questions that demanded resolution. Further sinister details emerged about Battistoni's pattern; descriptions of how he nurtured vulnerable girls with attention and gifts marked his predatory behavior (Ring, 2011). As his past unraveled, the specter of a potential link between Battistoni and Molly grew more pronounced. The proximity of his known criminal activities to Molly's circumstances drew renewed scrutiny from investigators. Investigative threads led back to the location of her remains three years after her disappearance, igniting hopes of closure.

It became abundantly clear that PI Malley's initial belief about Battistoni's intentions was misguided. The more their interactions were investigated, the more it became apparent that Battistoni was, in fact, not "protecting" the teenager as he had claimed. Instead, the layers of deception began to peel away, revealing a troubling truth that hinted at ulterior motives. Each conversation, every recorded encounter painted a different picture, one that suggested a far more complex relationship than mere guardianship. The question now loomed large: what was Battistoni really after, and how deep did this web of deceit truly run?

According to Kim Ring (2011) from the *Telegram & Gazette*, "The victim described in her statement how Mr. Battistoni would perform oral sex on her and eventually began 'having sexual intercourse with her whenever her mother was not at home,' according to Trooper Brendan M. O'Toole's report" (para. 8). Ring also stated, "He took her underwear, and raped her in her father's home, watching out the window in case he returned" (para. 9).

The past can most certainly weave itself through to the present in unsettling ways. PI Malley, delving into the foggy recesses of history, uncovered information that was impossible to overlook—evidence that could potentially implicate Battistoni as a suspect in the murder of 16-year-old Molly Anne Bish Stabile, 2011). The haunting proximity of past crimes and present lives laid a foundation for questions that demanded to be answered, intertwining destinies as cold and murky as the waters of the pond itself. Wait, there's more…

One of Battistoni's former wives revealed a haunting detail from their time in Ware, her husband frequently ventured over Whiskey Hill, a desolate rise that masked a darker truth beneath its surface, to procure drugs from a notorious dealer in nearby Warren (Ring, 2011). Then, three years after her disappearance, echoing through the community like a spectral whisper, Molly Bish's remains were discovered, hidden among the gnarled trees of Whiskey Hill, transforming a once-peaceful landscape into a haunting graveyard for secrets long buried (Ring, 2011). Recognizing the significance of Whiskey Hill as both a potential drug trafficking route and the location where Molly's remains were found, searching for additional evidence that could link Battistoni to her death was prominent.

According to Kim Ring (2011), "When she worked with a sketch artist to produce a drawing of the man, Mrs. Bish talked about the distinctive way the man held his cigarette and glared at her" (para. 23). Ring also reported that, "Mr. Battistoni's second wife said she used to get very annoyed with the way he 'effeminately' held his cigarettes" (para. 24). One pivotal moment stands out in 2011, following a series of alarming news reports detailing PI Malley's controversial work, Mr. Battistoni found himself in a state of deep distress. Hospitalized after a brutal act of self-harm, he had reportedly cut his throat in a desperate response to the mounting scrutiny (Ring 2011). Sources close to the situation hinted at a profound turmoil within Battistoni, suggesting that the weight of the revelations had driven him to the brink. This incident marked a significant turn in a narrative rife with unanswered questions and lingering consequences, leaving investigators and the public alike to ponder the intricate connections involving Battistoni and his past.

Within the walls of the Bridgewater State Hospital, a chilling chapter unfolded when Gerald Battistoni was transferred from the imposing walls of Walpole State Prison, following a harrowing incident that left the prison authorities rattled (Ring, 2014). Darren Duarte, appointed spokesman for the Department of Corrections, revealed in a terse statement that Battistoni was gravely ill, his condition deteriorating rapidly within the hospital's confines (Ring, 2014). Battistoni had succumbed to an illness, leaving behind a maze of unanswered questions.

In this ongoing investigation, a pivotal development emerged as Worcester County District Attorney Joseph D. Early Jr. announced plans to submit twenty-four pieces of evidence for enhanced DNA testing, most likely in

September 2016 (Croteau, 2016). The meticulous gathering of these pieces, cloaked in mystery and carefully preserved, may hold the key to unlocking the secrets of a case that has haunted the community for years. While Early confirmed that they will be dispatched to a specialized laboratory awaiting the arrival of upgraded testing technology in the fall, the authorities remain tight-lipped regarding the specific nature of the evidence involved (Croteau, 2016). According to Early, "The science is always getting better, we feel that the improved testing will help us in our efforts to identify Molly's killer or killers" (Croteau, 2016, para. 4). As the days pass, the hopes of rekindling the flame of justice rest upon the promise of modern science.

A meticulous gathering, shrouded in secrecy, held the potential key to unlocking the enigmas of a case that had haunted the community for too long. District Attorney Early expressed optimism about recent advancements in forensic technology improving their chances of solving Molly's case.

In recognition of the enduring pain experienced by families of missing persons, the Unresolved Case Squad was formed, inspiring law enforcement and families to persist in their quest for justice. Following a heartfelt meeting with the Bish family, Early committed to invigorate the investigative efforts that had long been stagnant (Croteau, 2016). This transformation sought to honor the continued hope of families yearning for closure.

According to Early, "John Bish had asked me not to call it a cold case squad because he felt it made it seem the cases were on a shelf somewhere collecting dust, so, I changed it" (Croteau, 2016, para. 8). He continued to say, "These cases are not forgotten, and they are being worked on continuously. We get tips on Molly's case every week and we track down every lead (Croteau, 2016, para. 8).

On June 2, 2021, Heather Bish, stood at the precipice of hope and dread, her heart racing with a mixture of anticipation and anxiety. Massachusetts State Police detectives were en route to her home, bearing the weight of a nearly two-decade-old enigma, the unresolved murder of her younger sister, Molly Bish (Baker, 2021). Because the Bishes didn't hear back from the detectives until 2021, it's likely that the DNA evidence submitted in 2016 was not successful in identifying a suspect at that time. Heather remembered that fateful day of June 27, 2000, when her vibrant sixteen-year-old sister disappeared without a trace, her laughter forever silenced, only to be found lifeless three years later, miles away from where she vanished. As the door creaked open to reveal the grim-faced detectives, Heather's breath hitched. They carried with them not only a trove of items retrieved from the initial investigation but also a photograph, an unspeaking witness to a story that had lingered in the shadows of uncertainty (Baker, 2021). The detectives' silence about the image was electric, a chilling promise that the past might yet surface to unearth truths long buried, but was Heather ready to see the picture?

As the detectives stepped into Heather's residence, they offered Heather a cardboard box. Inside lay the remnants of her younger sister's life, fragments she knew would haunt her thoughts long after they departed (Baker, 2021). Heather's hands trembled slightly as she sifted through the mementos, each item a ghost of happier times, a distressing reminder of everything she had lost. Meanwhile, in another part of the investigation, Heather and her mother, Magi Bish, watched from a distance, Magi's face illuminated by the glow of her phone screen as they were shown a haunting photograph. The image captured a man named, Francis "Frank" Sumner Sr., a face that sent shockwaves through their hearts, a chilling connection to the mystery that had shrouded their lives in darkness (Baker, 2021). Time seemed to freeze in that moment as the revelation settled upon them like a heavy fog. Heather responded, "We recognized all the characteristics that my mother has described for police sketches" (Baker, 2021, para. 7).

In the once-bustling parking lot of Comins Pond, where laughter and splashes echoed in the air, a darker undercurrent lurked just beneath the surface. It was there, on the eve of Molly's mysterious disappearance, that her mother encountered an unsettling sight, a man, seemingly out of place, sat alone in a white Chrysler, a plume of smoke curling from the cigarette clasped in his left hand (Baker, 2021). The tension in the air was palpable, igniting a flicker of recognition in Magi's mind, as she recalled the unsettling familiarity of that face, was it merely a trick of memory, or had their paths crossed before in the shadows of other unresolved mysteries? The clock was ticking, and with every tick, the churning waters of Comins Pond seemed to whisper the secrets of a cold case waiting to be unraveled. Magi remembered saying, "I'm kind of nervous, thinking, 'What's this guy doing? Why isn't he at work?" (Baker, 2021, para. 9).

Magi, in her thoughts said, "Because we're in a small town, people will kind of say hi, or just nod their head, but this guy just stared at me" (Baker, 2021, para. 10). For years, the unsolved case lingered in the shadows, with investigators sifting through a myriad of suspects, yet frustration mounted as not a single arrest materialized. However, on June 3, a seemingly ordinary day, an unexpected announcement shattered the stillness (Baker, 2021). Worcester County District Attorney Joseph Early Jr. revealed that, after receiving a significant tip in recent months, the investigation had taken a startling turn (Baker, 2021). The name at the center of this renewed inquiry was Francis P. Sumner, a convicted sex offender whose untimely death in 2016 had rendered him a ghost (Baker, 2021). As detectives probed deeper into his past, the chilling implications of the tip loomed large over the case, reigniting hopes of finally uncovering the truth that had eluded them for so long. District Attorney Joseph Early Jr. made a startling comment,

"Pictures they found of Sumner 'are strangely similar to the composite'" (Baker, 2021, para. 13).

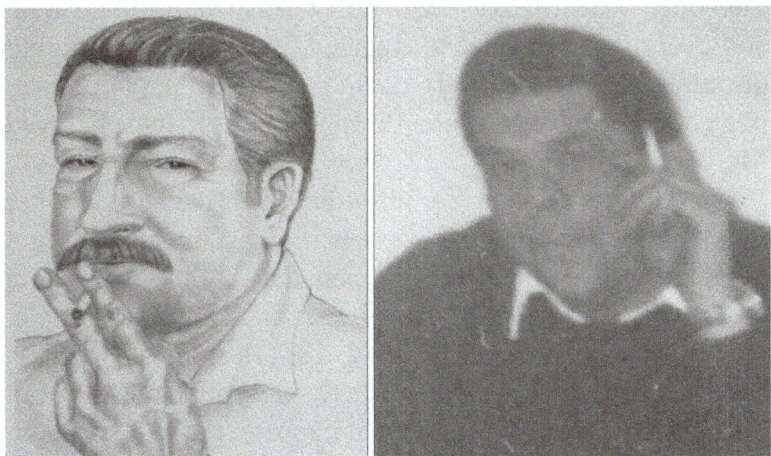

Left: This sketch, made available by the Bish family, shows the alleged abductor of Warren, Mass., lifeguard Molly Bish, was released during a news conference in Worcester, Mass., Monday March 19, 2001. Right: A photograph of her potential killer Frank Sumner released by the district attorney's office earlier in June 2021. (AP Photo/Charles Krupa)/ (Worcester County District Attorney's Office)

When District Attorney Joseph Early Jr was asked, "if he thought the sketch of the suspected abductor of Molly Bish resembles Frank Sumner, Sr." he responded, "I believe so. It's the same hairstyle, left-handed smoker. There are a lot of things that are similar" (Baker, 2021, para. 14). "We have growing confidence in the tip because a number of facts that have been corroborated to a continuing investigation have come through," he said, adding that he considers Sumner "a suspect" (Baker, 2021, para. 16).

An unsettling truth began to unravel. The chilling revelation hit Heather and her mother like a winter chill; they learned that Sumner was a registered sex offender (Baker, 2021). His past loomed large, stained by the heinous acts of rape and kidnapping against a young woman, casting a darkness over their once-peaceful lives. With every whispered conversation and every furtive glance exchanged in the dark, a haunting question lingered in the air, could this violent predator have played a sinister role in the disappearance of their beloved Molly?

The picture seemed so unsettling to Heather and her mother. Heather said, "It was terrifying, I mean, he's got aggravated rape and kidnapping charges; he brutally beat a woman, he stalked people, and he sexually harassed people. He is scary" (Baker, 2021, para. 18). Heather also added, "We might never know what exactly happened to Molly, but we can certainly conjecture what happened to her, based on some of the things he's done" (Baker, 2021, para. 19). "He was convicted of aggravated rape and kidnapping in 1982 after he locked a woman he'd hired to clean an apartment in the apartment" (Sudborough, 2023, para 6). As a result of his actions, given that he was a sex offender, he would most likely be placed on the sex offender registry today. This designation would identify him as someone who poses a moderate risk of reoffending.. This categorization not only serves as a grim reminder of his past but also raises unsettling questions about the implications of his conviction and the scars it left on the lives he impacted.

Heather's eyes roamed over the unassuming cardboard box, an artifact of a life once familiar and now faded. Among the mundane treasures lay a forgotten ChapStick, two prom mugs that whispered tales of youth and laughter, and an array of handmade candles, dulled by time (Baker, 2021). A sign, once bright with motivational mantras, leaned against the side, its words now barely legible (Baker, 2021). Four or five cassette tapes, relics of another era, hinted at the soundtracks of long-lost memories, while photographs captured fleeting smiles and moments frozen in time (Baker, 2021). Tucked into the depths, "two or three bags" of Bath

& Body Works products lingered, their scents dulled yet reminiscent of warmer days (Baker, 2021). These items, seemingly trivial, held the weight of nostalgia and the echoes of a life that once was, each piece a potential clue in the enigma that remained unsolved. In the midst of received Molly's possessions, Heather said, "I got at least a little bit of my sister back" (Baker, 2021, para. 21).

According to Francis Sumner's Obituary:

> Spencer, MA - Francis P. Sumner, 71, of Spencer, died Wednesday, May 4th, 2016 at his home. Survivors include daughters, Michelle Brown of Rutland, and Concetta Sumner of Leicester; two sons, Francis Sumner Jr, of Spencer and Steven Sumner of Worcester; several grandchildren; his sister, Cecelia Mason and her husband, Raymond of Worcester, several nieces and nephews. He was preceded by a son, Robert Sumner and a brother, John Powlics. He was the son of the late Francis and Evelyn (Cormier) Powlics. Frank graduated from South High School, and enlisted in the Massachusetts National Guard. Frank was the former owner of Sumner's Auto Repair. Francis was a loving father and will be greatly missed by those who knew him. (Worcester Telegram & Gazette, 2016, para. 1)

In a 2022 interview, Heather said the following:

> My mom in the past has often compared these feelings that we have right now to being on a roller coaster. You always have hope. Hope is an eternal blessing that I hope I never run out of. But it's disappointing. This has been a long journey. There's been a lot of errors in Molly's case. The crime scene wasn't preserved. Our local police did not know how to look for a missing person. There was some tunnel vision with Molly's boyfriend initially. There have

been lost samples in the past. And right up to learning about Mr. Sumner and his DNA not being in the coded (sic) system, there's been a lot of challenges in this case. (Becker & Madeja, 2022, para. 13)

Although her family stands at a crossroads of uncertainty, she feels an ember of confidence and disappointment by the latest flurry of leads. Heather continued in her interview and said:

It's very difficult to navigate, and I'm disappointed in the Worcester County District Attorney and state police because it's hard for us to understand why they feel so strongly about this particular person without any further reasoning. I don't even get the privilege of knowing what kind of DNA tests are being done...Instead they tell me they can't tell me about DNA. And that's been really hard. Over this time, I've earned a doctorate degree. I just feel like there's nothing that I can do that's enough to get the information so that I can sleep at night. I've always been told by the investigators, well they sleep at night, but the problem remains is that I don't. (Becker & Madeja, 2022, para. 13)

There is an unwavering sense of appreciation for those who continue to step forward with vital tips, the lifeblood of any investigation, Heather believes. Each piece of information, no matter how small, brings them closer to the truth.

When Early was asked if he believed if Sumner had killed Molly Bish, replied, "There's (sic) lot of evidence that leads to Frank Sumner, yes. That's why we first named him a person of interest and then a suspect" (Curran, 2024, para. 14). He continued and said, "We're not stopping, we're going to do everything we can to, you know, make sure that this case gets closed out" (Curran, 2024, para. 14).

In response to the comment regarding the investigation into Frank Sumner, a detective might clarify that a "person of interest" is different from a "suspect," as the former is someone being looked at more closely while the latter is believed to be involved in a crime based on evidence gathered. The detective would emphasize the importance of various types of evidence, such as physical evidence, witness testimonies, and surveillance footage, all of which must collectively create a coherent picture. The detective would assure the public that thorough investigations are paramount, involving further evidence collection, witness interviews, and potentially preparing for trial if there is sufficient evidence to charge an individual. They would underline their commitment to ensuring justice is served fairly, while also encouraging critical thinking about the investigation process by posing questions like, "What kind of evidence do you find most persuasive in a case like this?" or "How do detectives assess the credibility of their sources?"

This case has over 267 pieces of evidence for detectives to sort through, as well as more than 6,700 leads since Molly disappeared (Curran, 2024). You may wonder, Why hasn't there been any arrests in this case. Here's why… According to Early, "We don't typically name people of interest, and we don't name suspects, but we did in this case because we got some solid information that came in, we want to see a little bit more" (Curran, 2024, para. 17). Heather Bish and her family would like to see more done, and evidence sent to outside DNA experts to assist in Molly's case. Heather said, "My hope is to use my voice and stand up for Molly as much as possible and continue to look for resources available to support the investigation into solving her crime" (Curran, 2024, para. 19).

Molly's case had repercussions far beyond her hometown. It ignited discussions about safety protocols for young people and the importance of community vigilance. Parents became more acutely aware of the risks their children faced, and local officials took action to implement new safety measures in public spaces. Discussions around missing persons gained traction in the media, urging society to confront the vulnerabilities that children often face in everyday life.

The pain endured by the Bish family and others echoes in the hearts of communities, inciting conversations about safety, vigilance, and the safety of children. The Molly Bish story is a solemn reminder of life's fragility, and the unwavering spirits left behind in the wake of tragedy. As Molly's family's advocacy efforts spread, discussions about children's safety permeated local discussions, prompting community members to remain vigilant and proactive. As we reflect on Molly's disappearance, we are reminded that her legacy shines through those carrying forth her memory, working tirelessly to ensure that her story remains alive. The cold case remains unsolved, symbolizing the struggles endured by families of missing persons and the community's collective resilience in seeking justice.

Molly Bishes' murder remains unsolved primarily because the evidence collected at the crime scene, including DNA evidence, did not lead to identifying a suspect initially. Since the detectives did not receive any new information or breakthroughs until 2021, it suggests that the DNA evidence either did not match any known suspects at the time or was insufficient for a definitive identification. This delay and lack of concrete evidence contributed to the case remaining unsolved for many years. It raises important questions about the challenges forensic evidence faces, such as limitations in DNA databases at the time, the quality of the evidence, or possible investigative hurdles that prevented solving the case earlier.

As we reflect on Molly's disappearance, we are reminded of the fragility of life and the importance of vigilance in our communities. The haunting questions surrounding her case compel us to strive for a world where families can live free from the fear of losing a loved one. Molly's light may have dimmed, but her legacy continues to shine through the efforts of those who carry her memory forward, ensuring that she is always remembered.

Though the case remains unsolved, it serves as an important reminder of the ongoing struggles faced by families of missing persons and the importance of community support in these harrowing situations. Ultimately, Molly's legacy serves as a call to action for vigilance, compassion, and advocacy within society. In our quest for answers, we honor her memory, acknowledging her story's power in moving us toward awareness, action, and hope.

Anyone with information on Sumner or any additional information on the Molly Bish case is asked to call the district attorney's anonymous tip line at 508-453-7575.

The LORD is close to the brokenhearted and saves those who are crushed in spirit. ~ Psalm 34:18

CHAPTER 4

SHADOWS ON THE SHORE

Nestled along the shores of Palm Beach County, Jupiter, Florida, is a picturesque coastal town renowned for its stunning beaches, captivating history, and lively outdoor lifestyle. With its inviting neighborhoods and a palpable sense of community, Jupiter invites us to reflect on the themes of identity and belonging. The town's vibrant way of life is deeply rooted in leisure, with activities such as sun-soaked beach days, leisurely boating adventures, and an array of outdoor sports taking center stage. As a popular tourist destination, Jupiter harmoniously intertwines the richness of local culture with diverse influences from visitors, creating a unique tapestry that enhances its charm and character.

Among the spirited youth of this town was Rachel Hurley, a vibrant 14-year-old student at Jupiter Middle School with a passion for music. She would often fill her world with the joyful strains of "Oh, oh, oh, sweet child o' mine" (Ponushis, 2014). Her laughter echoed through the halls as she reenacted iconic scenes from *Top Gun*, her voice mimicking a confident "Talk to me, Goose" (Ponushis, 2014). With her captivating smile and enchanting spirit, Rachel was the heart of her friend group; pretty, silly, and undeniably popular (Ponushis, 2014). Rachel was the popular student that everyone wanted to hang out with.

However, on a fateful day in March 1990, the light that was Rachel flickered out, leaving behind a haunting void. Laughter and melodies came to an abrupt stop, and in the wake of her disappearance, a chilling silence settled over those who knew her. The carefree memories of her youth now serve as a stark contrast to the mysteries that linger, a reminder that the stories of Rachel Hurley end where so many open questions begin.

On a beautiful Saturday, March 17, 1990, St. Patrick's Day, the sun shone brightly over Jupiter Inlet as Rachel bid her friends farewell while they docked their boat on the beach. She promised to meet her mother at Carlin Park (Ponushis, 2014); the last time Rachel was seen alive. This day, filled with vibrant celebrations, would soon turn tragic; Rachel never reached her destination. Just a short distance away, in the tangled beach scrub, her lifeless body was discovered, a tragic end for a spirited eighth grader who once dreamed of becoming a fighter pilot (Ponushis, 2014). The brutality of her murder, marked by the heinous act of rape, sent shockwaves through the community, leaving behind an eerie mystery. What transpired in those fleeting moments between laughter and tragedy remains chillingly unexplained, and the search for answers continues to linger in the shadows.

On that sun-soaked afternoon, a seemingly carefree day among friends spiraled into a dark enigma in the quiet community of Dubois Park. Rachel, alongside her two closest friends, Erin and Maddy, spent the day on a 12-foot Boston Whaler, laughing and enjoying the warm breeze rolling off the Intracoastal Waterway. As the clock inched close to 3 p.m., a pivotal moment arose: the group, consisting of five girls and two boys, had just returned to shore when Maddy's urgent need for a bathroom interrupted their plans (True Crime Diva, 2023). Despite Erin's urging for her to wait, Rachel, feeling the time slipping away, made the fateful decision to set off alone, a little over a mile away from the Civic Center where her mother awaited. She ran into the shortcut path through the woods, unaware of the sinister turn her day would take.

Rachel's mother initially went to their house to see if Rachel had gone there. When she didn't find her daughter, she returned to Carlin Park, where an hour passed in agonizing stillness before Rachel's mother reported her daughter missing. What started as a casual outing quickly morphed into a frantic search. Friends and family scoured the neighborhood as the joyful echoes of laughter transformed into a profound, unsettling silence. The once-vibrant community grappled with a chilling uncertainty: how could a beloved girl simply vanish?

According to Andrea Cavallier (2021), a Digital Producer for *Dateline NBC*, "The Palm Beach Sheriff's Office (PBSO) was notified at 5 p.m. and launched a search that involved approximately 100 deputies, two boats, one helicopter, eight mounted deputies and three canine units" (para. 9). The night was thick with an uneasy stillness as the community hastily dismantled plans for a simple softball game, a pastime that once brought laughter and camaraderie. "They ended up canceling our softball game because everyone was out searching for Rachel," Sheri Duff recounted (Salzbank, 2022, para. 8).

An unmistakable tension replaced the energy that usually filled the field. Eyes that once focused on the diamond scanned the dimly lit streets, desperate to uncover the whereabouts of the girl whose laughter had been the heartbeat of their gatherings. This choice to shift focus was born not out of rivalry or weather but from a shared sense of urgency and a collective bond in the face of this chilling mystery.

As the night wore on, the search expanded into the surrounding woods of Carlin Park, where Rachel's lifeless body would ultimately be discovered—partially clothed and bearing the scars of horrific violence. According to PBSO, "Her nude body faced up and her clothing was nearby" (6:53-6:59). Each inquiry into her fate lingered like a shadow, haunting those who loved her and challenging the notion of security within their close-knit community. Rachel's friend, Sheri, recalled, "We got the call that they had found Rachel… they found her body. That moment still gives me chills. It's a moment I won't ever forget" (Cavallier, 2021, para. 11).

Rachel's body was found at precisely 8:15 p.m. lying among dense underbrush just east of the well-traveled path that wound south from Dubois Park. The area felt eerily quiet as investigators arrived, piecing together fragments of a life abruptly cut short. Nearby, remnants of Rachel's clothing were scattered, whispering tales of a struggle while raising haunting, unanswered questions. Who was Rachel in her final moments, and who was she with? What dark circumstances led to this tragic end?

Rachel's official cause of death was asphyxiation, caused by a deprivation of oxygen essential for survival. There was physical restraint in Rachel's case, the pressure applied to the neck or chest can restrict the airflow, which might occur in situations involving strangulation, much like Rachel's murder. In cases of asphyxiation, the body cannot get enough oxygen, which is vital for brain function and other bodily processes. Without oxygen, brain cells begin to die within a matter of minutes, leading to irreversible damage and eventual death. Understanding the precise mechanism and context of asphyxiation in a specific case, such as Rachel's, requires a thorough investigation into the circumstances surrounding her death.

The discovery site where Rachel's body was found harbored unsettling secrets; it often served as a refuge for the homeless. Amidst the investigation, a critical tip emerged from a high school student who claimed to have been in the park on the day Rachel died. The witness described a man in his mid-thirties with a sun-kissed complexion, dark blond hair, and a beard, approximately 160 pounds and six feet tall, a figure who seemed to blend into the shadows of the trees. This mysterious individual was seen lingering in the vicinity where Rachel's remains were discovered, becoming pivotal in the search for answers.

Four days following the tragic death of Rachel, an outpouring of grief enveloped the community as family, friends, and fellow students gathered at the First United Church to pay their final respects. Rachel, beloved by many and the youngest in her family, deepened the sorrow felt by those who knew her. Her father, a dedicated teacher, had touched the local community's heart, which further thickened the bond between those who mourned Rachel and the Hurley family. The atmosphere, heavy with emotion, reflected the profound impact Rachel had on everyone's lives, leaving a lingering sense of loss that would forever haunt the hallways of her school and the hearts of those who loved her.

In their relentless pursuit of justice, detectives interviewed over fifty homeless individuals, yet these efforts yielded few fruitful leads. The original investigators had been unwavering in their commitment, tirelessly exploring every avenue relating to Rachel's murder. In 2004, the Palm Beach Sheriff's Office established a specialized cold case squad, which took on Rachel's case with renewed vigor.

The emergence of various leads over the years faded into obscurity, leaving the mystery shrouded in silence.

Many individuals hesitate to report what they witnessed during a crime, often driven by a complex interplay of fear and uncertainty. The potential repercussions loom large in their minds, fear of retaliation from those involved in the crime, concern for their safety, or anxiety over being drawn into a legal process that could disrupt their lives. Additionally, some may question the effectiveness of law enforcement, doubting that their information would lead to justice. This reluctance creates a chilling silence where crucial evidence remains hidden, leaving crimes unaddressed and cases unresolved.

Detective William Springer of the Palm Beach County Sheriff's Office expressively remarked, "Someone deprived her of all the joys of life," as he revisited Rachel's haunting case, which he took over in 2004 (Salzbank, 2022, para. 10). Since then, he has relentlessly pursued new leads, testing the DNA of over 100 individuals to piece together the mystery surrounding her tragic fate (Salzbank, 2022). Initially, several suspects emerged, including a potential lead concerning a homeless man, given the nearby encampment at that time (Salzbank, 2022). As Springer continues to explore these avenues, the pursuit of justice for Rachel remains a steadfast commitment.

FBI profiling serves as a critical tool, designed to decipher the psychology of offenders. Through an intricate process that fuses behavioral analysis with investigative insight, profilers sift through unsolved cases, unraveling the complex layers of a criminal's mind. They scrutinize patterns of behavior, motives, and victimology, piecing together a portrait that transcends mere statistics. Imagine a detective looking through a kaleidoscope of clues—each twist revealing insights into the perpetrator's psyche. The goal is not just to catch a suspect but to understand their criminality, guiding investigators toward a resolution. As cold cases linger in the dust, the art of profiling emerges as a vital tool, bridging the gap between mystery and resolution.

In the ongoing investigation, authorities systematically tested DNA from over 127 men, ruling them out as potential suspects. Among these inquiries was Billy Fagan, a 17-year-old who notably matched the FBI's profile of a likely perpetrator. However, like many others, Fagan was ultimately eliminated from suspicion. Once charming, he displayed generous tendencies, often spending lavishly on friends; however, beneath this façade lurked a more sinister side—he exhibited violent tendencies under the influence of alcohol (True Crime Diva, 2023). Just two months after Rachel's tragic death, Fagan faced 31 felony charges related to the abuse of 13 girls and one boy (True Crime Diva, 2023). Despite the severity of these allegations, none linked him to Rachel's case. On the day of her murder, he maintained a solid alibi, leaving police to sift through the shadows of his complicated history without resolution.

As the anniversary of Rachel's murder approached, attention returned to Fagan, again thrust into the public eye after allegedly raping a young woman at a party, resulting in his arrest, a case still shrouded in uncertainty. Facing prior sexual battery charges, he served three years in prison, emerging in 2005, now classified as a registered sex offender. His past serves as a chilling reminder of unsolved crimes waiting to be unraveled.

On the fifteenth anniversary of Rachel's murder, a chilling clue resurfaced: a bloody shirt discovered in a garbage can near her lifeless body. The investigation accelerated when detectives tracked down the shirt's owner, Douglas J. Gross, serving time in prison (True Crime Diva, 2023). A DNA sample from Gross matched the blood found on the shirt, yet he maintained silence, never confessing to the horrific crime. However, whispers of guilt echoed within the prison walls; a fellow inmate claimed Gross boasted about his involvement in Rachel's death while implicating an accomplice, Franky

Washburn (True Crime Diva, 2023). Authorities contacted Washburn, who cooperated with a DNA test but denied any connection to Gross, fueling contradictions and unanswered questions within the cold case.

In prison, conversations flutter like moths drawn to a flickering flame. Inmates, dressed in faded uniforms, gathered in small clusters, their voices low and conspiratorial, as if the very walls had ears. These exchanges serve as a sanctuary, a fleeting sense of camaraderie amidst the harsh realities of confinement. Inmates talk about their daily grievances about prison food and laundry schedules to deeper, darker discussions about survival strategies within the unforgiving environment. Trust is a commodity as rare as daylight, and while some inmates forged alliances, others sought to manipulate vulnerabilities for personal gain, almost like the show, *Survivor*.

Amidst the barbed wire and concrete walls, each story carries a weight, tales of betrayal, loyalty, and the quest for redemption in shared narratives of confinement. Inmates form bonds and fracture them too, revealing the sophisticated web of relationships that could shift in an instant. The exchange of information, whether a whispered warning about a looming threat or a piece of advice on navigating the complexities of prison life, became a vital currency in the prison world, underscoring the profound impact of human connection, even in its most precarious state.

The case of Gross stands starkly unresolved. Despite ongoing investigations by law enforcement, the credibility of the lone inmate's testimony was met with skepticism, casting doubt on the validity of critical leads. The relentless pursuit of truth was overshadowed by uncertainty, leaving Gross untouched by the hand of justice.

In 2003, a pivotal lead emerged when Tami Rowell came forward with a harrowing account of being assaulted by a man named Paul Simon, just three years after Rachel's tragic death. Tami's testimony painted a grim picture: Simon had attempted to suffocate her, but fortune intervened when a brave friend rushed to her aid. Currently serving time for a rape conviction, the silence surrounding Simon's past looms larger; he was just 17 when shadows of his actions crept into the lives of those around him. The intersection of these narratives raises unsettling questions: could there be a connection between Simon and Rachel's untimely death, or do their cases merely share the same dark tapestry woven through their community? The investigation remains open, with unanswered questions pressing on the hearts of those seeking the truth behind Rachel's murder.

Rachel's mother, Andrea Hurley, had spoken in 2017, stating:

> Our Rachel, to her family, was a feisty, sassy, beautiful girl, who made us laugh with her silly antics. She was a force to be reckoned with, a charmer, who we often said could start out with a quarter, travel the world and return home with change. (Cavallier, 2021, para. 33)

PBSO's lead detective William Springer, stated, "Somebody murdered Rachel and is out there enjoying life, just went on with their life like nothing" (Idle, 2019, para. 9). The elusive perpetrator, a figure fitting the FBI's psychological profile of a likely unemployed young white male from an affluent background, remains at large, having never been apprehended. Despite extensive investigations, this individual has skillfully evaded capture, leaving a chilling void in the pursuit of justice.

It has now been 35 years. Even when suspects have come and gone, there still haven't been any arrests in Rachel's case. Sheri Duff continues to look through Facebook messages and posts on the page she helped create with her friend, "Justice for Rachel Hurley." The lay person needs to remember that even though the Palm Beach County

Sheriff's Office may have evidence, that doesn't mean that it is enough for a conviction. This just means that they are waiting for more information, possibly someone that saw or heard something.

The tragic case of Rachel Hurley represents the fragility of life and the haunting presence of unanswered mysteries. Despite years of tireless efforts by law enforcement, the truth remains elusive, casting a long shadow over Jupiter, Florida, a town once known for its vibrant spirit and tight-knit community. As investigators search for justice, the echoes of Rachel's laughter and the memories of her youthful exuberance linger in the hearts of those who loved her. Her story underscores the importance of vigilance and compassion, urging a collective commitment to ensure that no voice is silenced, and that the pursuit of truth continues until every unanswered question is met with resolution. Ultimately, Rachel Hurley's legacy inspires us to remain steadfast in our quest for justice, honoring her memory by striving to illuminate the darkness that sometimes envelops our world.

If you know anything or have any information, you are asked to contact Crime Stoppers at 1-800-458-8477 (TIPS) or Springer at 561-688-4013. Crime Stoppers is offering a $15,000 reward for anyone with information that leads to the killer's arrest.

"Do not take revenge, my dear friends, but leave room for God's wrath, for it is written: "It is mine to avenge; I will repay," says the Lord. ~ Romans 12:19

PART II

ECHOES OF ABSENCE

CHAPTER 5

THE VANISHING NEWS ANCHOR

Jodi Sue Huisentruit (pronounced HOO-zen-troot) was born on June 5, 1968, in Long Prairie, Minnesota. She was a white woman with blonde hair, brown eyes, and adorned with pierced ears. During her high school years, she proudly represented the golf team, leading the team to victory in the state Class A tournament in both 1985 and 1986. Growing up in Long Prairie, Minnesota, playing golf in high school was an experience that encapsulated both charm and the camaraderie of small-town life. On sunny afternoons, the local golf course became a sanctuary where students exchange laughter and friendly banter between swings, marking their journey from adolescence into young adulthood. The sport, often viewed as a rite of passage, taught invaluable lessons beyond the fairway learning discipline, patience, and the importance of teamwork.

Imagine the anticipation of tournaments, where classmates sported matching uniforms and gathered in the early morning dew, ready to navigate the challenges of the course. The thrill of competition was palpable, but so was the support of a tight-knit community that rallied around its young athletes, celebrating their victories and providing comfort in defeats. Yet, even in the midst of these cherished moments, there were unspoken rivalries, the pressure to perform, and the weight of expectations that came with being part of the team.

For those who played, golf was more than just a game, especially for Jodi, it was a lens through which to view their own growth, mirroring personal challenges and triumphs that echoed the broader experiences of coming-of-age in a changing world. What memories lingered long after the clubs were put away? How did those afternoons on the green shape their perspectives on life, ambition, and the pursuit of excellence? In reflecting on this formative period, one might uncover deep connections, both to the sport and to the community, illuminating the multifaceted journey of growing up in Long Prairie.

Following her graduation, Jodi enrolled at St. Cloud State University, where she pursued her degree and studied mass communications and speech communications, laying a strong foundation for her future career. In 1990, she earned her bachelor's degree and embarked on her professional journey with Northwest Airlines, marking the beginning of an exciting chapter in her life.

Jodi, a vibrant 27-year-old woman, with a very distinct Minnesota accent, was on the cusp of a promising career. At the time of her disappearance, she stood between 5'3" and 5'4" tall and weighed approximately 110 to 120 pounds. Her last known contact occurred on June 27, 1995. According to NamUs (2021), the details surrounding her disappearance are as follows:

> Jodi Huisentruit had left her residence at approximately 4:00 am (sic) for her scheduled shift at a local television station where she anchored the morning news. When investigators arrived at her apartment complex (sic) they found her red Miata convertible in the parking lot. Personal items were scattered around her vehicle. Witnesses indicated that they heard a scream that morning. Investigators are looking for a white mid 1980s (sic) Ford Econoline van. (NamUs, 2021, para. 3)

On the early morning of June 27, 1995, Jodi, a morning and noon anchor and producer for KIMT-TV in Mason City, Iowa, was set to begin her shift between 3:00 a.m. and 4:00 a.m. At 4:00 a.m., while most people were still tucked away in slumber, Jodi was preparing to head to the station. Recognizing that she might arrive late, Jodi was contacted by her colleague, Amy Kuns, her news producer. Jodi informed her that she was on her way and would arrive in a few minutes. Amy noted that Jodi had sounded like she overslept, which was why she was running late. Amy anchored the news broadcast that morning and tragically, Jodi never arrived, and her voice had been silenced forever; she vanished without a trace.

In the realm of broadcast journalism, the responsibilities of a news anchor extend beyond merely delivering the morning, afternoon, and evening news; they embody a sense of professionalism and reliability that audiences expect and trust. When a co-anchor fails to show up for their morning shift, it raises significant questions about duty and commitment. The absence can evoke frustration and concern for the missing colleague, compelling the present anchor to grapple with their own obligations while considering the implications of their co-anchor's choices. The absent anchor's failure to fulfill their role disrupts not only the broadcast but also the emotional and professional dynamic of the team.

The partnership between co-anchors is integral to the effectiveness of their performance, where collaboration and coherence create a polished delivery of news. The unexpected absence creates a rift, presenting challenges that require the present anchor to navigate a complex emotional landscape. The tension between professionalism and personal feelings could arise. The on-time anchor must adapt swiftly, yet their ability to maintain composure speaks to their resilience and character. Additionally, the audience's perception of the news is heavily influenced by this on-screen dynamic. Viewers often take for granted the seamless presentation of news, blissfully unaware of the behind-the-scenes realities that may unfold in the moment of broadcast.

Jodi's colleagues began to feel a sense of unease when they noticed her unusual tardiness; it was out of character for her to be late or to miss work altogether. As the clock struck 7:00 a.m., their concern deepened, prompting them to alert the police for a welfare check at her downtown residence in the Key Apartments in Mason City. Upon arrival, at approximately 7:16 a.m., the officers discovered a disconcerting scene. As the sun dipped below the horizon, casting long shadows over the parking lot, investigators approached Jodi's apartment, their senses heightened by the eerie stillness that permeated the scene. Parked conspicuously was a bright red Mazda Miata, its vibrant color a stark contrast to the unfolding mystery, an unfulfilled promise of a new beginning for the missing woman. Scattered nearby, personal belongings with a chalk line that circled them bore witness to a violent encounter: a bent car key lay abandoned, likely the last attempt to escape, while stylish red high heels, synonymous with her signature flair, were carelessly tossed aside. These items painted a harrowing picture of a struggle, hinting at the chaos that erupted moments before her disappearance.

Among the debris, an unidentified palm print on the vehicle offered a chilling clue, a silent testament to a presence that had crossed from the shadows into her life. Noting that there was conflicting information, the Mason City police investigator on Jodi's case said the palm print was on a light pole, which was revealed by SGT Terrance Prochaska in the Hulu docuseries on Jodi. Each fragment of evidence, a piece of the puzzle, awaited the keen eye of those determined to seek the truth buried within the remnants of that fateful night. Notably, there were no signs of a struggle within Jodi's apartment, suggesting that the circumstances of her disappearance may have begun in the parking lot itself.

Witnesses near the Key Apartments reported hearing a scream emanating from the parking lot shortly after 4:00 a.m. (The Charley Project, 2006). Investigators believe that Jodi was forcibly taken, since there were signs of a struggle in the parking lot by an unknown individual, or individuals, from the parking lot at that very hour. Since that fateful morning, there has been no trace of her. Pursuant to this scene, a missing persons investigation had to begin.

The sudden disappearance of a news anchor can leave a profound impact on both the audience and the community they serve. Viewers, who have come to rely on the anchor for trusted information and companionship, may experience a range of emotions, from confusion and concern to sadness and anxiety. The anchor is often seen as a familiar presence in their daily lives, providing not just news but also a sense of stability and connection during tumultuous times. This void can create an unsettling atmosphere as their absence raises unanswered questions and ignites speculation about their well-being. Additionally, loyal viewers may feel an overwhelming desire for updates, grappling with the uncertainty of what has happened to someone they have come to feel a personal connection with. In essence, the missing anchor represents not just a loss of a professional figure but also the disruption of a relationship built on trust and familiarity.

The next day, a thorough search was launched. A news anchor had vanished, and soon, the community would be reeling from the shocking news. Mason City Police Chief Jack Schlieper addressed the situation, revealing that investigators had few leads and scant clues to guide them in solving Jodi's disappearance. As he assessed the unfolding scenario, a growing sense of unease settled over him; he couldn't shake the feeling that something sinister was at play.

Two days had passed, and the investigation had intensified. Over a hundred individuals had been interviewed, yet no clear suspect had emerged in the case. In a powerful display of solidarity, the community united to honor Jodi with a heartfelt prayer service at Mason City Church, seeking solace and strength in their shared grief. Intriguing questions began to surface, casting a shadow over Jodi's life. Was she perhaps being pursued by a stalker? Did a stalker lurk in the shadows, fueled by obsession? Had she inadvertently angered someone within the community, an individual captivated by her on-screen persona? The unsettling possibilities lingered.

As July unfolded, the search for Jodi Huisentruit took on an increasingly urgent tone. With little to no progress in uncovering leads, Chief Schlieper addressed the community in a heartfelt statement, declaring that Jodi's disappearance was now being classified as an abduction. In an effort to engage the public, he shared critical details, hoping someone might hold the key to unlocking the mystery surrounding her vanishing.

Eyewitness reports hinted at a shadowy white van seen lingering in the parking lot of Jodi's apartment complex, and chillingly, a scream was heard around the time she disappeared. In a bid to spur vital information, a reward fund was established, swelling to an appealing $11,000, a beacon of hope for anyone who might have witnessed something out of the ordinary. With the clock ticking, the community banded together, each person acutely aware that even the smallest clue could lead to a significant breakthrough in the investigation and hopefully an arrest.

Every Sunday, the parishioners of Mason City Church gathered in solemn unity, their prayers rising like whispered hopes into the heavens for Jodi. Each plea was a thread woven into the community's tapestry of heartache and determination. Friends and family members stood alongside them, their voices joining in harmony as helicopters droned overhead, scouring the skies for any sign of Jodi or clues that might lead them to her.

Despite the relentless search operations, airborne and on foot, ceasing on July 3, 1995, the investigation pressed on. Detectives tirelessly sought answers, engaging with witnesses and piecing together fragments of a mystery that gripped an entire community. The pain of loss was palpable, but so too was the resolve to uncover the truth. Authorities successfully conducted an interview with a martial arts instructor from Mason City. During their discussion, the instructor shared that Jodi had attended a self-defense course he led in March. He recounted that Jodi expressed to the police, "She'd had an incident a few months back that she wasn't comfortable with" (Benson, 1996, para. 11). Chief Schlieper announced that there are no new updates regarding the investigation.

According to Benson (1996), a notable development occurred on July 10, 1995, when Chief Schlieper announced to the community that an FBI behavioral scientist had been assigned to assist in Jodi's case. The FBI aimed to explore potential links between Jodi's situation and other missing persons cases involving young women in the area. This move was seen as a crucial step, as it brought national attention to the case and instilled hope among the community that their concerns were being taken seriously. While the investigators received over 700 tips, Benson (1996) notes that, unfortunately, no significant leads had materialized. Many of the tips were vague or unsubstantiated, highlighting the challenges law enforcement faced in sifting through such a high volume of information in search of actionable insights. Moreover, this lack of progress added to the community's anxiety, underscoring the urgency of finding Jodi and the emotional toll the situation took on her family and friends.

On July 25, 1995, Benson (1996) reported that Chief Schlieper revealed the unfortunate news that, despite over 800 interviews conducted, the investigation was still without any solid leads. In the weeks that followed, extensive ground searches were conducted, but unfortunately, no new leads or evidence came to light. Special Agent John Lang from the Iowa Division of Criminal Investigation (IDCI) revealed that the suspect in this case likely had been stalking Jodi, indicating a familiarity with her daily habits and behavior patterns (Benson, 1996). This troubling insight raised further concerns about Jodi's safety and underscored the urgency of the investigation. As investigators continued to piece together her last known movements and interactions, they urged the community to come forward with any information, no matter how small, that might assist in uncovering the truth. The pervasive sense of unease only grew as time went on, highlighting the importance of vigilance and community support in the fight against such disturbing criminal behavior.

A growing sense of unease began to envelop the community as over two hundred individuals gathered for a candlelight vigil in honor of Jodi at the local swimming pool. This powerful assembly served as a poignant reminder of their collective concern and support for her well-being. The atmosphere was charged with emotion, as flickering candles illuminated the evening, casting a warm glow over the somber faces of friends, family, and neighbors united in their hope.

Throughout the community, signs emblazoned with "Find Jodi" lined the streets, and vibrant yellow ribbons adorned tree branches and storefronts, symbolizing both solidarity and the desperate longing for her safe return. These displays served not only as a call to action but also as a visual testament to the community's commitment to rallying together in times of crisis. Such elements of communal support reflect the deep connections that bind people together, illustrating the role of shared values and collective effort in navigating troubling circumstances.

As the weeks turned into months, Jodi's family from her hometown felt an increasing sense of urgency and concern. In September 1995, they took a decisive step in search of clarity by hiring a private investigator to delve deeper into the circumstances surrounding Jodi's mysterious disappearance. Their commitment to uncovering the truth was further underscored by the substantial reward money that had accumulated, now exceeding an impressive $30,000. This growing sum reflected not only the desperation of her loved ones to find answers, but also the community's willingness to rally behind their cause, demonstrating the profound impact Jodi's case had on those who knew her.

Three months after Jodi vanished without a trace, her case gained national attention when it was featured on the television program, *America's Most Wanted*. This broadcast prompted a significant outpouring of public interest, resulting in over 60 tips that could potentially aid in solving her case (Benson, 1996). This situation underscores the powerful role that media can play in criminal investigations. When high-profile cases are shared with a wide audience, it not only raises awareness but also encourages community involvement. The tips generated from the show illustrate how collective memory and vigilance can contribute to uncovering vital information that might otherwise remain hidden. The involvement of the public can often serve as a catalyst for new leads, which is a critical aspect of solving missing person cases.

In a perplexing development, local authorities reported that a man was questioned regarding the disappearance of television news anchor, Jodi Huisentruit, and has been charged with stalking another anchorwoman in St. Louis Park, Minnesota (Benson, 1996). This unsettling revelation added a new layer to the ongoing investigation into Jodi's case; however, Mason City police have clarified that, despite the charges against him, the man is not currently regarded as a suspect in Jodi's disappearance. As the mystery surrounding Jodi's vanishing continues to unfold, the connections between these incidents remain unclear, emphasizing the complexity of the case and the pressing need for further inquiry.

In a haunting twist in this cold case of Jodi Huisentruit, her family sought the insights of three psychics during a trip to California, filming their session for the television show, *Psychic Detectives* (Benson, 1996). The psychics presented a chilling theory, suggesting that Jodi's abductor may have been an individual who developed an unhealthy obsession after watching her on television (Benson, 1996). Despite this intriguing perspective, the family's hope for resolution remained dim. In November, three private investigators were hired to delve deeper into the mystery of Jodi's disappearance have yet to uncover any substantial leads or identify a suspect, leaving the truth about Jodi's disappearance frustratingly elusive (Benson, 1996).

As December settled in, bringing with it the chill of winter, Jodi's case continued to grow colder, much like the stark landscape around Mason City. Days turned into weeks, and despite exhaustive searches, there remained an unsettling silence: no clues, no leads, no evidence to point towards her whereabouts. The frigid waters of the surrounding dams yielded nothing but stillness, leaving investigators grasping at the shadows of hope. Each fruitless search deepened the mystery, as the community held its breath, yearning for answers that remained frustratingly out of reach.

For families enduring the trauma of a loved one missing, the Christmas holidays, traditionally a time for joy and celebration, can become a period fraught with heartache and sorrow. The absence of Jodi during what should be a festive season amplifies the feelings of grief and loss. Families often find themselves grappling with deep sadness as they are reminded of the joyful gatherings that once were. The chair left empty at the dinner table serves as a stark reminder of their missing loved one, turning what is meant to be a celebration into a painful reminder of their loss.

During the holidays, families of missing persons may honor their missing loved one. Families may begin to create new traditions that acknowledge their memory. Lighting a candle in their honor, sharing cherished stories, or engaging in acts of kindness could serve as rituals that reinforce her presence in spirit, even in their physical absence. Through these rituals, families strive to keep their memory alive while also finding a way to reclaim some semblance of joy during a difficult time.

As the six-month anniversary of Jodi Huisentruit's mysterious disappearance arrives, the weight of unanswered questions hangs heavily in the air. Christmas has now come and gone. Despite the relentless efforts of investigative teams, no new leads have emerged, leaving friends, family, and the community in a state of perpetual worry and uncertainty. Meanwhile, KIMT staff members heroically step up to fill the void left by Jodi, maintaining the spirit of her work even in her absence. The Jodi Huisentruit reward fund continued to grow, now surpassing an impressive $34,000, reflecting the community's unwavering commitment to finding answers and bringing Jodi home. Each dollar represents hope, each day underscores the struggle for closure, and the case remains a haunting reminder of the fragility of life and the persistence of mystery.

On February 18, 1996, a segment about Jodi's disappearance aired on *Unsolved Mysteries* (Benson, 1996). Jodi's family had never given up hope and tirelessly sought answers regarding her mysterious disappearance, prompting them to collaborate with the television program that specialized in highlighting cold cases. As the episode aired, it became a critical moment in their search for justice and closure, allowing them to share their emotions and the details of Jodi's case with a national audience.

The response from the viewers was both overwhelming and encouraging. In just a few days following the broadcast, *Unsolved Mysteries* received an astonishing 186 calls and 97 actionable tips for law enforcement (Benson, 1996). This surge in engagement revealed the public's deep interest in unsolved cases and demonstrated how community involvement can significantly impact the resolution of such tragedies. Each call represented a potential breakthrough, a piece of the puzzle that could unveil what truly happened to Jodi.

Law enforcement faced the challenge of sifting through these tips to identify credible information among what could potentially be false leads. This task is vital in cold cases, as the accuracy of new leads can often determine the direction of an investigation. The airing of Jodi's case on *Unsolved Mysteries* served as both a cry for help and a testament to her family's unwavering hope.

As the weeks turned into months, Jodi's family remained resolute in their search, driven by an unwavering hope to uncover the truth behind her disappearance. They organized a grassroots search party, tirelessly scouring the area and diligently marking suspicious items with bright flags for the police's attention. Despite their efforts, when law enforcement conducted searches in the flagged locations, they came up empty-handed, further deepening the mystery and frustration surrounding Jodi's case. Each negative result fueled the family's determination, but also their despair, as they grappled with the haunting absence of their loved one and the countless questions that lingered without answers.

A year has slipped by quietly since Jodi vanished without a trace, leaving behind an unsettling void that haunts both her family and the small community she called home. In that time, investigators interviewed over a thousand individuals, and waded through more than 1,500 tips, yet the murk of uncertainty lingers, shrouding her disappearance in darkness. Ground and air searches have turned up nothing; a landscape once teeming with hope now lays barren of leads. Witnesses remain elusive, casting an even longer shadow on an already bleak narrative. Just minutes away from the bustling news station, Jodi's apartment sits as a stark reminder of her absence, nestled less than five miles from where she was last seen. Neighbors recalled the haunting echo of a possible scream and brushed with the unnerving presence of a white van lingering in the parking lot where her red Mazda Miata was parked, a chilling clue that, like so many others, led only to further questions. The clock ticks on, and with each passing day, the trail grows frostier, leaving all those who knew her grappling with a painful uncertainty that refuses to dissipate.

Let's revisit the case as we piece together the chilling details that linger like shadows over Jodi's abrupt disappearance. On that fateful day, her apartment parking lot bore witness to a scene of confusion and distress, a scattering of her personal items around her parked red Mazda Miata. Among the evidence were a striking pair of red dress shoes, a blow dryer, a bottle of hairspray, a set of earrings, and a singular car key, notably bent and abandoned on the asphalt. This bent key raises alarm bells; it suggests a struggle, a moment of panic, perhaps Jodi had the key poised to unlock her car when she was attacked from behind. The rest of her belongings tell a curious story as well. One cannot imagine a young woman, dressed elegantly, maneuvering through the world with her arms full. She must have had a bag or large purse to carry her things. But the haunting question lingers: where is that bag now? What secrets might it hold?

The red dress shoes remained a peculiar detail in the investigation, out of place, yet telling. In my experience with female lawyers during my years in law enforcement, it was customary for women in the business world to carry their polished footwear, opting instead for something more comfortable for their commutes. These shoes, vibrant and striking, suggested a deliberate choice, raising questions: Who does this pair belong to? Why were they left behind? We know they were Jodi's shoes, and we know why they were left behind. We just don't know the reason yet. This small detail could unlock a deeper understanding of the crime scene, hinting at the presence of a woman who straddled the line between professionalism and personal life, leaving us to ponder the circumstances that led to her abduction.

The connection between the red dress shoes and Jodi's clothing at the time of her abduction creates a compelling thread in unraveling the case. If we consider that the red shoes were indeed hers, we must explore their significance in relation to her overall appearance and the circumstances surrounding her disappearance. When Jodi chose to wear those red shoes, they may have been more than just a fashion statement; they could signify a specific occasion (news broadcast) or mindset. Perhaps she dressed with a polished look, contrasting sharply with a more practical outfit suited for daily life on the television.

Moreover, understanding the clothing Jodi wore alongside the red shoes could shed light on her state of mind. We know she had overslept. Was she feeling empowered and in control, or was she simply maintaining appearances despite waking up late? No one knows what Jodi was wearing that morning, but we do have the red shoes. Ultimately, the red shoes are not just a piece of evidence; they are deeply intertwined with Jodi's identity and the layers of her narrative leading up to her abduction.

Jodi's case effectively displayed the social contract theory, where the community felt an inherent responsibility to care for one another. The gatherings, prayer services, and public vigils underscore the idea that our well-being is interconnected; her disappearance impacted not only her family and friends, but the broader community that had come to rely on her presence. Much of the community's concern centered around theories of stalking and obsession, revealing dynamics of a fearful society. Jodi's perceived vulnerability as a public figure may have generated a discourse on gender-based violence and the societal obligations to protect individuals from potential harm.

In the days leading up to Jodi's mysterious disappearance, Jodi was immersed in the joys of life, engaging in activities that painted a picture of a young woman enjoying her summer. A dedicated television news anchor, Jodi, spent her early mornings preparing for work, demonstrating her commitment to her profession. The Friday before her disappearance, she followed her routine, arriving at work between 3:00 a.m. and 4:00 a.m. to prepare for her noon newscast. Later that day, she joined friends for a weekend trip to Iowa City, where they indulged in waterskiing, a sport that Jodi cherished.

Jodi's weekend was filled with laughter and adventure. Alongside her friend Tammy Baker, she enjoyed the sun-drenched waters of Coracle reservoir, reveling in the thrill of waterskiing behind a boat whimsically named with the same name as Jodi. The group of friends bonded further that night, hitting various local hot spots, including a lively establishment known as Vito's, creating memories that would soon become bittersweet. After a weekend brimming with joy, Jodi took a moment to express her affection, penning a letter to her mother that read, "Mom, look forward to seeing you this weekend. It will be fun." (The Huisentruit File, 2004, 1:44-1:48). The note concluded with a heartfelt "love you, Jodi" (The Huisentruit File, 2004, 1:57-1:58), capturing her vibrant spirit and excitement for the days to come.

Upon returning to Mason City, Jodi attended a golf tournament at the Mason City Country Club on Monday, where she interacted briefly with her then-news director Doug. This event marked the last known sighting Doug had of Jodi. That evening, she visited John Vansice's apartment to watch a video of a surprise birthday party organized for her weeks prior (The Huisentruit File, 2004). Friends recall an easygoing atmosphere filled with talk of their beloved water skiing. After the video, Jodi bid farewell and left the apartment, heading down the stairs and out to her car, her demeanor still light and cheery. This was John's last time seeing Jodi.

In the investigation of Jodi Huisentruit's disappearance, her older sister, Joanne Nathe, offered a poignant reflection on Jodi's character, describing her as someone who "had the most beautiful personality" and "really lit up" any room she entered (The Huisentruit File, 2004, 0:27- 0:31). This vivid portrayal not only highlights Jodi's warmth and charisma but also raises further questions about how such a vibrant presence could vanish without a trace. As the case remains unsolved, Joanne's memories serve as a haunting reminder of the life lost and the mystery surrounding her sister's fate.

Joanne recalled her sister as a remarkable young woman, someone who embodied kindness and reliability. She described Jodi as a good kid who consistently made positive choices and adhered to the right path in life. However, Joanne also noted that her sister's trusting nature may have been a double-edged sword, her innate kindness and willingness to see the best in people might have left her vulnerable. This poignant reflection raises questions about the complexities of character and the impacts of trust in an uncertain world, highlighting how her sister's strengths may have inadvertently led her into risky situations.

Joanne looks to the heavens and often asks Jodi what happened, knowing she can't answer back. Joanne's heart holds on to the hope that one day, the truth will surface, shedding light on the shadows of uncertainty that cling to her family. In May 2001, Jodi Huisentruit was declared legally dead. Legally, a person may be declared dead by a court if they have been missing for a prescribed duration, usually seven years, although this can vary by jurisdiction. This status allows the missing person's estate to be settled and provides closure for the family. Joanne described her life as being frozen, and that you become a robot, saying everything just gets sucked out of you (The Huisentruit File, 2004, 2:23-2:30).

It now has been almost three decades since Jodi vanished without a trace, her voice echoing only in the memories of those who loved her. Despite the passage of time, law enforcement remains steadfast in their pursuit of answers, following every lead and piecing together the fragments of a case that remains open and unsolved. Determined to bring closure to a haunting mystery, the investigators refuse to relinquish hope of uncovering the truth behind her disappearance. According to Declan Desmond (2024), Mason City Police Chief Jeff Brinkley stated the following:

> MCPD recently worked with Minnesota law enforcement officials to follow up on a lead in Winsted. MCPD continues to receive, evaluate, and follow up on information it receives related to Jodi Huisentruit's disappearance on a regular basis. Information gleaned from this effort will be used in the ongoing investigation. At this time, there is no additional information for public release. We do want to encourage anyone with information about Jodi's disappearance to contact the MCPD or the Iowa Division of Criminal Investigation. (para. 3)

After nearly three decades of unanswered questions and lingering heartbreak, Jodi's family finally spoke out on June 27, 2023. Their statement, infused with deep emotion, resonated with the community, revealing the profound impact Jodi's disappearance has had on their lives. As they shared their unwavering hope for resolution and justice, they called upon the community to remember Jodi and to assist in keeping her case alive, reminding everyone that behind the cold case files and faded memories, there exists a stark emptiness that only the truth can fill. Here is the family's statement to the community:

> It's now been 28 years since our Jodi went missing, and it is so hard to put into words the emotions we are feeling as we mark yet another year without answers and justice in her case.
>
> 28 years since we last saw her smile, heard her laugh, or had a chance to hug her and tell her how much we love her. 28 years of not being able to share in experiences and make memories together with her.
>
> 28 years of pure anguish dealing with the loss of our dear Jodi and trying to find answers to what happened to her on June 27, 1995.
>
> We, Jodi's family, would like to say a big thank you to all of you who have shown up here today and who continue to show interest in Jodi's case. We know that along with us, you feel the pain and agony over Jodi's case still being unresolved. Jodi lived her life as an optimist, and she had a great passion for living life to the fullest. She was a bright light in this world, and you would often hear her exclaim "I love life!" We know that she would want us to be happy, be positive about the future, and to make the most out of our lives. However, we have to admit that, as much

as we remind ourselves to do so, sometimes it is just too hard to feel this way. We have our moments when we feel very sad, bitter, frustrated, and angry that this happened to our sweet Jodi and to our family. Jodi had such a bright future ahead of her, and she should be here every day enjoying it. She deserves better, and we continue to pray that someone will come forward with the missing piece that will finally solve this case and give Jodi the justice she deserves.

Our sincerest gratitude to all who have worked tirelessly on Jodi's case over the last 28 years and continue to do so, including law enforcement and FindJodi.com. There are simply not enough words to thank you, and we wholeheartedly appreciate your dedication to finding Jodi and solving her case. Thank you also to Jodi's Network of Hope for the great work you do in Jodi's name, including the scholarships and safety training. We know that Jodi would be so proud and grateful for everything you have done and continue to do.

We never thought a tragedy like this would happen to our family. Please do not make us wait another year for answers. We implore you, if you know something, SAY something. The pain of not knowing where Jodi is or what happened to her is a pain we would never wish on anyone. Please, help us bring Jodi home.

Sincerely, Jodi's family (Fuller, 2023, para. 1-7)

In the ongoing investigation of the cold case surrounding the disappearance of Iowa news anchor Jodi Huisentruit, new developments have emerged. Following a recent influx of tips from the public, investigators from Mason City, Iowa, undertaken a search in Winsted, Minnesota, an area that may hold crucial evidence related to Jodi's vanishing.

This operation, conducted in November of 2024,in the rural outskirts, northwest of the Twin Cities, highlights the relentless pursuit of leads that continue to offer hope in unraveling the mystery that has lingered for years. Despite the passage of time, the search for answers remains steadfast, as detectives work to piece together the fragments of a case that has captivated and confounded many. Like any ongoing investigation, the chief did not give too much information regarding the active investigation they were working on.

Winsted, Minnesota, a three-hour drive from Mason City and 104 miles from Long Prairie, Minnesota, Jodi's hometown, has become a haunting backdrop in a case that has lingered in the shadows for nearly three decades. For Jodi's family, friends, and former colleagues at KIMT-TV, each new report of tips and searches stirs a profound and painful hope, only to be met with the crushing weight of unanswered questions. Nothing was found. This relentless cycle of searching and waiting continues to cast a sadness over their lives, as they navigate the emotional turmoil of a case that remains tormentingly unresolved, a chilling reminder of the mystery that surrounds Jodi's disappearance.

Despite exhaustive efforts in the search for Jodi, including various investigative techniques and community outreach, the case remains a haunting mystery. As pain and frustration continue to mount for those who seek answers, the reward for information has now swelled to an astonishing $100,000. Each lead has yielded nothing but heartbreak, as hope and desperation intertwine in the relentless pursuit of closure.

As Jodi's case file remains open, we are reminded of the power of community and the vital role that media plays in prompting new leads and encouraging individuals to come forth with information. Continued public outreach and engagement are crucial in unsolved cases; every voice and every shared piece of information can potentially lead to breakthroughs that might bring the missing home or unveil the truth behind their disappearance. Could you be the one with the critical piece of information? Stay vigilant and keep Jodi's story alive.

Anyone with information in Jodi Huisentruit's case should call the Mason City Police Department at **641-421-3636**. Every tip counts!

"Fear thou not; for I am with thee: be not dismayed; for I am thy God: I will strengthen thee; yea, I will help thee; yea, I will uphold thee with the right hand of my righteousness."
~ Isaiah 41:10

CHAPTER 6

THE GHOST THAT TOOK HER

On July 10, 1944, in the serene town of Newton, Massachusetts, Carol Louise Wilson was born to Dr. Clinton Leroy Wilson Jr. and Louise Flodin Wilson. Her formative years played out against the backdrop of Newton until 1958, when the family moved to Wayland, where they remained until 1966. Most of the information in Carol's story came from her case file.

In January of 1966, during this time of significant change, Carol married Roberto Grau Rodriguez in an intimate ceremony at her family's home. Roberto, a man of many trades, balanced jobs ranging from digging holes to pouring concrete foundations, many secured through connections to Carol's father. However, the stability of his employment was short-lived; he mysteriously stopped going to work. Rumors of trouble surfaced after he was fired due to allegations of missing money. As Roberto grappled with the challenges of his erratic employment, Carol took on the role of provider, finding work cleaning motel rooms. What began as a promising life soon spiraled into one shadowed by uncertainty.

On May 9, 1966, Carol welcomed her son, Robert Anthony Rodriguez, into the world amidst the quiet of Wayland, watched closely by their friendly neighbor, Jane. However, the joy of a new life stood in stark contrast to the instability that plagued their family. Roberto, affectionately known as Bob, had a tumultuous past marked by repeated separations, including a notable disappearance between 1967 and 1968 that intensified the family's struggles. His absence was further compounded by his ongoing failure to attend important family events and holidays, forcing Carol to face the complexities of parenthood solo. Through the intricate tapestry of their lives, Bob's unpredictability added a troubling chapter, raising questions about his influence and the repercussions of his choices on their family's fate.

In the dimly lit town of Wayland in Massachusetts, a second child emerged into a turbulent family narrative, John Daniel Rodriguez, born on January 16, 1969. Speculation swirled around his parentage, casting doubt on whether he truly belonged to Roberto, or if his father was another man, now believed to be deceased. Amidst this uncertainty, Carol, a struggling mother, sought solace in the arms of another, Richard, around 1971. Their relationship, however, would prove to be as complex as her past; whispers of Richard's association with the Hells Angels hinted at a more sinister undertone to the household. As the years pressed on, Carol's struggles with alcohol and prescription pills deepened, painting a portrait of a woman grappling with her demons.

Ultimately, the shattered remnants of her marriage to Roberto were formally declared over on June 10, 1973, closing a chapter that was fraught with chaos and emotional turmoil.

On August 3, 1973, Carol returned home, her presence marked by a sense of anticipation as she prepared for a wedding. She chose a striking purple mini dress adorned with an intricate Chinese pagoda print, richly embellished with subtle decorations that hinted at a cultural fusion. The dress featured a crisscross V-neck bodice that flattered her figure, complemented by long sleeves that gathered elegantly at the waist, emphasizing her grace. She paired her ensemble with sheer stockings and carried a pristine white leather clutch, its gold-colored closure and clasp gleaming softly in the light. On her feet were white sandals, their braided straps leading to a modest two-inch heel, combining comfort with style. Adding a touch of sophistication, her prescription glasses bore tinted lens encased in a delicate wire rim, framing her eyes with an understated elegance. Little did she know, this seemingly ordinary evening would become entwined in a mystery that would remain unsolved for decades.

On the following day, August 4, 1973, Carol found herself in an unsettling situation as she accepted a ride to a wedding from her ex-husband, Roberto. Though their past was tinged with affection, having once deeply cared for each other, the remnants of their relationship were marred by unresolved tensions that ultimately led to their divorce. As the evening unfolded at the reception, a simmering jealousy ignited within Carol when she witnessed Roberto's flirtatious interactions with another woman. In stark contrast to the celebratory atmosphere around her, Carol's emotional turmoil escalated; she remained composed, devoid of intoxication or rage, yet unable to suppress her unease. Amidst the celebratory chaos, Roberto's response to her distress, commanding her to calm down and remain quiet, only served to heighten the palpable tension between them, marking a significant moment in a story still shrouded in shadows.

What followed became a dark and perplexing mystery that remains unsolved. It was an ordinary evening, following a reception, when Carol found herself in Roberto's car, journeying toward a friend's house in Brookfield. They were the last vehicle in a convoy of six, the air thick with tension as arguments erupted between them, swirling around unresolved grievances. In a moment of frustration, Carol exited the vehicle, storming away roughly 50 feet into the dusk, seeking distance from the escalating confrontation. In an unexpected twist, she accepted a ride from a stranger passing by, yet unbeknownst to her, Roberto had his sights set firmly on her. He trailed the new vehicle for approximately three miles, a shadow vigilant in pursuit. Once again, Carol disembarked, walking about 100 feet before resuming her search for a new ride, her vulnerabilities exposed to a world that had taken an unnerving turn. Each decision she made seemed to amplify the eerie sense of isolation, forever altering the course of a night that had begun with promises of camaraderie but spiraled into the unknown.

The timeline surrounding Carol's second pick-up reveals critical yet puzzling details in her mysterious case. Witnesses later reported sighting her being driven to a payphone situated in the dimly lit parking lot of Cumberland Farms, conveniently located across from the Town Hall. Here, Carol placed a collect call to her roommate, Susan, who also assumed the role of caretaker for Carol's young children. During this call, Susan was introduced to a mysterious figure named "Paul," identified as the driver of a light-colored foreign vehicle. Carol assured Susan that this man would ensure her safe return to Framingham. Curiously, whispers circulated that Paul might have ulterior motives, potentially seeking an invitation to a party in the area. The two women planned to reunite by 7 p.m., found the clock ticking slowly as the evening shadows deepened, and dusk crept in, obscuring what had happened to Carol after that fateful conversation.

As the investigation unfolds, the questions loom larger, who was Paul, and what truly transpired during those lost hours?

As evening descended on North Brookfield, the alarms began to ring. Carol Rodriguez was reported missing, stretching the shadows of uncertainty long over her absence. The North Brookfield State Police were summoned, along with the local hospital, as concern grew among those who knew her. Susan's outreach to the Wilson household echoed through the serene walls of their summer home at Baboosic Lake, where Carol's family had gathered. The weight of that communication fell heavily on Scott, Sandy's boyfriend, who answered the phone with palpable dread. Sandy, Carol's sister, felt the void left by her sister's disappearance seep into their summer retreat.

Carol's friends grew increasingly worried; one had called the family when she failed to arrive at his Brookfield residence, setting off a chain of events that would unravel the fabric of their lives. Notably, Roberto, the ex-boyfriend entwined tightly in her social circle, remained a troubling figure, having neither sought out Carol's family for answers nor made any effort to visit them since she vanished. The silence he left behind raised unsettling questions about his role in Carol's life and the secrets that lay buried amidst the chilling depths of her mystery.

Dr. Wilson had reached out to the police, his voice tinged with an urgency that betrayed his calm demeanor. Yet, the officer's response was a chilling dismissal, "She was 29; she can take off if she wants to." In that moment, the weight of her disappearance settled like a fog over the small town, an unsettling reminder of how easily a life could vanish, and how often those who disappear are simply brushed aside as if they had the freedom to choose. Her age offered no comfort; rather, it cast a shadow over the investigation, revealing the complacency that often shrouds cases where the missing are perceived to have the autonomy to disappear at will. As Dr. Wilson pondered this callous logic, he couldn't shake the feeling that there was more beneath the surface, a hidden truth waiting to be uncovered concerning his daughter's disappearance.

The day after Carol's unsettling absence, Dr. Wilson returned home, intent on gathering his two grandchildren, a lively seven-year-old and an energetic four-year-old. Together, they began preparations for a New Hampshire trip, a venture meant to escape the impending storm that loomed on the horizon. Yet, as shadows lengthened, Dr. Wilson felt the weight of mundane tasks burdening him, organizing Carol's possessions, from her cherished car to the apartment that had once echoed with her laughter. Little did he know that these seemingly ordinary tasks would intertwine with the unsettling mystery soon to unfold.

An officer from the Spencer Police Department had initiated an inquiry into the whereabouts of Roberto Rodriguez, only to discover that Rodriguez was absent from his residence at the time of the visit. The officer's investigation led him to Roger's home, a key figure in Rodriguez's past, as he had sponsored Roberto's perilous escape from Cuba during the tumultuous era of the 1960s. The officer was determined to unravel the connections that might shed light on Roberto's current circumstances, unaware that this seemingly routine visit would unearth shadows from a past long buried, waiting to be uncovered in the labyrinth of an unresolved cold case.

When Carol Rodriquez vanished on August 4, 1973, she was last seen in Spencer, Massachusetts, at the young age of 29; today, she would be 81 years old. Carol is a small, petite woman with a height of 5'5" and 129 pounds. According to the Charley Project (2016), she was last seen wearing:

> Taupe-colored stockings, white sandals with braided straps and a chunky two-inch heel, possibly a gold locket and chain, a purple long-sleeved minidress with a gathered waist, a back zipper, a crisscross V-neck bodice, and Chinese pagodas and other

Chinese decorations printed on it. Carrying a white leather rectangular clutch-type bag with a gold-tone closure and clasp. (para. 8)

On August 15, 1973, the Massachusetts State Police made their initial appearance at Carol's residence, a seemingly ordinary day that would soon unfurl layers of family tension and unresolved mystery. Inside, Carol's mother and sister, Sandy, hurried to pack the remnants of Carol's life, her cherished belongings strewn about like shattered dreams. The atmosphere was thick with unease as the police pressed for answers. Sandy, her voice laced with anger and desperation, insisted on clarifying to all present that Carol's maiden name was Wilson, not the name Rodriguez that had become synonymous with their current predicament. This assertion, steeped in defiance and perhaps a desperate bid to distance themselves from the unfolding tragedy, raises an unsettling question, did this familial discord alter their demeanor, or even cloud their judgment on that fateful day? As the investigation progressed, would this tension reveal secrets best left unspoken, or merely exacerbate a tragedy that had already woven itself into the fabric of their lives?

Days later, after Carol's residence was cleaned out, Mr. Wilson took to the pages of the *Evening Gazette*, posting an ad that would become a pivotal moment in the investigation. He offered a $100 reward for any information regarding her whereabouts, a significant sum that, when adjusted for inflation, would equate to roughly $721 in today's currency. This gesture not only illustrated Mr. Wilson's desperation but also highlighted the societal context of the early '70s, where such an amount spoke volumes about hope and urgency. In a world where every penny mattered, this reward became a beacon of promise, calling upon the community to engage in the search for answers.

Carol's devoted parents, willing to fight for the care and well-being of their grandchildren, and Roberto, the estranged father, were seemingly indifferent to his parental responsibilities. The question hangs in the air, why did Roberto, the biological parent, refuse to pursue custody, leaving his children in the hands of his in-laws? Was this a deliberate attempt to distance himself from his family's life, or a cry for help, masked by apathy? The court's decision to grant Carol's parents full custody serves as a pivotal turning point.

On the chilly autumn afternoon of September 14, 1973, the air was thick with uncertainty as Mr. Wilson sat down with journalist Frederick Smock for an interview with the Evening Gazette. The conversation was centered around an increasingly dire situation, the mysterious disappearance of his daughter, Carol Wilson. The haunting absence of their loved one led the Wilson family to reach out publicly, not only through the printed word but also via a televised plea, desperately seeking information that could illuminate the shadows surrounding her case. Mere weeks later, Roberto, maybe grappling with the weight of loss, would sign legal documents transferring custody of his children to Dr. and Mrs. Wilson, a stark reminder that in the stillness of sorrow, life must continue, even as the search for Carol remained unresolved. The echoes of that day lingered, foreshadowing a cold case that would chill the hearts of those who sought answers.

In the years following the tragic events that shook the family to its core, the grandchildren's lives took a significant turn. To ease their social integration and to alleviate the confusion stemming from their disparate last name, a decision was made to legally change their last names to Wilson. This transformation offered a semblance of normalcy amidst the chaos, enabling the boys to navigate the complexities of their new environment with greater ease. Families searching for the boys in local phone books, grappling with the disconnect of an entirely different surname linked to their guardians, found relief in this change. However, the question lingered, in a search for identity and belonging, what ties were severed in the pursuit of a fresh start?

As the years slipped by, the shadow of Carol's disappearance loomed larger, shrouded in a veil of contradiction and suspicion. Her ex-husband, Roberto, became a reluctant figure at the center of this cold case, spinning a web of inconsistent narratives at the local bars where he sought solace in drinking. Among these tales, one conspired to capture the attention of unsuspecting listeners, a story in which he claimed to have spirited Carol away himself, meticulously packing her belongings and whisking her off to the airport for a flight to the sun-drenched shores of California. Yet, this assertion crumbled under scrutiny, unraveling in the light of facts, as her family had already taken charge of her possessions, rendering Roberto's account not just improbable, but a blatant fabrication. As investigators sift through the shards of lies and half-truths, the question persists, what really happened to Carol, and why did Roberto feel the need to construct such a distorted narrative?

On September 15, 1985, the somber atmosphere surrounding Carol's mother's funeral was shattered by the unexpected arrival of Roberto. His presence was met with palpable disdain, slicing through the grief of the mourning family like a jagged blade. Witnesses observed in disbelief as he approached the hearse and took hold of the casket, a shocking act perceived as both intrusive and profoundly disrespectful. The family, in a shared silence that spoke volumes, chose to ignore his presence entirely, their backs turned to a man who had once been a part of their lives. Questions lingered in the air. Was Roberto's defiance a reflection of guilt, or was it something far more sinister? As the day unfolded, the complexities of emotions and unspoken histories began to intertwine, casting a shadow over an already tragic farewell.

Carol's disappearance remains an open wound in the hearts of those who loved her. While the official records never marked her as deceased, the weight of uncertainty pushed her family toward a somber yet hopeful act of remembrance. Encouraged by well-meaning relatives yearning to find solace, they organized a memorial service in her name, an emotional gathering that sought to honor her spirit amid the silence. At the heart of this endeavor lay a memorial garden at the local church, a tranquil space dedicated to remembering Carol, a place where flowers might bloom as a metaphor for healing. Yet, as the years slipped by, that garden became a bittersweet testament to a life uncharted, a lingering reminder of the love they held and the questions that still haunt them.

> As a reminder, the Massachusetts State Police is the current investigating agency for this missing person's cold case. At the time of her disappearance, Carol had long bangs and shoulder-length hair with blonde highlights. Like living in the 1970's, she also wore round, tinted eyeglasses. During that time, Carol had a scar on the bridge of her nose and right cheek. According to the NamUs website (2023), under "Circumstances of Disappearance," she was:

Last seen making a phone call at a pay phone in the parking lot of Cumberland Farms across from the Town Hall in Spencer, MA. She argued with the person driving, got out of the car she was in, and started hitchhiking. She called her roommate to say the person who picked her up would bring her home to Framingham, and they would be there at 7 pm (sic). She has never been seen or heard from since. (para. 3)

The last vehicle Carol was seen in was a beige-colored sedan. As of today, Carol is still missing, and there is still hope. If you have any information or the whereabouts of Carol Rodriguez, please contact the Massachusetts State

Police at (508) 832-9124, Agency Case Number 2014-115-0085.

"My flesh and heart may fail, but God is my heart's strength and portion forever." ~ *Psalm 73:26*

CHAPTER 7

PUTTING OUT FIRES

Firefighting is a profession steeped in history, and its narrative stretches back far before any of us can recall. Yet, what is often overlooked is the significant and groundbreaking role that women have played in this field, a history that deserves recognition. One of the earliest documented female firefighters was Molly Williams, a remarkable figure from the early 19th century. As a slave in New York City, Molly later became a member of the Oceanus Engine Company #11 around 1815. Lorraine Dowler (2018) recounts that

"Williams was a black woman enslaved by a wealthy New York merchant who volunteered at the firehouse. Williams would accompany the merchant to the station to cook and clean for the all-white, all-male crew" (para. 8).

One night, when an alarm sounded at Oceanus No. 11, the men were incapacitated by the flu. Without hesitation, Molly seized the hand-pumped hose and bravely responded to the call alone. Her strength and determination so impressed the firefighters that they offered her a position among them (Dowler, 2018, para. 9). This act was not just a moment of heroism; it marked the beginning of a new chapter in the history of women in firefighting, as the men of the firehouse began to respect and acknowledge the one who had once merely fed them.

Fast forward to 1926, at the age of 50, Emma Vernell became a member of the Westside Hose Company #1 in New Jersey after her husband, a fellow firefighter, died in service (Dowler, 2018). As more women joined the ranks, they formed teams alongside men, volunteering during World War II to establish women-run fire departments in the absence of the men who went off to war.

As time progressed, so too did the presence of women in firefighting. Dowler (2018) observes, "Like soldiers, firefighters are viewed as proud warriors working on dangerous front lines. That image comes with powerful stereotypes about who's best suited to do the work" (para. 23), a sentiment that is echoed in the fight against cultural norms that perpetuate the image of men as heroes and women as mere onlookers or victims.

Women firefighters play an essential role in challenging these stereotypes, showcasing their strength, courage, and unwavering dedication in a historically male-dominated field. They not only break gender barriers but also serve as inspiration for future generations of female firefighters. Despite facing discrimination and obstacles, women in firefighting remain committed to serving and protecting their communities. Their contributions diversify the fire service, bringing unique perspectives and skills to the team. By embodying resilience and fearlessness, these women contribute to a more inclusive society, proving that courage knows no gender.

However, the reality of the profession can be hauntingly sobering. When considering the case of a missing female firefighter, we are forced to confront profound questions of sacrifice, courage, and the value of human life. The case of Brandy Lynn Hall, a dedicated volunteer firefighter, highlights these challenging realities. Brandy, who went missing on August 17, 2006, in Malabar, Florida, was just 32 years old at the time. People often associate the Space Coast with palm trees and NASA, yet, beneath the surface, a tragedy unfolded that linked this vibrant region to the heart-wrenching mystery of a missing firefighter.

Brandy Lynn Hall was born on September 14, 1973, and would be 52 years old and stood between 5'4" and 5'7" tall. At the time of her disappearance, she weighed between 120 to 140 pounds. According to the Charley Project (2019), she was last seen wearing: "An off-white long-sleeved shirt with the Malabar Fire Department logo over the left breast and the words 'Malabar Fire Department' on the back, dark-colored work pants, and mid-calf work boots" (para 9).

Brandy is a white female with shoulder length strawberry blonde hair and green eyes. Some distinguishing features about her are that her tongue and navel are pierced, she has a tattoo of a fishing scene on her lower back, and Tweety Bird with a fire hydrant on her ankle. As far as scars are concerned, she has one on her right eyebrow and one on her abdomen. Brandy also has a breast implant. The investigating agency is the Palm Bay Police Department. According to the NamUs website (2021), "Brandy Hall is a 32-year-old mother of two and a well-liked and dedicated Fire Fighter. She has been missing since August 17, 2006, when she was last seen leaving work at the Malabar Fire

Department around 10:45 pm (sic) in her dark green Chevy truck" (para 2).

When a firefighter goes missing, terror begins to taunt the town. The last time Brandy was seen was on August 17, 2006, when she was leaving the Malabar Volunteer Fire Department, located on the 1800 block of Malabar Road in Malabar, Florida in Brevard County at approximately 10:45 p.m. One interesting point was that she said she needed to go home early even though she was supposed to work a full shift that night. Brandy was seen driving away in her dark green Chevy Silverado, not knowing she would later vanish. As a detective, we ask the question as to why she said she "needed to go home early." We also ask who would possibly want her dead? It's almost a guiding principle to look at those close to the victim.

In missing person cases, detectives are often tasked with solving mysteries surrounding those missing persons, which is a complex and challenging aspect of their job. In these types of cases, detectives must carefully investigate the circumstances surrounding the disappearance, gather evidence, and follow leads to help uncover the truth. Detectives start to work backwards. They may use various tools, such as surveillance footage, witness interviews, and forensic analysis, to piece together a timeline of events and determine the whereabouts of the missing individual.

One crucial aspect of the detective's role in these cases is the ability to think critically and creatively, considering all possible scenarios and motivations that could have led to the disappearance. In this case, why did Brandy need to go home before her shift ended. They must also maintain empathy and sensitivity towards the loved ones of the missing person, understanding the emotional toll that such an event can have on families and communities. This can be even more difficult because Brandy was a first responder, and her firefighter family is still wondering what happened when she left their firehouse.

Detectives working on the case of Brandy's disappearance frequently face immense pressure to solve such mysteries and provide closure for those affected, including her family and friends. Their unwavering commitment to justice and truth underscores the vital role they play in society, offering hope to families and communities in distress. Ultimately, the work of detectives is crucial in the search for missing persons, as they skillfully piece together the puzzle that leads to resolution in challenging cases. The Palm Bay Police have never relented in their pursuit of answers and continue to work diligently on Brandy's case, remaining vigilant in their hope for justice.

Journalist John A. Torres of *Florida Today* has thoroughly investigated this case. Like many, I was captivated by Brandy Hall and the circumstances of her disappearance. Torres's podcast, *Murder on the Space Coast Season 3*, features a segment titled "Where is Brandy Hall?" In his pursuit of understanding Brandy's story, he interviewed her mother, Debbie Rogge, and the detectives involved in the case.

When Brandy was born in Central Florida, her mother, Debbie Rogge, described Brandy's birth as being fast. According to Debbie in an interview, Brandy was born six weeks early (Torres, 2018, 5:54). Brandy and her family later moved to Bull Creek, west of Melbourne, Florida. Her family wanted the best for her since she was Debbie's only daughter; however, Brandy had a half-sister on her father's side. Brandy loved the outdoors, and her father did too. With an adventurous spirit, she and her father bonded over outdoor activities, learning to ride dirt bikes and airboats and embracing a lively appreciation for life.

Understanding Brandy's upbringing is crucial to this investigation. Growing up in the spacious land of Bull Creek, she thrived as a tomboy, relishing activities like fishing, off-roading, and hunting. Riding horses and teaching them tricks brought her joy, and with friends, she played freely in the woods, creating a happy childhood. Brandy was a natural leader among her peers, often dreaming up creative ways to enjoy the outdoors. Her husband, Jeff Hall, affectionately referred to her as a "true country girl" (Torres, 2018, 9:28). In her formative years, Brandy developed a love for adventure, frequently enjoying airboats and target shooting.

When Brandy was a child, 12 years old, she was in a bad ATV accident that almost killed her. Her mother recalled the accident and said she was at work when it happened. Debbie remembered that day like it was yesterday. The accident occurred on March 30, 1985, while Brandy's mother was at work. Upon returning home, she was confronted by the harrowing sight of her daughter gravely injured (Torres, 2018, 10:39). Debbie walked in the house and saw Brandy all bloody. She described the accident stating:

> The neighbors, they were riding a three-wheeler out in front of our property, they went down in a ditch and didn't come back. They just fell right on top of her head and smashed her whole head. Smashed it all back in. At the time, I guess everyone didn't realize how badly it hurt her. So, then we realized, he (her father) went and put her in the shower just to try and get rid of the blood. (Torres, 2018, 10:56-11:28)

Fortunately, Brandy survived the ordeal, but the experience left a lasting impact. Debbie recounted the extensive surgery Brandy endured, emphasizing the fragility of life in her daughter's recovery. These experiences highlight the overwhelming emotional journey for any mother. A mother's attachment can lead to profound pain when her child suffers, exposing vulnerabilities and fears regarding their well-being. This can be a humbling and deeply challenging experience as she navigates her own emotions and fears for her child's well-being.

The philosopher Jean-Paul Sartre famously stated, "Hell is other people" encapsulating the existential struggles encountered when we deeply care for others, especially when their suffering mirrors our own (Binder, 2023). A mother grappling with her child's injury may be confronted with the existential questions of meaning, purpose, and the nature of human suffering. Ultimately, Debbie's only child was badly injured. She may have undergone a profound emotional journey watching Brandy heal. For Debbie, Brandy's mother, witnessing Brandy's healing process may have reshaped her beliefs and values, fostering resilience and a deeper understanding of life's complexities. This may be the very reason why Debbie is waiting for Brandy to walk through her front door. Brandy's mother described the surgery her daughter went through:

> They cut her from ear to ear. Pulled her face all the way down and did major surgery. They had her in there, I think it was 11 to 13 hours or whatever it was. They had to restructure all her bones. Her jaw bones were broken, her eye was broken, and they said she was a hair from being dead. It was just a hair, so God didn't take her then. And that's what I hang on to. (Torres, 2018, 12:05-12:37)

Brandy remained tough and showed perseverance through her healing. She didn't let the accident take her down. While the scars on her face remained, they did not diminish her spirit; however, they did make her self-conscious. Brandy returned to her adventurous nature, navigating life with headaches, migraines, and her growing reliance on medications for anxiety. Once Brandy overcame her injuries from the accident, she was back to herself, the Brandy everyone knew, the outdoors kid. She fought through headaches, migraines, and pain in her adult life, having anxiety if she didn't have her medications close to her. This dependence potentially cultivated sentiments of vulnerability, underscoring the relationship between personal well-being and external factors. As Brandy matured, she learned to manage these challenges while prioritizing her family.

As Brandy grew older, she grew as a person; however, she never forgot the scars on her face. Physical appearance can certainly impact our self-esteem, so I'm sure she fought through that tough time. We can overcome this by examining how we see ourselves and how our perception of ourselves may be influenced by societal norms or personal beliefs. It's important to question whether our value as individuals is truly defined by our physical appearance or if there are other aspects of ourselves that hold greater importance. Brandy's greater importance was to her children and family.

Brandy wanted to give back to the community when she became an adult. She never forgot the people who helped her recover from the ATV accident. Brandy thought that there was no better way to serve her community, so she decided she wanted to be an EMT/Firefighter. She wanted to help people. Her passion to save lives became her career path. In 1990, while still in high school, she volunteered for a fire department and a year later she graduated and went on to college taking fire classes. Brandy's mother truly believes that Brandy's accident served as the driving force behind her vocational choice.

While Brandy volunteered at the fire department, she met Jeff Hall, who was an officer with the Osceola County Fire Rescue and EMS. Within 10 years of working as a fire fighter, Jeff had risen to the rank of Fire Chief. Brandy and Jeff, both fire fighters, would end up meeting several times on service calls. Both Brandy and Jeff started talking and began liking each other and eventually started dating. Brandy's life was fighting fires, much like Jeff's. Perhaps that's what brought them even closer. For dates, the two would go to rodeos, go airboating, or go to the movies. Sounds fun, doesn't it? Brandy was just that type of girl.

In 1993, Jeff and Brandy tied the knot; Brandy was just 19, while Jeff was 30. Some might question the ethical implications of their age difference, while others assert that as consenting adults, it is ultimately a matter of personal choice. Nonetheless, the potential for power dynamics exists, as Jeff's greater life experience could influence their union. Brandy's parents held a favorable view of Jeff, appreciating how he took care of her and supported her passion for life. Brandy thrived in her adventurous pursuits, such as working on airboats, and ultimately earned her EMT certification, joining the Palm Bay Fire Department on October 10, 1994, as one of only four female firefighters.

Regarding Brandy and Jeff's marriage, Brandy's parents really liked Jeff. He excelled in the Fire Department and took care of Brandy; why wouldn't her parents love him. He let Brandy do what she loved to do, be free. One of Brandy's jobs was working on airboats spraying weeds near ponds. She loved being on the airboat and even more so being on the river. She later earned her EMT and went to work for Palm Bay Fire Department on October 10, 1994, after applying for several other fire departments in the area (Torres, 2018, 21:09). She became one of four female firefighters in Palm Bay. Brandy didn't mind being in a man's world. She remained humble and talked to the guys about hunting, fishing, and all that "boyish" stuff.

Gender significantly influences opportunities and experiences. In the 1990s, women in traditionally male-dominated professions such as firefighting faced numerous challenges, often needing to prove themselves more than their male colleagues to earn respect. Yet, Brandy appeared undeterred, navigating her role as a female firefighter with confidence. While many women in her profession encountered discrimination and harassment, Brandy was accepted as "one of the guys," maintaining bonds with her male counterparts.

Female firefighters in the 1990s may have also grappled with internal struggles related to their own sense of identity and self-worth. Brandy had her own struggles, but it wasn't about work. Female firefighters might have had to reconcile societal expectations of what it means to be a woman with the demands of a physically demanding and traditionally male profession. Fortunately, Brandy was just one of the guys in her eyes and the male firefighters felt the same. The only dynamic thing that changed was that she was allowed to sleep in a separate area than the men, which was reasonable.

For any EMT or firefighter, ongoing training and certifications are crucial. In April 2000, Brandy achieved her certification as a paramedic and earned a promotion to driver engineer. Her dedication to her craft was evident; she would often climb her mother's deck stairs in full gear, honing her agility and readiness. Brandy's passion for firefighting was unmatched, as she would train rigorously, even in the sweltering Florida heat that made the weight of her gear feel even more burdensome. Over the course of her career, she garnered numerous accolades and commendation letters, which she proudly kept in her administration jacket, affectionately referred to as her "file." Her willingness to volunteer for additional duties and challenges only solidified her reputation as a dedicated and skilled professional in her field.

After Jeff retired, he and Brandy decided to open a welding and fabrication shop in Melbourne, Florida, further establishing their shared life together. Their combined income facilitated a comfortable lifestyle, allowing them to raise their two children well. It opened a whole new world for her. Since Jeff retired, more friends had entered their firefighter family, especially from owning a business. Imagine the get-togethers they had during the holidays.

Like police officers, firefighters rely on each other in life-threatening situations, forming strong bonds and a deep sense of camaraderie. These relationships are built on honesty, trust, and a shared sense of purpose in risking their lives to save others. Since their family and friends were very close, several firefighter families went camping together within the different state parks. One family that joined Jeff and Brandy's family was the Richmond family.

One thing about Brandy that was certain, she took care of her two children. She ensured they had the best life like she did when she grew up. She and Jeff made good money and they both provided for their family. She liked the finer things in life; to her it was gold jewelry and her big Chevy truck. Everyone knew Brandy was around when they saw her truck. But all good things eventually came to an end.

Jeff and Paul Hirsch, another fellow firefighter, were friends and business partners; partners in the drug business. Tragedy struck on July 2, 2005, when Jeff Hall, Brandy's husband and a retired fire chief, was arrested in connection with a large-scale marijuana cultivation operation. This was so large that Jeff was arrested for trafficking marijuana, possession with intent to sell, plus manufacturing a hallucinogen. This shocking event devastated Brandy and her family. In the interview with Brandy's mom, Debbie, described that day:

> It was more than devastating. We didn't know anything about it. I was on my way home and I always call my husband and tell him I'm on my way home, and he was watching the news. He told me, "You're not going to believe what just came on the TV. (Torres, 2018, 3:32-3:47)

Jeff was arrested on his property in Bull Creek with his partner, Paul Hirsch, and according to John Torres (2018), "Agents confiscated 18 pounds of marijuana and hundreds of plants, in what was described as a million-dollar operation" (4:03-4:09).

It all began with a modest operation that started with just ten marijuana seeds, purchased from *High Times* magazine. This endeavor quickly escalated, taking place in a barn and a mobile home located on their Bull Creek property.

The setup was ingeniously crafted, with electricity sourced from generators, cleverly designed to mislead both law enforcement and the utility company. The operation featured advanced irrigation and ventilation systems, marking it as a significant grow operation in the eyes of the agents involved in the case.

On July 5, 2005, headlines for Firehouse.com said: "Ex-Osceola, Florida Fire Chief Arrested in Pot-Growing Bust." This was much worse than expected for the family. This article explained a lot as to how bad this was going to be for Brandy and her family. According to Christopher Sherman and Erin Cox (2005), who wrote the article reported the following:

> A tip led deputies to a house owned by former Fire Chief Jeffrey Ray Hall, 42, who now lives in Melbourne. Hall's partner in the operation told investigators the two were taking in $15,000 a month by growing and selling an especially potent variety of pot known as "crippy," which fetches a higher street value, the Osceola Sheriff's Office said. The sheriff's community-response team found 460 marijuana plants, 18 pounds of pot and several grow rooms with watering and high-tech lighting systems in the house, sheriff's spokeswoman Twis Lizasuain said.
>
> A $23,000 generator ran the lighting and sprinkler system, she said. Officials said the evidence seized had a value of $1 million, partly because of the price that "crippy" marijuana, with its high content of THC -- the chemical component that creates the "high" fetches on the street. The variety is known on the Internet as the most potent available in Florida. (para. 3-7)

The tip received by law enforcement proved to be a windfall. Following the lead, deputies began tracking Paul Hirsch as he exited the property. What's even more staggering is that Jeff and Paul initiated their expansive grow operation while still active firefighters just a few years earlier.

This incident raises significant ethical considerations, particularly in relation to the moral standards associated with the firefighting profession. When a local firefighter, the former Fire Chief, no less, faces arrest, it prompts us to examine the ethical dilemmas at play. Jeff and Paul's actions may suggest a breach of the ethical code expected of those in their profession. Even though they were retired, questions arose regarding their character, integrity, and how they were regarded by the community.

From a criminal justice perspective, the arrest of a firefighter raises several questions about how the legal system is functioning. It was reported that Jeff and Paul were both still active firefighters when they started the marijuana grow operation. Are the laws being applied fairly and consistently to everyone, regardless of their profession or social status? Is there transparency and accountability in the judicial process? What are the moral responsibilities of individuals in positions of authority, such as firefighters?

Reflecting on his involvement in the drug operation, Jeff openly acknowledged the foolishness of his decisions, especially considering his background. In an interview following his arrest, he recounted the day when everything changed:

> Oh my God...me and the kids, Brandy was on duty, me and the kids came back from a movie in Viera and pulled in and two dirtbags walked up to the apartment, walked up and they pulled a little badge out and said they were with Osceola Game and Drug Enforcement Unit and started asking me questions

and said they got Paul Hirsch sitting here, we got him arrested on your property and we'd like to take you out there. (Torres, 2018, 7:02-7:34)

This obviously did not go well. Did they know the consequences, such as legal repercussions and damage to their reputation as firefighters? Both officers drove Jeff out to his property and later arrested him. Jeff, I'm sure, was embarrassed, getting arrested, booked, and bonded out by Brandy. The question is, did Brandy know about the drug operation on her own property?

Brandy's fury was palpable, especially regarding the fallout for her family's reputation. As we know, she was thriving as a firefighter at the Palm Bay Fire Department and Jeff was a retired fire chief. As a dedicated firefighter at the Palm Bay Fire Department, she could not fathom how her husband, a retired fire chief, had landed them in such a predicament. What the heck happened here? Jeff asked Brandy to bail him out of the Osceola County jail. Here is the interesting part of this, Brandy had to borrow money to bail Jeff out of jail. She went to her friend, Charles McClellan, to borrow $1000, which was not uncommon for these arrangements. Normally, if Brandy couldn't pay, she would build him an airboat and perform other welding jobs.

Where, then, had all the money from the marijuana operation gone? Did Brandy have any inkling of her husband's involvement in such illicit dealings? Reports indicated that money from the operation was spent on jewelry and various expensive items for their children, as well as educational tools like computers and recreational gear such as motorcycles and camping equipment. The critical question lingered, Did Brandy know about Jeff's marijuana growing operation, despite her apparent financial awareness? Randall Richmond claimed she did, as noted by Torres (2018).

Jeff insisted Brandy was unaware of the operation, while Randall and investigating agents argued otherwise. So, whom should we trust? One arresting agent, Justin Boutilier from the Osceola County Sheriff's Office, recorded in his report:

> Brandy Hall told me that she knew that her husband was manufacturing cannabis, but she just looked the other way. He also wrote this: Jeffrey Hall told Sgt. Devlin that his wife had warned him that he would eventually be caught by law enforcement for manufacturing the cannabis. (Torres, 2018, 11:08-11:35)

Justin Boutilier also wrote, "I asked Brandy if I could talk to her about her involvement in the grow operation. She stated, 'I don't want to talk to you guys, people will do anything to get even' (Torres, 2018, 11:54-12:04). Wow! What does this mean exactly? Is the cartel involved? We know what happens when people talk when they worked for the cartel. Obviously, Brandy feared someone or feared something was going to happen to her.

Brandy's greatest fear manifested just days later—being embroiled in the marijuana growing operation led to the loss of her job at the Palm Bay Fire Department. Merely a week after her husband's arrest, on July 8, 2005, Brandy turned herself in to the police on drug charges linked to Jeff's operation. Debbie later remarked, "When she got arrested that was just so devastating. Everyone was crying. I saw Jeff crying the night she got arrested. We were all crying a bit and then she's like 'Mom, I can't lose my job' (Torres, 2018, 12:44-12:59).

What other devastating events could befall Brandy's family? In December of 2005, Brandy faced a life-altering setback when she lost her dream job as a firefighter and medic for the City of Palm Bay. Rather than allowing this loss to shatter her spirit, Brandy redirected her energy toward volunteering at the Malabar Fire Department. However, the circumstances surrounding her job loss were particularly devastating. As Jeff describes it:

> She lost her job and that was the most devastating thing to her how they played that out. They already had the charges but they waited until she got on duty and went and dragged her off of work in front of all of her friends. I said that's a pretty shitty move. (Torres, 2018, 15:14-15:25)

I firmly believe that law enforcement should embody humility. Mistakes can happen, and it's crucial to remember that everyone, including police officers, is human. Given what they knew about Brandy, and recognizing she was likely not a threat, did they really need to arrest her at her workplace, surrounded by colleagues in uniform? Brandy was well respected and a mother of two; why did the police choose such a public and humiliating method of apprehension? Perhaps they acted preemptively. Had they opted for a less public approach, Brandy might have been able to maintain her administrative role until her court proceedings were resolved. This is not an isolated incident; similar situations have occurred within police departments before. Brandy's mother, Debbie Rogge, echoed these sentiments with her own reflections:

> They made a public spectacle out of her, which she didn't do anything to deserve that. I mean they should have known that. You shouldn't be accountable for what somebody else did even though your name is on the property. They didn't need to do all that. That was uncalled for. They shouldn't have done that to her. They knew what kind of person she was and bad for you people who did that to her. You know, karma, karma comes around. (Torres, 2018, 15:26-1601)

The aftermath of Brandy's arrest was painful. Although the charges against her were eventually dropped, the ramifications lingered. She had not only lost her dream job but also now carried an arrest record involving drugs, something that would undoubtedly hinder her in future background checks. The emotional toll of such an arrest can be overwhelming. Many individuals find themselves caught in a whirlwind of confusion and anxiety after being arrested, even when charges are ultimately dropped.

This experience can raise profound questions regarding justice, perception, and our understanding of freedom. Being taken into custody, questioned by police, and potentially spending time in jail can lead to feelings of fear, confusion, and powerlessness. This can have a significant impact on a person's mental well-being, leaving them feeling vulnerable and anxious. Imagine being in a 12 by 12 room with solid concrete or metal bars. I know I'd have anxiety, especially if I was innocent.

When the charges are dropped, the individual may feel a sense of relief that they are no longer facing potential legal consequences; however, this relief may be accompanied by confusion and frustration about why they were arrested in the first place. The sudden change of fortune can lead to a range of conflicting emotions, including disbelief, anger, and gratitude. The stigma of being arrested, even if the charges are later dropped, can have lasting effects on a person's self-image, reputation, and mental state. They may struggle with feelings of shame, embarrassment, and mistrust towards others. This can raise questions about the nature of identity, social judgment, and the impact of past experiences on our sense of self. The individual was labeled while serving time, sometimes that label follows them.

Brandy's experience exemplifies how society labels individuals based on past actions. Even once the charges were dropped, she found herself burdened by a label that may never fully fade. Furthermore, being a victim of an unjust arrest can shake one's confidence in the legal system. It prompts communities to reassess the fairness of police actions, the motivations behind those actions, and the reliability of the evidence presented. It begs the question: Is there a rift between law enforcement and fire services? Ideally, they should function as a cohesive team, except perhaps during their friendly competitions in hockey, softball, or basketball.

Brandy was a dedicated professional, intent on being the best firefighter she could be. Her brisk work ethic and rigorous training had always served her well, and even after losing her job, she remained steadfast in her commitment to her profession. As Jeff noted:

> First and foremost, my concern was to clear her of wrongdoing in the hopes of getting her job back. I had already retired and whatnot and so it's who she was. Like I told you earlier. She lived and breathed the fire department. I mean you can see that just going through her records. And that was what she was born to do, I think, to help people on and off of duty because she was always helping people. (Torres, 2018, 16:34-1702)

In a 2007 Florida Department of Law Enforcement interview, Randall Richmond stated:

> I only know what she told me about the whole growing organization. Whatever she told me, which basically was she swore up and down telling me that she had nothing to do with it. That she was aware of it. That she had knowledge of it, but she never did anything, you know. (Torres, 2018, 9:44-10:08)

Jeff contradicts what Randall stated to the police, Jeff was adamant that Brandy knew nothing about the marijuana grow operation. John Torres interviewed Jeff and asked Jeff if Brandy knew where the money was from. Jeff had told Torres that a story was made up about renting the property to tenants. Jeff stated, "That was one of the reasons we moved out here so that the kids wouldn't be around that stuff." (Torres, 2018, 10:26-10:33)

What did losing her job truly mean for Brandy? It meant fewer comforts and luxuries for her and her children, no more opportunities for recreational activities or educational tools like computers. Yet, there was a silver lining, Brandy's welding business provided some financial relief while she was struggling without her position at the Palm Bay Fire Department. For many, a job is a central component of their identity, and its loss can lead to profound feelings of inadequacy or failure. Nevertheless, Brandy pressed on, undeterred by her setback, volunteering at Malabar Fire Department and keeping her skills sharp.

Her former Fire Chief, Joe Gianantonio, said the following about Brandy:

> Brandy is the kind of person that comes around only once in a lifetime that is truly genuinely sincere about helping others. If you were going to be anyone in the fire service, you'd want to be like Brandy Hall. (Torres, 2018, 17:56-18:07)

Eventually, Jeff pled guilty, and his sentencing was scheduled for Friday, August 18, 2006. His lawyers felt optimistic that he would be out on bail pending appeal, but life was becoming increasingly daunting for Brandy. Life was getting serious now, the reality of managing bills and caring for the children loomed heavily on her. Her friend, Cher Ryder had this to say about Brandy:

> The last time I saw Brandy she seemed ok to me, but she seemed like she was a little stressed out to me. The most (sic) thing that was weighing on her mind was her bills. You know, she just kind of felt

like she was getting buried. It's like she felt like she was working and working and never getting ahead. We didn't talk about Jeff's sentencing hearing a lot because the kids were around that day, but she did mention that she was nervous about the outcome and what was going to happen. (Torres, 2018, 21:11-2140)

Brandy had a lot to think about. She was stressed, she was angry, and she blamed everything on Jeff. Understandable I guess, but was she planning on divorcing Jeff if he went to prison? Brandy spoke to her mother every day. Here was her last conversation according to her mother:

Like I said, I talked to her every day or saw her every day and I talked to her the night before and she was at work at the time and if she was working that day, she would always call me and call the kids and say their prayers and I told her I'd see her in the morning. She asked me if we were going to be at the courthouse and I said yes and that's the last time I talked to her. (Torres, 2018, 22:24-22:50)

She was trying...she was OK. I think she was trying not to let me know anything was wrong. Like when all this happened, she always tried to make sure the kids had a normal life so it wouldn't disrupt them. So maybe that's what she was doing with me too, trying to make me think that everything was OK. (Torres, 2018, 22:58-23:25)

As we approach the final hours of Brandy's life, it becomes increasingly haunting. On August 17, 2006, Brandy spoke one last time to her family. She routinely called home to say their prayers and good nights to Jeff and the children, ages 10 and 5. Jeff recounted his last phone call with Brandy:

I spoke to her that night. She had called to say her prayers with the kids. And I forget what show was on, it was like the finale of Big Brother or something, or you know one of the shows that was on back then, I forget. They said their prayers and I said I'll talk to you later and I said I love you and she said I love you and the kids were lying in bed with me, you know watching TV. (Torres, 2018, 23:40-24:00)

Perhaps to ease her mind that night, she and Jeff spoke about the inevitable future after the sentencing hearing the following day. It was up in the air if the Judge would allow Brandy to testify as a character witness for Jeff. Let's not forget, she was charged as well, but the charges were eventually dropped. According to the lawyers, she was the number one witness for Jeff's case. Let's not forget about spousal privilege, which is commonly discussed when considering whether a husband and wife should be compelled to testify against each other in a trial. Spousal privilege is the legal right that protects marital communication from being disclosed in court proceedings.

Yes, many people ask questions concerning why we have spousal privilege. The reasoning behind this privilege is to foster trust and intimacy within marriages, and to prevent conflicts between spouses when the husband or in this case, the wife, may be forced to provide testimony that could harm the other. No, Brandy wasn't being forced in this particular scenario. Spousal privilege is based on the idea that spousal relationships are inherently private and should be protected from outside interference.

However, the concept of spousal privilege also raises questions about justice and fairness in legal proceedings. Should the truth be prioritized over the protection of marital relationships? What happens when one spouse is a victim, and the other is the perpetrator of a crime? Did Brandy really know about Jeff's money-making marijuana scheme?

Now we approach the point of Brandy's tragic disappearance. Among the secrets yet to be unveiled lies a critical question, did Brandy's knowledge of her husband's illicit activities play a role in what happened to her? One of the last conversations Brandy had the night before her disappearance was with Jeff, according to Torres (2018), "At 9:45 p.m., Brandy calls home and speaks to Jeff and the kids to say goodnight. She told Jeff she would see him in the morning and be at the sentencing hearing. They said, 'I love you'" (2:46-3:00). Another interesting fact, Jeff also spoke to retired Palm Bay Fire Captain, Randall Richmond a little less than an hour prior to speaking to his wife.

Jeff wanted Randall to testify on his behalf at his sentencing, which Randall said he would. "According to phone records, that call from Randall to Jeff took place at 9 p.m. Brandy calls home at 9:45 p.m." (Torres, 2018, 4:36-4:47). The fire station's security cameras showed Brandy walking around the fire station in a possibly confused manner around 10:32 p.m. Brandy's truck was seen leaving the fire station at 10:50 p.m. It was learned through investigations that Brandy had used her mobile phone to check her voicemail after her departure from the fire station.

Brandy's next move was to get gas at the Sunoco gas station. She filled her diesel truck up and then she made a phone call around 11:06 p.m. Here's an investigator's trick, 10:50 p.m. plus 11:06 p.m. equals 16 minutes. This was 16 minutes after leaving the fire station and checking her voicemail. The phone call was between Brandy and Randall and lasted a few seconds past 10 minutes. John Torres (2018) in his podcast stated the following:

> It wasn't the first time they'd talked that day. According to phone records they'd also spoken at 2:49 p.m., 4:24 p.m. and 6:36 p.m. In fact, investigators said that it wasn't uncommon for the pair to talk either by text or on the phone, averaging

52 calls or texts a day. Yes, you heard that right. 52 times a day. It turns out that Randall Richmond was a little more than just a close family friend. Randall and Brandy had been having an extramarital affair and, well, it wasn't just a one-off, according to detectives and Randall. (6:10-6:56)

This just got interesting, didn't it? Apparently, this had been going on for 10 years or so. In an interview with one of the detectives, John Torres (2018) mentioned that Brandy and Randall were often called "Brandell" by Brandy's friends and other firefighters. Did Jeff not know about this? Apparently, their friends and her co-workers knew. They were always together; how did Jeff not know about any rumors at least?

The two people in the world that didn't know about the affair were Randall's wife and Jeff. Maybe they were oblivious to their surroundings or just enjoyed their life with their spouse. As mentioned before, Brandy and Jeff had two children while Randall and his wife had three boys. I'm sure there were thoughts or possible discussions made between Brandy and Jeff and Randall and his wife about the affair, at least questioning it.

Whether Jeff had believed there was an affair or not, here's what he said:

We joked about it. You know but, I never, but you know you always hear things. Saying oh yeah they're… Well, that's bullshit, because Randall's actually right here at the shop. I'd get a call saying Randall and …they're at the Motel 6 and I'd say well he's right here with me at my shop. I'd take a picture and send it. It was just a rumor. It's typical fire department, you know? There's tell tell-a-fireman, teletype, telegraph. It's typical fire department. (Torres, 2018, 7:53-8:22)

According to Jeff, he didn't believe the rumors. Brandy may have played it off; if you believe she was having an affair with Randall. Whatever the odds, Randall was supposed to be a close family friend to Jeff and Brandy Hall, and he was always around.

Let's talk about Randall's wife, Annmarie, for a minute. Like any spouse, especially a female spouse, she had heard of the rumors and confronted Brandy in a public setting. Do you blame her? Six months before Brandy went missing, she and Annmarie had an exchange of words at the Grant Seafood Festival. The firefighters were there working the beer tent so it wasn't a surprise that Randall and his wife were there along with Jeff and Brandy and every other firefighter.

Randall denied that his wife knew about the affair or that there was a heated argument between the two wives. Jeff was pretty confident that the exchange was pretty serious. Randall even goes on to say the following, "Yeah so, my wife didn't actually know about the sex part. Ok, she knew that we had no sex. She didn't know that we had sex. But my wife called that an affair of course" (Torres, 2018, 12:45-12:59). Jeff Hall rebutted what Randall said and stated:

> I heard about it from, whew…Brandy said something to me, um a bunch of firemen said something to me, a bunch of people I knew said something to me, a lot of people who witnessed this. And she just got into her shit. And um, now we know that Annmarie's assumptions were correct. (Torres, 2018, 13:07-13:32)

Jeff knows now about the affair because of a retired detective that worked on the case. Detective Sid LaDow stated:

> After he got out of prison, he did about 14 months, he found one of her telephones at home. He got into

it and there it was right there. There was no doubt left in his mind. He took the telephone to his lawyer and the lawyer had it transcribed and gave us a transcription. (Torres, 2018, 8:42-9:07)

Regardless of the he said-she said bit, there were witnesses that saw Randall's wife and Brandy having some sort of argument at the Grant Seafood Festival, only a few months before her disappearance. There were multiple entries made about this incident in the missing person report regarding Brandy's case. The community was so close that everyone either knew about the incident or was present and witnessed the incident that day.

So, the plot thickens. In his podcast, Torres (2018) spoke of that incident:

> According to one eyewitness in Sid's notes, it started when Brandy asked Randall why he was wearing a wedding ring. He asked her to lower her voice and Brandy just got louder and louder until Annmarie heard what was going on. Sid's notes also contain a short transcript of an interview with Annmarie herself. Here's what it quotes Annmarie as saying: "Brandy made a scene at the Grant Seafood Festival. She told me that I was nothing more than a two-year-old piece of shit. She asked why I was wearing a wedding ring." (13:49-14:22)

None of the witnesses reported witnessing a physical fight, but there was a beer tent nearby, suggesting that alcohol may have played a role in the incident. If the ladies in question had consumed alcohol, their capacity for a reasoned debate or discussion would have likely been impaired. Substances can distort judgment, alter perceptions of reality, and provoke impulsive or emotional reactions that divert from logical thinking. This raises the possibility that a confrontation with a lover, particularly in the presence of his spouse, could have occurred—yet the true events of that day remain shrouded in uncertainty.

Randall denied having an affair, yet he also made admissions that contradicted his denial. Meanwhile, Annmarie grew increasingly concerned about the alleged relationship between Randall and Brandy. The truth surrounding the affair didn't emerge until after Brandy went missing, which is significant given the police's intent to conduct a thorough investigation into her personal life. During the investigation in 2007, Wayne Ivy, who would later become the Brevard County Sheriff, interviewed Randall Richmond. Their dialogue shed light on Randall's absence from Jeff's sentencing:

Randall Richmond: Well, you know, she was a little upset, you know, 'you told Jeff that you were going to be there, and he's counting on you,' and I said yeah I know he's counting on a lot of people to go out there and stand up for him and say something, but I said you know you've got to remember the position I'm in as a public service employee, a captain at the fire department and everything else. I just can't do it. I don't think it's going to look good, and I don't think it's going to do my career any good. And I think she was let down that I wasn't gonna help.

Wayne Ivey: So, she wanted you to help him.

Randall Richmond: Yeah, she wanted me to help him.

Wayne Ivey: Why do you think that was?

Randall Richmond: I'm sure she didn't want her husband going to jail, I don't know. I would think that would be the, she didn't want her husband to go to jail. I mean she had comments to me before, you know, during the course of stuff like that if Jeff goes to jail, I don't what I'm gonna do and I said what do you mean? She said what do I do with the kids? I said gee, you got your mom, the kids are in school during the day. There's lots of things that can be juggled around with the kids.

Wayne Ivey: OK, so she's obviously not happy, you guys are talking back and forth and then what happens.

Randall Richmond: Gosh, I guess we talked about all the normal stuff, about the business you know, 'cause I always talked to her about business. What's going on at the airboat shop, what's going on with your business? How are things progressing with builders? And I'm sure that's where the conversation went then, and the biggest part of the conversation is where are you and what are you doing? (Torres, 2018, 15:17-17:22)

Was Brandy concerned about money in the event that Jeff went to prison? Let's not overlook an intriguing twist in this narrative. Brandy was also entangled in an affair with a married firefighter, Captain Randall Richmond. John Torres (2023) points out that "He is the last person known to have spoken with Brandy. Initially, he lied to the police, denying any contact with her for weeks before her disappearance. However, phone records revealed a different story" (para 10). Additionally, Torres notes, "There is video footage of Brandy leaving the Malabar fire station at 10:51 p.m. Moreover, Brandy and Richmond exchanged texts or had phone conversations more than 80 times prior to her departure from the fire station that night" (para 11). According to Torres (2018):

> Their communication continued even after she left the station, supposedly to go home. Brandy texted Richmond at 10:53 p.m.. Richmond texted again at 10:56 p.m. and 10:57 p.m.. He then called her at 11:06 p.m. and they spoke for 10 minutes and 46 seconds until 11:17 p.m. . (para 12)

In that same 2007 Florida Department of Law Enforcement interview with Randall, Wayne Ivey ends up pushing some buttons with Randall. Here is that interview:

Wayne Ivey: And she tells you that she's leaving.

Randall Richmond: Yeah, I'm leaving. Where are you going? What are you doing? She wasn't real clear about it, you know. I said well what are you doing right now? She said I'm waiting on money. What do you mean you're waiting on money? I'm getting money. Where are you getting money from? Who are you getting money from? Never was there any answers to those questions. Never.

Wayne Ivey: And where was she at during that call?

Randall Richmond: Well, she told me she was at the Sunoco.

Wayne Ivey: OK, which Sunoco?

Randall Richmond: I'm assuming it would be the one, which is what I told in the interview and everything before, it would have been on the west side of 95, the big one. Because there's another one on the other side that used to be called The Store but that is a Sunoco also. I'm assuming that's where she would have been. She never really said.

Wayne Ivey: Now that conversation became pretty emotional right? Between you and her? Her saying she's leaving?

Randall Richmond: Well, it became confusing. What do you mean you're leaving? Where are you going? You can't leave. Aren't you violating something to do with what has happened with your drugs? I didn't know, I thought I remembered something at some time about how she couldn't leave the area. Maybe I'm wrong, I didn't know. You know, you can't leave, aren't you going to be violating something.

What are you going to do about the kids? What about Jeff? How are you going to take care of the kids? You can't leave. You know, things like that. And like I said, nothing was ever answered whether she was leaving for an hour, three hours.

Wayne Ivey: So, she wasn't answering anything?

Randall Richmond: No, she was very vague in all of it.

Wayne Ivey: So, she didn't tell you she wasn't coming back?

Randall Richmond: Nope, nope.

Wayne Ivey: She just said I'm leaving? OK, like you said just now, for all you knew she could have been leaving for a day or three hours or whatever. OK, alright, now, you hang up the phone with her and that's it?

Randall Richmond: No, I told her do I need to come down there? No, you don't need to come down here. Don't come down here. And pretty much I left it at that. (Torres, 2018, 17:34-20:04)

Inaction carries significant weight in the realm of investigation, particularly when examining an individual's life patterns. Each person's journey is uniquely defined by their experiences, choices, and values, creating a singular trajectory. Envision your life as a winding road, marked by its own twists and turns, as well as moments of both triumph and challenge. Each day is filled with decisions, the formation of relationships, and new experiences that collectively shape who you are and where you are heading. Over time, these events and choices weave a distinct rhythm into your life, continuously evolving as people come and go. You may face setbacks, but you also experience victories and accomplishments. Your life story is not a static narrative; it is vibrant and ever-changing.

In this context, the pattern of life becomes critically important. Consider the phone call between Randall and Brandy: it lasted 10 minutes and 46 seconds, concluding at 11:57 p.m.. The investigation revealed that Brandy and Randall typically communicated an average of 52 times a day through calls and texts. If someone you deeply cared about suddenly went missing, wouldn't you flood their phone with calls and messages? Personally, I know I would. This makes Randall's inaction particularly troubling.

Let's think rationally. Brandy had two children at home. If Jeff was heading to prison, would we truly believe she would simply "leave" and escape the situation? Her kids were her life. This raises an interesting question: Why would a married woman and mother of two just vanish? People don't usually disappear without reason. Although we often tend to think the worst, it's essential to remember that Brandy wasn't a child, she was an adult. Adults are generally expected to handle their lives independently, right? As a firefighter, she was trained to be tough. So, what could have compelled her to leave so abruptly? Was it her children? Her husband?

For nearly two decades, this case has captivated the Space Coast, leaving many to ponder the mystery surrounding Brandy's disappearance. According to Torres (2018), his team reached out to Randall in search of answers. However, Randall's lawyer indicated that responses would be provided via email. Torres also reported that Randall mentioned Brandy "seemed a bit apprehensive" during their last late-night conversation. Additionally, in the same email from Randall, Torres noted that she told him, "She was waiting on someone she was borrowing money from" (Torres, 2018, 21:04-21:07). What are your thoughts on this? I have my own opinions, but let's focus on the facts.

Jeff Hall's attorney called him with an important update: his sentencing hearing had been rescheduled to an earlier time. Knowing Brandy's routine, he was aware that she worked the morning shift. Concerned about the change,

Jeff decided to reach out to her at 11:48 p.m. to ensure she was informed. However, his call went unanswered. He tried contacting her via Nextel, but again, there was no response.

In an unexpected turn, Torres, a Palm Bay police officer, was on patrol when he noticed a striking sight, a red Chevy Suburban belonging to a Palm Bay fire captain parked at a Hess gas station. The officer made a mental note of the vehicle, driven by a natural curiosity, as this station was conveniently located near I-95 on Malabar Road. Retired Palm Bay Detective Sid LaDow stated the following:

> A couple of minutes later, along came a Palm Bay police officer and saw that vehicle there. And wondering what it was doing there she got out and looked around and said well, I guess some firefighter is out there checking something. She got back in her vehicle and drove around to the back of the place she saw over there at the Home Depot but where they sell trees and stuff, she saw a big pickup truck. So, she went down there. She could tell as she neared it and turned her lights on high. The driver was a lady, had long blonde hair, and there was another person in the front seat with her. She drove around to the back and was going to call in the tag. (Torres, 2018, 22:10-22:55)

It is not uncommon for a police officer to investigate a vehicle that appears "suspicious." In this instance, it is presumed that the large pickup truck in question is Brandy's green Silverado. When officers encounter such a vehicle, they engage in a quick, instinctive assessment of the situation, weighing various factors to determine if the vehicle presents a legitimate threat or is merely an ordinary sight.

The officer's initial instinct often draws on their training and experience, prompting them to consider questions like: "Is this vehicle out of place? Does it seem unusual for this location?" They may take note of the vehicle's make, model, and color, as well as any distinctive features, such as tinted windows or a modified suspension—that could indicate something amiss.

In Brandy's case, the officer noted that the driver was a woman with long blonde hair and that a second person was seated in the front passenger seat; however, the identity of that individual remains unknown. It is crucial for the officer to consider the context in which the vehicle was encountered. For instance, they might ask, "Is this vehicle parked in an area known for high crime rates or recent criminal activity?"

The officer should also closely observe the driver's behavior for any signs of nervousness, evasiveness, or suspicious activity. Questions may arise in the officer's mind: "Is the driver acting normally? Are they hesitant to provide information or exhibiting signs of anxiety?" It's worth noting that the officer never made contact with the driver, or the other occupants of the truck parked behind the Home Depot.

Throughout the investigation of the suspicious vehicle, the officer will continually weigh and reassess various factors to determine the appropriate course of action, whether to approach the vehicle, conduct a more thorough investigation, or move on to another priority. There's a reason why the officer didn't call in the tag or possibly investigate further; that reason was because there was a foot pursuit going on and the radio channel had to remain clear for those officers involved in the pursuit. It is also normal not to change dispatchers until the air is clear.

My question is: why didn't the officer change channels to run the truck tag? While I can't provide an answer to that, I do know what I would have done in her position. The officer appeared to assume that nothing was amiss, especially since the fire captain's vehicle was parked out front. It wasn't until she had completed her shift and heard the missing person report the next day that she turned in a tip sheet.

The officer had done her duty. During the investigation of Brandy's disappearance, one of the detectives interviewed another officer who was handling administrative tasks due to an injury. This officer distinctly recalled writing and submitting the tip sheet that day. And just like that—poof—Brandy was gone.

As hours passed, no one seemed to notice her absence. It wasn't until the following day that anyone began to realize Brandy was missing. Meanwhile, Jeff waited at the courthouse, but Brandy never arrived. His attempts to reach her by phone went unanswered. As previously mentioned, this was not typical behavior for Brandy. Concerned, Jeff reached out to her friends in search of answers. In his growing desperation, he confided his worries to John Torres:

> So, I was in a panic. I tried to call Brandy that morning and she didn't answer her phone. Unlike her. It was unlike her because she had two phones. She had a Nextel and an ATT. Then I called the fire station and they said that she had left last night, that she went home sick, and I started freaking out. So, I started calling everybody. (Torres, 2018, 5:05-5:21).

As you can imagine, Jeff called Randall because he was a close friend. However, at that time, he had no idea they were having an affair. Here is what Jeff had to say about that conversation:

> I said have you talked to Brandy, and he said I haven't talked to her, I didn't even talk to her yesterday was what he told me. I haven't talked to her. I haven't talked to her. I said, OK, well that's kind of weird because I can't get a hold of her and everybody's calling now, we're calling everybody. (Torres, 2018, 5:35-5:49).

Along with Jeff, Brandy's mother, Debbie, began to worry. Everyone was at the courthouse, except for Brandy, and of course, Randall. Like any mother connected to her child, Debbie felt that something was wrong. The "what ifs" started to creep in, and her mind raced with the worst-case scenarios. Debbie knew it wasn't like Brandy to not show up. Meanwhile, Jeff received his sentence: 18 months in prison and 42 months of probation for drug charges. After the court hearing, Debbie and her family went to a friend's house to try and figure out where Brandy might be.

As the investigation unfolds, the police find few clues about Brandy's disappearance, and the case may not be as straightforward as it initially seemed. As we know, this situation is becoming more and more complicated. Here is what we know so far:

- Brandy was having an extramarital affair with Randall, the Fire Caption for Palm Bay Fire Department, who was also a family friend for many years.

- The affair was only a secret to Jeff and Randall's wife, everyone else knew.

- There was a heated exchange at the festival six months prior between Brandy and Randall's wife. There were several witnesses.

- Randall spoke to Jeff the night prior to his sentencing hearing and told him he'd be there for him in court, but he never showed up.

- Randall stated he spoke to Brandy and told her that he wasn't going to go to Jeff's sentencing to support him as a witness.

- Brandy told Randall that she was leaving, but that may or may not be true.

- Brandy's truck was last seen at a gas station with a blond female inside and another unknown individual.

- Brandy owned a gun and always had it in her truck, the gun was never recovered.

As we can see, the complications in this case continue to grow. Who is telling the truth? Who is being honest? Who might be avoiding the police? There are so many questions, and so few answers.

Now, it's the following day, August 18, 2006. Twelve hours have passed, and it's early Friday afternoon. Imagine yourself out fishing on a peaceful lake, enjoying the serenity of nature. As you reel in your catch, you notice something unusual, a truck hidden in the water, surrounded by trees. As you get closer, you realize it's a newer pickup truck. Suddenly, it hits you: this could be a missing person's vehicle.

That's essentially what happened. An individual was fishing near Eastern Florida State College, formerly Brevard Community College, at a pond that wasn't well known. His fishing line got snagged on something. When he looked closer, he saw that the line was caught on bunker gear belonging to a firefighter. The good citizen brought the gear to the Palm Bay Fire Department, which was very close to where he was fishing.

The name on the gear said Malabar Volunteer Fire Department—the same volunteer fire department where Brandy had worked the night before she went missing.

Initially, some time was spent searching the area without law enforcement involvement. However, after a few hours, someone realized that it was necessary to bring law enforcement into the search. Detective Mike Pusatere had been supervising Brandy's case. When they finally searched the pond more thoroughly, they discovered that the bunker gear wasn't the only thing near the water. According to John Torres (2018), "Along with her bunker gear, Brandy's cooler with a few cans of beer and a few sodas still cool to the touch, were found floating as well" (Torres, 2018, 8:48-8:58).

Now, the official investigation begins. Detectives learned that Brandy's husband and family had tried to contact her, but no one could find her. They also discovered that she never showed up to Jeff's sentencing and had not made it home (Torres, 2018). As in any case, the detectives called in their forensics unit to process the scene. Here is what Crime Scene Investigator John Hollister said when he arrived at the scene that day near the pond:

> When I arrived on scene, I spoke with Cpl. Aiello, who advised that the fire department had found an area on the west side of the lake where it appeared that a vehicle had gone into the water. They surmised from a cooler that was floating in the lake and also the bunker gear that the firefighter's vehicle may have gone into the water. Whenever we have a scene that is a potential crime scene, they would need to restrict the access to that. We will rope it off as a crime scene using yellow crime scene tape. At that point, someone is assigned to that scene and documents anybody's comings and goings out of that scene: who they are, what time they came in,

what time they left, what they're doing there. When the vehicle is recovered from the water, we have no idea what has gone on in and around this vehicle. All we know is that a vehicle has gone into the water. We don't know why. We don't know whether it's an accident. We don't know if it's an attempt to conceal a stolen vehicle. We don't know whether it's a suicide, a homicide. (Torres, 2018, 9:24-10:24)

Debbie was obviously worried about her daughter, as anyone in her position would be, thinking the worst, like any normal human being. Perhaps Brandy had been in a car accident and was in the hospital. While that seemed less likely now, a mother's mind tends to go to these possibilities. The mother-daughter bond can be seen as a unique and intimate connection that transcends language and logic. This bond is often rooted in a deep emotional and instinctual understanding that's difficult to put into words.

Realistically, mothers have a kind of sixth sense when it comes to their children. They may instinctively know when their daughter is upset or needs comfort, without needing to be explicitly told. This sense of care isn't necessarily based on logical reasoning or clear communication but rather on a deep emotional connection, one rooted in shared experiences and a natural, instinctive understanding. Any mother would recognize this innate awareness.

Have you ever had a feeling that something was wrong, especially when you share a deep connection with someone? Not to go off-topic, but I remember when I was a teenager. My mother and I were out getting pizza when we heard a fire engine with sirens blaring. I saw the ladder truck head toward our neighborhood, and instinctively, I told my mom we had to leave, immediately.

As we hurried home, we discovered that my best friend's house across the street was engulfed in flames. Everyone had already gone to my house, worried about me because I was always over there. That moment was life-changing for my best friend at the time, but it also made me realize just how strong the connection was between me and my neighbors. Sometimes, our instincts and feelings can reveal truths that words cannot fully express.

Don't forget, Brandy was involved in a terrible accident when she was younger, and her mother's instincts immediately came into play when Brandy didn't show up for Jeff's sentencing hearing. Imagine this: your daughter's friend approaches you, breathless, and says, "We found the truck." How would you react?

Here is what Debbie said when that happened:

> I was coming up to the stop sign and that's when I met one of her friends. She got out of the car and come running to me and she said they just found Brandy's truck. They just pulled Brandy's truck out of the pond. And I was like, "What?" and so we went over to the fire station and that's when we learned what was going on. (Torres, 2018, 10:45-11:03)

Remember, Brandy loved her truck, she cherished it as one of her prized possessions. Many people knew Brandy and her truck; it was almost like one and the same. Family and friends knew that when they saw her truck, Brandy was either coming or at that location. Her dark green 2002 Chevy Silverado was found submerged in the pond where the fisherman had been fishing. The last time anyone saw the truck was when an officer discovered it parked behind the Home Depot.

The pond where Brandy's Chevy was found wasn't a well-known spot. So, how did her truck end up in the water? This area was secluded, one of the hidden "spots" where Brandy and Randall, yes, Randall, would meet. To back up a bit, the fire academy is located near the pond, so most of those familiar with it know how to find this secluded area. The pond itself is used to supply water for firefighting purposes, which explains its existence and why it's sometimes used as a quiet meeting spot.

The location where Brandy's truck was found had a damaged tree nearby, most likely from when the suspect put the vehicle into the water. A helicopter had flown over the pond and was able to see the top of Brandy's truck submerged beneath the surface (Torres, 2018). With the truck now located, authorities faced the challenge of figuring out how to recover it.

Experts from various fields, such as engineering, environmental science, fire and rescue, and law enforcement, were called in to assess the situation. They examined the truck's condition, the water quality of the pond, and the surrounding environment to determine the best course of action.

Deciding how to proceed involved careful consideration of potential risks, costs, and the possible environmental impact, including effects on local wildlife and nearby communities, even though the area was secluded. A team of specialists was assembled to coordinate the recovery efforts. This team likely included salvagers, divers, environmental experts, and emergency responders.

The recovery team took steps to minimize environmental impact. They would have worked to contain any spills, protect nearby water sources, and prevent further pollution, especially since the truck could contain fuel or other contaminants. Using specialized equipment and techniques, they carefully extracted the truck from the pond to ensure safety and environmental safety. Once the truck was removed, the team would proceed to clean up any remaining debris or pollutants from the pond, if any were present, to restore the area as much as possible.

Let's take a moment to remember Jeff. He was convicted and sentenced to 18 months in prison the day before Brandy's truck was discovered. However, his attorneys appealed the decision, and the judge granted Jeff bond, allowing him to be released while awaiting his appeal. During that time, Jeff had to wait in a holding cell at the Osceola County jail until his bond was processed. Imagine being locked up, with your wife missing, and then glancing at the television. Here is what Jeff had to say about that moment:

> Yeah, I'm in a general population holding cell, you know, still in my clothes from court and stuff like that and I see them pulling Brandy's truck out and they start talking about me on the TV and then they came and got me and put me in another room. Then they put my co-defendant in the room with me, you know. So, yeah, I saw it breaking on the TV and I started making phone calls and I just called my mom, and they were crying and then we started talking. They said what's going on Jeff? And I said, 'you tell me.' I see, I can't hear it, but I can see it. I couldn't hear what was going on. They had my name flashing on the TV. I was freaking the hell out, yes, and then within about 15 minutes, it was like every five minutes they came in with a media request, media request. I said no, no, no, no. Because I'm knowing now, putting two and two together they got the truck up and out, the door open and water's pouring out and the little scroll is along the bottom you're trying to read, they got my name plastered all over the TV and stuff like that. So, I'm freaking out and everyone is saying, oh ok, well it's this dude right here. And yeah, so it was kind of freaky. (Torres, 2018, 13:47-14:55).

Word spread quickly across Palm Bay and Malabar that Brandy was missing, and her beloved truck was found in the pond. What were the odds that a well-known person in the community would go missing? When the truck was finally pulled out of the water, it left behind some intriguing evidence, most notably, Brandy's cooler with floating cans that were still cold to the touch. And of course, everyone loves DNA evidence, right? Well, the evidence recovered included blood, quite a substantial amount of it, raising many questions about what had happened.

The crime scene investigators found blood inside Brandy's truck, located on the driver's side door and beneath the steering wheel. The amount of blood was significant, and the truck's windows were rolled down. It appeared that the person who pushed the truck into the pond wanted to ensure it filled with water, sank, and destroyed any potential evidence.

Another critical detail that the suspect may not have considered was the blood itself. The blood had been allowed to mostly dry before the truck was pushed into the water. This was a forensic "touchdown"—meaning the truck wasn't pushed into the pond immediately after the blood was shed.

This raises troubling questions: Did someone kill Brandy while they were meeting her at the pond, leave the blood evidence behind, then dispose of her body separately, only to return later and push the truck into the water? Was there enough blood to cause her death? Many questions remain.

Here is what retired Detective Sid LaDow said about this discovery:

> In looking at the photographs, I never got to see the truck. There was a big clot of blood directly underneath the steering wheel and a bit to the left over toward the door. And that got me curious, and we called around and we were told that if that truck had went into the water immediately um the blood wouldn't be there. But the truck sat out long enough for that to coagulate. And when it went into the water, 15 feet of water, it stayed there, it did not

melt. That told me something there. (Torres, 2018, 16:56-17:35)

And here is what Sid's partner, retired Detective Doc Jones, had to say about those same findings:

> It appears to me that the truck sat on dry land at least six or eight hours. And that is based on blood inside the cab. That wasn't washed away when the truck was under water. It had to dry, ok? Blood doesn't dry in 15 minutes. So how long does it take? Best estimate is 5, 6, 7 hours. And there was enough blood on the inside of the door panel to show that it was there; that means to me, no one else has said this but that means to me that the truck sat on dry land for several hours before going into the water, ok. Where is her body? I don't know. (Torres, 2018, 17:56-18:37)

When discussing blood drying, it refers to the process of evaporation—a complex event influenced by various factors. In the case of blood, drying occurs when the liquid component loses water and transitions into a solid state. The rate at which this happens depends on several key factors.

First, temperature plays a significant role. Higher temperatures accelerate evaporation, while cooler temperatures slow it down. For example, blood left at room temperature (around 20°C or 68°F) might take several hours to dry, whereas in a hot and dry environment (say, 30°C or 86°F), it could dry in just a few minutes.

Second, humidity affects drying too. Air with low humidity allows for faster evaporation because there is less moisture in the air to compete with the water in the blood. Conversely, high humidity slows the process down, making the blood take longer to dry.

Third, air circulation is important. Good airflow can speed up evaporation by increasing the surface area exposed to air and by reducing the concentration of water vapor near the blood's surface. In Brandy's case, the open windows might have aided this process by promoting better air circulation.

Finally, the volume of blood itself matters. Larger amounts of blood contain more water and thus require more time to dry completely. So, the more blood there is, the longer the drying process takes.

It might sound like simple math, but understanding these factors helps forensic investigators piece together timelines and events. Now, let's ponder a hypothetical scenario: a large amount of blood is spilled on the surface. How long does it take for it to dry? Assuming a moderate temperature (around 20°C/68°F), moderate humidity (around 50%), and average air circulation, here's a rough estimate of what it would take to dry:

- Small amount of blood (e.g., 1-2 mL): 1-2 hours

- Medium amount of blood (e.g., 10-20 mL): 2-4 hours

- Large amount of blood (e.g., 100-200 mL): 4-6 hours

Keep in mind that these are rough estimates and can vary significantly based on the specific conditions discussed earlier, temperature, humidity, air circulation, and blood volume. Forensic experts often employ specialized techniques and equipment to analyze bloodstains and more accurately estimate their age.

In this case, Detective Doc Jones was considering a timeframe of approximately five to seven hours for the blood to have dried. August in Malabar, Florida, is typically a hot month, with high humidity levels from June through August, and it often experiences the most rainfall of the year. Daylight hours are just over 13 hours, which provides more time for the suspect to move through the night under the cover of darkness. All these factors, hot weather, high humidity, extended daylight, could influence how quickly the blood dried and, consequently, how much time the suspect had to act before the blood evidence was no longer fresh.

The crime scene investigators did an excellent job processing the truck, especially in collecting the blood evidence. However, there was one crucial piece of evidence that was missing: Brandy's gun. Brandy always kept her gun in her truck and never went anywhere without it. Most people who knew Brandy were aware that she carried her firearm with her regularly. This raises important questions: Could Brandy have been shot by her own gun? Was the blood found in the truck her own? Here is what Detective Mike Pusatere had to say about the DNA found in Brandy's truck:

> One of the windows was down, I believe it was the back passenger window was down so that when the water comes in it would have a washtub effect and there was some blood found in the truck that we had tested for DNA, and it was tested positive to her parent's biological daughter, and they only had her so it wasn't like a sister or somebody else, it was her blood. (Torres, 2018, 20:27-20:46)

Now that Brandy's truck had been recovered and blood was discovered inside, the investigators needed to locate her body. It was time to notify the dive team. When a police dive team searches for and attempts to recover a body from a pond, it is often a painstaking and meticulous process. The water in such ponds is almost always murky, making visibility limited. The dive team carefully navigates the waters, searching for signs of human remains by waving their hands in front of them and feeling around. They may also utilize specialized equipment, such as sonar devices or underwater cameras, to aid their search.

If human remains are found, the dive team proceeds with great care, extracting the body slowly and deliberately to avoid causing further damage or disturbance to the deceased. This process requires patience, precision, and a deep respect for the gravity of the task.

Here is what retired Palm Bay Lt. Joe Eakins said about the search of the scene in 2006:

> When we pulled the truck out, we checked the vehicle, we're not finding anybody in the vehicle. It wasn't a stolen vehicle so we were concerned with suicide, homicide, so at that particular point given the characteristics of the lake and the nature of the investigation itself, we decided we wanted to be 100 percent she wasn't in or around that lake, and we may have missed something because once again the conditions were, they were deep, and it was dark. So, we decided at that point we figured we would try to figure out a way to drain the lake.
>
> We had public works come out, they built a dam, we were able to block that off and then we were able to pump out the water, it took about two days to get the lake completely drained. And at that point we confirmed that she was nowhere in that search area we were looking. We are looking for anything. Anything that's out of the ordinary, anything that looks suspicious; we won't overlook anything. (Torres, 2018, 21:30-22:22)

The detectives understood the importance of thoroughness at the scene. Their decision to drain the lake to ensure they hadn't missed anything demonstrates a strong commitment to meticulous investigation and attention to detail in the search for Brandy. The detective's acknowledgment that some evidence might have been overlooked due to the deep and dark water highlights the inherent limitations of human knowledge. No matter how careful we are, there is always the possibility that certain aspects of reality remain beyond our complete understanding, reminding us of the bounds of certainty and the importance of relentless pursuit of the truth.

As the police continue to investigate Jeff's potential involvement in Brandy's case, initially believed to be a missing person case, but now possibly a murder, they are not only seeking physical evidence of a crime but also trying to assess the moral implications of Jeff's actions. They are asking themselves whether Jeff's conduct was morally justified or if he bears responsibility for Brandy's death, should she have been murdered. It is common practice to begin investigations by examining the husband and close friends, as they are often the most immediate persons of interest.

Retired FDLE agent Tom Davis shared his insights on the investigation into Brandy's close family and friends:

> I said, 'We probably should talk to the husband. Where is he? They said, 'Oh, he's over in Osceola Jail.' I said, 'Fine." Nobody seemed really enthusiastic. Well, he was in jail. And I said 'How about I go over and talk to the husband? He may have something for us. Let's see what's up.' So, I did, I traveled over to the Osceola County Jail that evening, it was dark or near dark. It was after the six o'clock news because as they brought Jeff Hall down to me to meet in the interview area, I remember he's like, 'It's on the news, pictures and talking and all kind (sic) of crap. What the hell's going on?" And I said 'Obviously, you haven't heard,' and I proceeded to explain to him what happened. And he was shocked.
>
> As I went through, I did not want to hand up any names. I wanted to extract that as much as anything because at that point honestly, other than the affair and Randall Richmond, I didn't know a whole lot. So

anyway, I talked to the husband, and I felt genuinely that he didn't have anything to do with it. You know all these years, John we've spoken all these years and it's just trust your gut and it's usually prevailed for me.

And he was more shocked or confused. I didn't see, which I didn't expect from a guy who was in shock, you know crying, weeping or wailing. He was more astonished than anything. What happened? I don't know. So, I left there and felt comfortable. I didn't spend a lot of time with Jeff. (Torres, 2018, 3:52-5:41)

The spotlight now shifted to Randall, Brandy's secret lover, at least a secret from Jeff and Randall's wife. Meanwhile, Jeff was also being questioned, but he eventually began to refuse to speak to the police, possibly due to ongoing appeals in his case. Initially, Randall was cooperative and discussed Brandy with investigators. Detective Pusatere noted that Randall claimed he hadn't spoken to Brandy in weeks, a statement that we now know was false. During the 2007 Florida Department of Law Enforcement (FDLE) interview regarding Randall's lies, here is what he said:

Yeah, and I told the police. I told Kevin and Jess that all didn't look good. I knew that didn't look good. I know I lied. I walked in there and told them I lied. I told the guys flat out, look what I told you on Friday, I lied. (Torres, 2018, 7:16-7:32)

During the 2007 FDLE interview with Randall, he appeared to be emotional. According to Agent Tom Davis, Randall was weeping, crying, and displaying extreme emotion during the interview (Torres, 2018). A friend of mine once told me that if someone is overly emotional, they are most likely guilty of something that happened between the two. When a person is in an "over emotional state" over someone missing and possibly dead, it's important to consider and understand certain aspects.

First, let's talk about emotional responses. Emotions are natural reactions to significant events or stimuli. In this case, it is possible that Randall's emotions are likely driven by a deep concern for Brandy, since they were having an affair. The intensity of his emotions could have been overwhelming, leading to an "over emotional state." Next, let's understand Randall's cognitive dissonance. The discrepancy between his expected outcome, Brandy being alive, and the reality of the situation, Brandy missing or even dead, can cause cognitive dissonance. This discomfort can lead to heightened emotions, such as anxiety, fear, or even anger. Everyone's brain works differently, even when emotions are involved. Randall was married and had a sexual affair with Brandy. Was he feeling guilty about the affair coming to light, or was it something else?

What was Randall's moral responsibility in Brandy's missing person case, now believed to be dead? As a person of interest, Randall's emotional state may influence his moral responsibility in this situation. If he's genuinely distraught over Brandy missing, it could indicate an emotional investment in her well-being. However, if he's feigning emotions to manipulate others or hide his own guilt, this could be a red flag for investigators.

Finally, what was Randall's motivation and intent? Understanding the motivation behind Randall's emotional state is crucial during this interview. Was he truly concerned about Brandy missing, or was he trying to distract himself from his own actions or motives? Investigators should consider whether Randall's emotions were a genuine response or a tactical maneuver to avoid suspicion.

To enhance your understanding of this concept, let's consider the following scenario: Imagine your friend has suddenly gone missing, and you find yourself at the center of the investigation as a suspect. In a state of profound distress, you display visible emotions that could easily be interpreted as genuine concern for your friend's safety. However, if investigators uncover a history of deceit or manipulation on your part, they may begin to question the authenticity of your emotional display, suspecting it might be a strategic facade designed to deflect suspicion.

It's also important to consider the underlying dynamics in relationships, such as the long-term affair between Randall and Brandy, which remained hidden from their spouses for years. This complexity adds another layer to our understanding of human emotions and behaviors, especially in high-stakes situations like criminal investigations. Grasping these nuances can be crucial, because during interviews, the lines between genuine emotion and calculated performance often blur.

During my interviews with suspects, an intriguing pattern emerged, approximately 70 percent of them broke down in tears during our conversations, ultimately leading to confessions. Each of these confessions was supported by compelling evidence I had gathered. This phenomenon, often referred to as the "crying confession," has sparked significant debate among psychologists and legal scholars regarding its ethical implications and reliability. A suspect's emotional outpouring can indicate a deep vulnerability, making them more susceptible to manipulation during interrogation. In such moments, an interrogator might exploit this emotional fragility by employing heartfelt appeals or tapping into feelings of empathy and guilt. As a result, these confessions raise important questions about their authenticity, especially when the suspect's guilt is not entirely certain.

The dynamics of interrogations are complex, with an interrogator's choice of words, tone, and body language playing a crucial role in creating an atmosphere of pressure that can lead to a confession. When a suspect is visibly distressed, often crying, they may feel an intensified urge to meet societal expectations, such as the belief that they should be forthcoming and truthful. This emotional turmoil can generate an overwhelming drive to confess, even if they are not genuinely guilty. Such "crying confessions" present significant ethical and legal challenges, as they risk producing false admissions of guilt. Innocent individuals, under the weight of emotional coercion or psychological pressure, might confess to crimes they did not commit, sometimes resulting in tragic wrongful convictions. I have witnessed this unsettling phenomenon firsthand. Do you trust your gut when you ask someone a question and they give you an answer that doesn't seem right? Agent Tom Davis said this in an interview with Johne Torres:

> My gut feeling was it was more of a fear because you see I didn't see the genuine "Oh my God, I lost someone I love." My gut, my years of this didn't tell me that, John. What it did was arouse suspicion. (Torres, 2018, 8:36-9:00)

As the investigation unfolded, the police faced the daunting task of narrowing down potential suspects. The case began to resemble a tangled web of deception and silence, complicating the detectives' efforts. Randall's fabrications obscured the truth, while Jeff's refusal to speak only deepened the mystery. It was understandable that Jeff had been advised by his attorneys to remain silent due to his ongoing appeal; yet one couldn't help but wonder about Randall's reasons for withholding information. In society, there's a common tendency to assume guilt over innocence, which presents a significant challenge for investigators. To uncover the truth, they must approach the case with an open mind, considering all perspectives instead of succumbing to bias, lest they miss crucial details that could lead to justice.

Liars are liars, and cheaters are cheaters. Randall Richmond was back at the police station, this time to change his story again, less than two days later. John Torres, who has provided much of the information about this case, was able to obtain the 2007 interview between Randall and FDLE Agents Tom Davis and Wayne Ivey. This interview was never made public until John released it. Here is the 2007 Florida Department of Law Enforcement interview:

Wayne Ivey: Back then. You gave a statement back then that was totally different than the statement you gave on Sunday. Why?

Randall Richmond: Because she had asked me…this is what I want you to do, don't tell anybody.

Wayne Ivey: OK

Randall Richmond: and then, of course, when Sunday rolls around and all of this stuff is in the news and there hasn't been a page that she told me she'd page me. I'm thinking well, what in the hell has happened. Has she really left? Has she staged all of this? Has something happened to her? (Torres, 2018, 13:26-14:00)

We have Randall, who initially denied talking to Brandy on the night she disappeared. However, a year later, he admits that he did indeed speak with her. He claims his initial denial was because Brandy was planning to leave town and didn't want anyone to know, so he says. Here are a couple of questions to consider: Is it morally justifiable to lie in order to protect someone's reputation or secrets? Should we prioritize honesty over loyalty or discretion? What are your thoughts?

Randall's initial denial led to a cover-up, which may have caused harm or delayed the investigation into Brandy's disappearance. Should we judge Randall's actions based on his original intentions, "protecting Brandy," or on the consequences of his deception? We are faced with a complex moral dilemma here. While Randall's actions may have been driven by a desire to protect his friend, his deception also potentially caused harm and may have even contributed to guilt. This scenario raises important questions about the nature of truth, morality, and the human condition.

The recorded audio from the 2007 FDLE interview with Agent Wayne Ivey and Randall Richmond took place a year after the incident involving Randall and the police. In this recording, he recounts details about Brandy's disappearance. Interestingly, two days after Brandy went missing, Randall spoke with the police about the incident and provided false information. During an interview with the Palm Bay Police, Randall's wife, Annmarie, arrived and reportedly slapped him, causing his glasses to cut his face. This event adds a layer of complexity to the case, hinting at potential further details that will be explored later.

When Randall Richmond said, "I don't know. Ten, eleven o'clock?" during the 2007 FDLE interview, it raises some concerns, or perhaps even hints at something more. When does one consider inaction a clue? Randall and Brandy communicated quite frequently, and then suddenly, their conversations stopped. He even mentioned the time of eleven o'clock. From what the documents reveal, it appears that Randall lied for nearly a year after Brandy went missing. This inconsistency could be significant and warrants closer examination. To give you a better understanding, let's continue that 2007 FDLE interview between Agent Wayne Ivey and Randall Richmond. Here is what was said:

Wayne Ivey: Without any hesitation from you are you in love with her?

Randall Richmond: Are you asking me then or are you asking me now?

Wayne Ivey: Then.

Randall Richmond: No.

Wayne Ivey: As you reflect back on it were you in love with her?

Randall Richmond: After I've been to see my wife's therapist, after I've been to see my therapist, they all said it's called love. Affairs of the heart.

Wayne Ivey: I want to ask you a question.

Randall Richmond: Yes sir.

Wayne Ivey: I'm from the country and I shoot straight from the hip. Alright?

Randall Richmond: Go.

Wayne Ivey: Did you kill Brandy?

Randall Richmond: No sir. I did not.

Wayne Ivey: Do you believe Brandy is dead?

Randall Richmond: I honestly do not know. I honestly do not know. That's what we were talking about, you know. Is she laying on the beach somewhere in Mexico or did something happen to her? You think about a lot of things and a lot of things, you know, I have not formulated an opinion.

Wayne Ivey: If you did kill her, what would have been your reason for doing it?

Randall Richmond: I had no reason to kill her. None whatsoever. I had none.

Wayne Ivey: OK, I'm gonna tell you a theory that's been thrown at me and I want you to, devil's advocate if you will. Brandy wanted you. You and her (sic) had obviously had a relationship. And when things started heating up with you not going to testify and everything else, there was the possibility that the cat was going to be out of the bag that Ann (sic) was going to find out the real truth about everything. (Torres, 2018, 19:44-21:16)

Throughout my career in law enforcement, I've noticed that when a person begins a statement with the word, "honestly," it often raises a red flag regarding the truthfulness of their account. In this case, Randall uses this phrase twice in quick succession. Police are trained to approach interviews with a healthy dose of skepticism, an essential skill developed through experience with subjects who may not be fully truthful. This skepticism leads officers to operate under a baseline assumption that individuals might withhold or distort information, especially in situations involving potential conflicts of interest. Suspects often navigate a gray area, revealing only fragments of their stories; such selective disclosure can be just as misleading as outright lies.

Speaking of deception, it's important to note how Randall shifts blame to Jeff during the 2007 FDLE interview. When questioned about Brandy's disappearance, Randall suggests that Jeff might have had a role or at least some knowledge about what happened. This attempt to deflect responsibility and implicate another person is a classic tactic in deception, trying to create doubt and divert suspicion away from oneself. Such statements can be motivated by a desire to lessen personal culpability, but they also raise questions about Randall's honesty and motives. Examining this blame-shifting provides insight into how suspects manipulate narratives, especially when they feel cornered or guilty.

> **Randall Richmond**: I only knew what I read and that he wasn't gonna talk to anybody about unless he got immunity…he wanted immunity from the drug charges to talk with anybody about her case. I didn't, you know…

> **Tom Davis**: yeah, you got the same question mark we would.

Randall Richmond: And that's what makes me think that what was the connection there between him and her? Is there somebody really looking to do harm to him or her and that's why he's not talking or and (sic) that's why he's asking for immunity, and I don't know…I don't know. (Torres, 21:26-22:24)

The debate over the existence and reliability of psychics in criminal investigations, especially in homicide cases, is as old as the practice itself. On one side, proponents argue that psychics possess extraordinary intuitive abilities that enable them to access information beyond the reach of conventional investigative methods. This perspective prompts us to consider deeper questions about the nature of intuition, the potential existence of extrasensory perception, and whether there are cognitive abilities that remain outside our current scientific understanding.

Conversely, skepticism is a persistent element in this debate. Critics argue that the insights claimed by psychics often lack specificity and reliability and are sometimes easily explained by common cold reading techniques, general statements that seem accurate but are actually quite vague. They caution that relying too heavily on psychic input can divert resources and attention away from more established, evidence-based investigative methods that have a proven track record of effectiveness.

This presents a compelling dilemma for law enforcement: Should they strictly adhere to empirical, proven practices in evidence gathering, or is there any value in considering unconventional sources of information like psychic insights? The outcome of this debate could not only shape future investigative strategies but also challenge our understanding of intuition and the nature of knowledge itself.

In the investigation of Brandy's case, a notable psychic medium, Gale St. John, was consulted for her unique insights. As the author of *Missing and Presumed Dead*, St.

John has gained recognition through her appearances on various crime shows that highlight her work. Psychics like her often rely on their intuition to provide insights into the circumstances surrounding a missing person, potentially offering valuable guidance to investigators. They may reveal details about the individual's last known location, their emotional state, or possible suspects involved. St. John's revelations regarding Brandy's case were particularly intriguing, as they introduced an unexpected layer to the already complex narrative of her disappearance.

Gale St. John recounted a perplexing story to John Torres about her unexpected involvement in the investigation. She revealed that someone connected to the crime—or perhaps even the perpetrator, had reached out to her via a cryptic email. The unsettling message left her with a lingering sense of apprehension, as if the sender possessed intimate knowledge of her connection to Brandy's disappearance. This raises an important question: was her reaction driven by a mere "hunch," or could it be considered "intuitive evidence"?

Intuition, often viewed as a double-edged sword, has both advocates and skeptics. On one hand, it can be a powerful tool, guiding us through complex challenges by tapping into instincts that sometimes surpass logical reasoning. On the other hand, it can mislead, fostering misconceptions rooted in fear, anxiety, or bias. Consider the profound bond of a mother's love, how often does it instinctively guide her to sense when something is wrong, prompting a protective response that defies rational explanation? In the realm of mystery and intuition, where should we draw the line between genuine insight and mere speculation?

Gale's intuition appears to have played a significant role in her involvement in Brandy's disappearance. Her immediate and strong reaction to the email led her to suspect that the sender was indeed involved in the crime. This situation underscores the importance of examining the reliability of our perceptions and experiences, especially when they influence our judgments. It also prompts a provocative question: what are the odds that someone closely connected to this case, perhaps even the individual involved, would reach out to a psychic in an attempt to aid in solving it? This possibility raises intriguing questions about motive, awareness, and the ways in which individuals may seek unconventional assistance in complex or unresolved cases.

This case has captivated countless individuals, yet it remains a haunting mystery. Given the web of lies and deception that has surrounded it, one might reasonably expect that a suspect or at least a person of interest would have emerged by now. However, the journey to uncover the truth is far from over; there are still pieces of this puzzle waiting to be discovered. What could have motivated someone to take Brandy's life? While we have unraveled many threads of this story, I am certain that, like me, you have your own theories and suspicions. Did Brandy threaten Randall or disrupt his relationship with his wife? The answer, shrouded in uncertainty, remains elusive.

Authorities conclusively determined that drugs were not a factor in Brandy's disappearance. They began closely monitoring her bank accounts and thoroughly examining all possible avenues she might have pursued. It is important to recognize that the circumstances of her case suggest that Brandy was unlikely to have chosen to abandon her children voluntarily. Here is what Debbie Rogge had to say regarding the possibility of Brandy leaving:

> I know that she would not leave on her own. She would never leave her family or her kids, her job, us, her kids. She would not do that in a million years. That was not her. She either had to have had to have (sic) amnesia or some reason, someone would have had to force her to leave. I don't know what it is or what? I don't know but. (Torres, 2018, 13:48-14:13)

Jeff shared the same conviction as Brandy's mother: there was no way Brandy would have willingly abandoned their children. They were her constant companions, the very center of her world. The profound, unconditional bond between a mother and her children is something that flows naturally, fiercely, and without hesitation. Those who knew Brandy well echoed this sentiment, firmly believing that she would never have chosen to leave her children behind, especially in light of the looming threat of Jeff's potential imprisonment. For Brandy, her kids were not just part of her life; they were her very essence. Here is what Retired Detective Doc Jones had to say about what may have happened:

> Somebody had some help. That's what I'm saying. I don't think one person, one person probably killed her. I think that person had some help moving her out of the truck into a vehicle and hauling her away and getting rid of her. I don't think that was a one-person deal. I don't think that. Can I prove that? No.

> That's a feeling I have. And that's the reason I think there's a second Charlie that you can if somebody (sic), "I didn't really want to get involved in this but..." and what that person may have done would not constitute a murder charge and I think it's a bit long in the tooth to be charging somebody with obstruction or aiding and abetting or something of that nature. But...

> I would like to be able to put my finger on the event, OK? But I can't tell you with any degree of certainty how she died. I know what I think but is that the only way? No, I don't think so. I can't tell you what happened to her body. I think the body was hauled away. Is that true? I don't know. We haven't found a body yet. If we find a body in Fellsmere then I'll say "See, I told you so." But other than that, there are

just too many unknowns in this thing. (Torres, 2018, 18:28-20:04)

Let's take a moment to consider the nature of deception. A lie, at its core, is a form of deceit, an intentional act designed to mislead or manipulate others. Whether it's a small untruth or a more significant fabrication, lying often serves a specific purpose: to achieve a desired outcome, evade accountability, or, in the most extreme cases, avoid serious legal consequences such as a murder charge. Those who believe they are skilled at deception may become overconfident, but the truth has a way of surfacing inevitably. Ultimately, even the most adept deceivers are likely to reveal their true intentions, whether through a slip of the tongue, a nervous gesture, or an involuntary expression. The inevitable exposure of a lie underscores the fragile nature of falsehood in the face of unwavering reality.

During my tenure as a detective, I found particular value in the insights offered by the book, *You're Lying! Secrets from an Expert Military Interrogator to Spot the Lies and Get to the Truth* by Lena Sisco. This illuminating read provided practical techniques that proved invaluable for those of us on the frontlines of uncovering the truth. She explains lies and deception very well. Lena Sisco (2015) wrote that "The body can 'leak' deception through the face (expression), the head, the eyes, the mouth, the hands, signs of uncertainty, and the nose (what I call the Pinocchio effect)" (p.136).

Now, let's explore the crucial concept of alibis. An alibi is a person's account or justification for their whereabouts and activities at the time a crime occurred. Essentially, an alibi functions as a defensive tool, aimed at disproving allegations of involvement in a particular incident. It plays a vital role in many defense strategies and can be highly effective if the alibi is genuine. Personally, I believe in the importance of maintaining records, whether it's saving receipts, sending a quick text to a spouse when I leave home, or using other forms of documentation. In an age where surveillance cameras are ubiquitous, having a well-documented time stamp can be invaluable in establishing innocence and clearing one's name.

To further illustrate the concept of alibis, consider this example: Imagine you're at a party, and someone accuses you of stealing their phone. You didn't take the phone, but you were in the same room when it went missing. You have two options: deny taking it, which might lead to more questioning, or provide an alibi, such as, "I was talking to someone else in another room." In this scenario, do you view your response as an honest answer or as a form of deception? What's your perspective?

Lying to the police ultimately costs time and resources, and sooner or later, the truth tends to surface. When it does, it rarely reflects well on the person who lied, especially once they reach court. For example, when Randall told police that Brandy was pretty much going to run away, do you believe that was an honest answer or a deception? Here is Randall's reasoning for his statement, as explained during the 2007 FDLE interview with Agent Wayne Ivey:

Randall Richmond: What didn't I answer honestly?

Wayne Ivey: Not all of them. But that's all right. We'll go into that at a later point. You're coming in on a Friday night and giving one statement and coming back on Sunday. I have some obvious issues.

Randall Richmond: Yeah, and I told police. I told Kevin and Jess that that all didn't look good. I knew that didn't look good.

Wayne Ivey: And when you're working a homicide investigation, you look for who had motive, who had opportunity and who lied.

Randall Richmond: Oh, I lied. I mean I walked in there and, I mean I told them I confessed it all. I walked in there said, look guys I lied. I admit to that. (Torres, 2018, 4:00-4:45)

Jeff, who lost his appeal a few months later, was facing an 18-month prison sentence for drug manufacturing. His lawyer, Kepler Funk, firmly believes that Jeff is innocent and had nothing to do with Brandy's disappearance, but he advised Jeff not to speak to the police during his appeal. This raises an important question: between Jeff, the husband, and Randall, the paramour, who was telling the truth? The presumption of innocence is a fundamental principle of the United States criminal justice system. It states that individuals are considered innocent until proven guilty beyond a reasonable doubt. This principle is designed to protect against wrongful convictions and to ensure that innocent people are not punished for crimes they did not commit. However, sometimes society fails to fully uphold or recognize this essential safeguard.

In Jeff Hall's drug case, there was strong evidence against him, making it challenging to uphold the presumption of innocence. However, his lawyer, Kepler Funk, firmly believes that Jeff is innocent in Brandy's case and is actively working to prove it. After all, police often focus their initial investigations on close relatives and friends. About two weeks after Jeff's appeal concluded, Palm Bay police detectives sought to speak with him regarding Brandy's disappearance. They went to Jeff's current location at the Central Florida Reception Center, where he was awaiting transfer to prison. The detectives informed Jeff that he could face the death penalty, but Jeff insisted on his innocence and claimed he had never lied to the police (Torres, 2018).

Returning to the topic of alibis, Jeff didn't have a particularly strong one. He claimed to have been at home sleeping with his children when Brandy disappeared. But who could verify his story? His sleeping kids? Given that it was 2006, we didn't yet have the widespread technology we have today, such as real-time surveillance footage or smartphone location data. Jeff stated the following about that night:

> They (the kids) actually slept in the same bed with me that night. We were watching, I forget what was the show that was on, I think it was the Amazing Race or something, the final episode of that. Then they were getting tired, so you know, I was trying to spend some time with them. They said let's call mommy so we can say our prayers and I didn't watch the end of that show so and then we fell asleep, so. (Torres, 2018, 7:05-7:33)

Jeff wasn't naive; he understood why the police were interested in him. Determined to demonstrate his innocence to both law enforcement and the community, he volunteered to take a polygraph exam. Here is what Jeff said about the polygraph examination:

> I took a polygraph test, and they asked me, "Do you know what happened to Brandy?" And you know, my mind says 'yes, I do,' I clearly, you know, I said "Well I didn't do nothing to her, and they were like 'yes or no' so."

> I said no because I truly don't know but my mind tells me yeah, because based on what I'm hearing and this is, um, this is not just hearsay stuff. (Torres, 2018, 9:10-9:34)

To clarify, what Jeff was hearing from the community and the police was that Brandy and Randall were indeed having an affair. Jeff also knew that Randall had initially lied to the police. Given this context, could the polygraph exam Jeff took that day be completely accurate? Were the right questions asked? Perhaps the police had the same suspicions and offered Jeff a second polygraph, which he reportedly passed.

Let's not forget that the last person Brandy spoke to the night she disappeared was Randall, not her husband, Jeff, or her children. If detectives rely on false or misleading information, they risk focusing on the wrong leads, wasting valuable time and resources. This can hinder their ability to identify the true perpetrator and bring them to justice. While the police may have been satisfied with excluding Jeff, they were also scrutinizing Randall, who had lied to police a few times. Randall's alibi was that he never left the fire station because there were no calls that night, as he told Agent Wayne Ivey during the 2007 FDLE interview. That alibi seems more plausible than Jeff's. Here is part of that interview:

Randall Richmond: I never left the station. Why are you guys, why are you still pointing the barrel at me like you just said. I know there's a lot of people out there who said we know he's the one who had to do it because him and her had the affair.

Wayne Ivey: Well, I'll give you some exact reasons. You, on average talked to her or text message her 52 times a day.

Randall Richmond: Whoa!

Wayne Ivey: Yeah, all those things, all the things I asked you are in the telephone records, and I already had the answers to... (sic).

Randall Richmond: Did I answer them honestly?

Wayne Ivey: No.

Randall Richmond: What didn't I answer honestly?

Wayne Ivey: not all of them. But that's all right. We'll go into that at a later point. You're coming in on a Friday night and giving one statement and coming back on Sunday. I have some obvious issues.

Randall Richmond: Yeah, and I told the police. I told Kevin and Jess that that all didn't look good. I knew that didn't look good.

Wayne Ivey: There's a phone call to Jeff at night telling Jeff that you would be there for him. The next phone call you make is to Ann (sic) from the station.

Randall Richmond: I called Jeff that night, OK

Wayne Ivey: Then you make the phone call to Ann (sic). And then you make a phone call to Brandy. And then a series of phone calls occurs between you and Brandy and text messages. She leaves at 23:06 you talk to her at 23:06 that phone call lasts 11 minutes. At 23:17 that phone call terminates. At 23:38 her husband starts trying to call her and she's never been heard from again. Now, everybody and their brother has called her and called her and called her. But not Randall. You never called her again. You talk to her on average 52 times a day. And you never called her again. (Torres, 2018, 13:07-14:55)

Wayne Ivey's accusations are based on phone records and timing, which suggests that he believes the sequence of events is crucial to understanding what happened. I would agree with him. Ivey is also accusing Randall of being involved in Brandy's murder, and Randall appears to be trying to deflect blame or justify his actions. His denial of involvement, despite having a significant history of communication with Brandy, illustrates how people can rationalize their actions and deceive both others and themselves about their involvement in wrongdoing. It seems

Randall is actively trying to conceal the truth about what really happened.

Remember when I discussed inaction earlier? Here, inaction refers to Randall's failure to call or contact Brandy after her disappearance. If you were close to someone and suspected something was wrong, wouldn't you keep reaching out? Despite their extensive prior communication, Randall never contacted her again after their last conversation, almost as if he knew she no longer existed. This inaction can be just as revealing as explicit deception, serving as a form of silence that can be equally damning.

According to Detective Mike Pusatere in an interview with John Torres, here is what was discussed regarding Jeff after he was released from prison and cleared of involvement in Brandy's disappearance:

When he got out of prison, I met up with him and offered him the opportunity to take a polygraph, which is what he did. Which did not show indications of deception. So, we were pretty much able to rule him out as a focus of the investigation. Based on his actions – if I kill somebody am I going to continuously call them, leave voicemails for them, leave a note for them? You know, I may do one or two to make it look like I'm not guilty but I'm going to go through the pattern of calling her parents, calling her friends, calling other people saying, hey if you see her tell her to meet me at court, I really need her here. Those are things that somebody that committed a crime is not going to do. Jeff's behavior was consistent with someone who was not involved with her disappearance. (Torres, 2018, 15:29-16:14)

During the 2007 FDLE interview with Agent Wayne Ivey, Randall refused to take a polygraph, and to this day, he continues to refuse. This part of the interview was particularly interesting:

Randall Richmond: We were just talking about that, I tried, just you know one of them things that gets in your head. I was telling him it was sometime this year in 07. But you know, after everything that happened and got called in here and talked with the police and all of that stuff, no, I never did. To tell you the truth I was scared to. You know, as bad as I wanted to, I was scared to. You know.

Wayne Ivey: I want to ask you a question.

Randall Richmond: Yes sir.

Wayne Ivey: I'm from the country and I shoot straight from the hip. Alright?

Randall Richmond: Go.

Wayne Ivey: Did you kill Brandy?

Randall Richmond: No, sir. I did not.

Wayne Ivey: Do you believe Brandy is dead?

Randall Richmond: I honestly do not know. I honestly do not know. That's what we were talking about, you know. Is she laying on the beach somewhere in Mexico? Did something happen to her? You think about a lot of things and a lot of things, you know I have not formulated an opinion.

Wayne Ivey: If you did kill her what would have been your reason for doing it?

Randall Richmond: I had no reason to kill her. None whatsoever. I had none.

Wayne Ivey: OK, I'm gonna tell you a theory that's been thrown at me and I want you to, devil's advocate if you will.

Brandy wanted you. You and her (sic) had obviously had a relationship. And when things started heating up with you not going to testify and everything else, there was the possibility that the cat was going to be out of the bag that Ann (sic) was going to find out the real truth about everything.

Randall Richmond: OK.

Wayne Ivey: Tell me your feelings about that. Tell me why that theory is not right.

Randall Richmond: What do you mean not right? I mean, if she was going to do that, if she was going to do that to me, I would have to go to Annmarie and say, look, this is what's happened. Guys, I have to go get (sic) to my dad.

Wayne Ivey: We're getting close here. Let me tell you what's important to us. Anytime you work a homicide investigation what's important is obviously to prove who did it, alright, but also to prove who couldn't have done it. And that becomes important at a number of different stages. A. It helps you focus in on who your primary suspect is. And B, when we get that suspect to court the defense is going to try to say this person did it, that person could have done it and do everything they can to make their person not appear guilty. So, for us it's not only important to prove who did it but also to prove who couldn't have done it. And that's one of the reasons why we wanted to sit down with you today is to be able to go over some of these things that there were some gray areas on and be able to work some of them out.

Randall Richmond: To prove that (sic) didn't did (sic) it, do it.

Wayne Ivey: Exactly. Now, one of the steps that we take, one of the tools that we use is a polygraph examination and it's an easy thing to do and…

Randall Richmond: I already did one of those.

Wayne Ivey: No, you didn't do a polygraph you did that voice stress. We don't use voice stress. We use a polygraph. It's very very good at what it does. I'd like for you to take a polygraph. That would help me eliminate you and allow me to focus on who I really believe did this. We can get it done, get you out of the picture and I know this has been a burden on your saddle for a long time as well. There's a lot of people, and this is no secret, there's a lot of people who have pointed the finger at you because of you and her's relationship. You've gone to more counselors than you probably care to go to. I would like to get you polygraphed and get you out of my picture. It would be my wish to do um (sic). Do you have a problem in doing that? (Torres, 2018, 16:25-20:18)

Is Randall hiding something, or is he simply exercising his Fifth Amendment constitutional rights? Jeff believes that Randall was involved, somehow, some way. Here is what Jeff had to say about Randall's potential involvement:

> I don't give a shit which way you play this, you know, run away or death, he knows he had something to do with it. Period. Period. Because there's no reason to lie. And I'll take a thousand polygraph tests every day and he won't even take one. And they got other ways, voice analysis, I'm sure they did the voice analysis on him, I know they did it on me without me knowing it. (Torres, 2018, 21:22-21:47)

John Torres did an excellent job covering this case. He spoke with retired Detective Sid LaDow about the Voice Stress Analysis test conducted on Randall Richmond. Here is John's conversation with Sid LaDow:

> He apparently did. Randall Richmond has never taken a polygraph examination in the case, despite being

asked to numerous times. A Voice Stress Analysis test was done earlier, and he failed. According to Sid LaDow, he failed quote, "Miserably." According to the report, the "hot" questions Randall failed on included "Do you know who killed Brandy?" "Did you kill Brandy?" and "Do you suspect anyone of killing Brandy?"

After the test, Randall was informed of the blood found in Brandy's truck and started to cry. It was during this time, again, according to the report, that Randall's wife Annmarie was calling him over and over again on the telephone. He did not take the calls.

The polygraph thing really irks Jeff Hall even to this day. He doesn't understand why his former friend and his wife's lover refuses to take one. (Torres, 2018, 20:19-21:21)

Let's take a moment to explore the core idea here. We're dealing with the concepts of truth-telling and deception. Randall Richmond has been asked by the police to take a polygraph examination to determine his involvement in Brandy's disappearance and murder. However, he refuses multiple requests. His refusal, along with his failure on the Voice Stress Analysis test, may suggest he's hiding something. But it's also possible that he's telling the truth and simply feels uncomfortable with the idea of taking a lie detector test, after all, who really enjoys taking one? Jeff Hall, Brandy's husband, is frustrated by Randall's refusal, which seems to imply that he believes Randall should be held accountable. Remember, Randall was considered a "family" friend.

Jeff is doing his best to care for the kids in their mother's absence. His greatest fear is that he may never find answers about her disappearance. To support them, he has taken them to counseling and has been fairly open when they ask questions. One comment Jeff made resonated with me when he spoke about how their children are coping. He said, "I asked the lady, how do you tell your kids their mom is dead when you don't know? She said, Jeff, it's been 8 months or whatever, realistically she probably is" (Torres, 2018, 22:48-22:57).

Let's revisit Randall's alibi. He claimed he never left the fire station that night, and there were no calls during that time. If he had left, his fellow firefighters would have heard the fire captain's diesel vehicle and seen the bay doors open. Additionally, the police officer reported seeing two people in Brandy's truck and noted a fire captain's vehicle parked at the nearby Hess gas station, based on the tip sheet she submitted.

Police are currently at a standstill, with no leads and no evidence to charge a suspect. In law enforcement, we often say that there are no coincidences. On June 24, 2007, in Vero Beach—about 30 miles south of Malabar, some teenagers were out doing typical teenage things near one of the many canals. Like the fisherman who found Brandy's truck, these teens discovered various items: clothing, steel squares, porno DVDs, and erection cream (Torres, 2018). Among these items was an address book that displayed the name "Brandy Hall." This was particularly interesting because the ink wasn't heavily smeared, as it would have been if it had been in water for a long time. The teenagers did the right thing, they called the police—but unfortunately, the police never arrived. So, was this just a coincidence, or could it have been a lead?

Imagine you're in this situation. You've stumbled upon something unexpected, something that feels significant. That's what happened when a group of teenagers found a backpack. But this wasn't just a backpack. One of them, driven by curiosity or maybe a sense of unease, looked up the name "Brandy Hall" and made a startling discovery, she'd been missing for nearly a year.

Armed with this crucial piece of information, they called the police again. This time, the response was different. The backpack, it turned out, belonged to Brandy and contained her medication. The condition of the bag told a story too; it hadn't been submerged for long. This discovery throws a new set of questions into the mix, questions that touch on human intention and the nature of chance. Was the placement of this backpack a deliberate act, a calculated attempt to mislead investigators? Or was it a random occurrence, the result of someone finding the bag, perhaps taking something, and then simply discarding it?

Meanwhile, Brandy's family and friends, desperately seeking answers, had increased their reward to $10,000 on June 29, 2007. At the time, the lead investigator was Retired Palm Bay Detective Ernie Diebel. Let's hear what he had to say about the finding of this pivotal piece of evidence:

> Several detectives plus FDLE went down there to talk to the people who recovered it and talked to the people who managed one of the canals. It was more like a lock, a little dam, and it was hung up on the dam. The person who manages that area said that shortly after Brandy went missing in 2006 there was a hurricane, Ernesto, was coming to the area, so they drained the canals in preparation of a lot of rainfall so they wouldn't have flooding. So, he feels like that backpack was not there when that happened because it would have been found. So, this is now a year later it's there and with personal items like her wallet, videos and there were a couple of metal parts in there, pieces of metal that had been cut. She did a lot of welding; she had the shops. There was a couple of larger pieces of metal, in her backpack, which shouldn't have been there. The only thing I can think of is that someone put those in there to weigh it down.

The backpack, to me, is one of the most interesting parts in this. It's camouflaged, it's like a hunting backpack. The thing that's kind of strange is that she used to keep her prescription medicine and a firearm in this and neither of those were ever found. Plus, she had a radio from the Malabar Fire Department that also was never found. It wasn't in the backpack, it wasn't on the scene, it wasn't in her truck. So, it's kind of strange, so where's her prescriptions?

Why wasn't this in the truck? Did she go and meet somebody and put it somewhere and leave it some place and they got rid of it later? It doesn't make sense. This is someplace else, and we still don't know where her body is. That's very curious. And why would somebody try to weigh this down and try to get rid of it? (Torres, 2018, 3:20-5:29)

The backpack. It should have been a clear path forward, a collection of clues. Instead, it presented a series of contradictions. No cameras to show who left it, but evidence of a deliberate act. Brandy's connection to metal, but the purpose of those heavy plates remained a chilling question. Were they simply scraps, or were they specifically chosen to drag the bag to the bottom? And the most glaring absence: the gun. The one item almost always with Brandy, missing from the very place it should have been. The backpack offered pieces of a puzzle, but they didn't fit together, leaving us with nothing but a dead end.

Approximately five months after Brandy's backpack was discovered, FDLE Agents Wayne Ivey and Tom Davis sat down with Randall. The year was 2007. This was the first of several interviews they would conduct with him regarding the backpack. Here's how that initial conversation unfolded:

Wayne Ivey: We now have the backpack that was found down in Indian River County. We've got the cellular telephone companies working with us triangulating all of everybody's telephone records. We've got a number of things that are coming to the table now. DNA, the backpack and everything else is being tested for DNA because being submerged in water doesn't do it. It doesn't get rid of it. There's a lot of things, even down to DNA that's being taken from some Mandelay erection cream that was found in the backpack.

Randall Richmond (whispers): Mandelay erection cream?

Tom Davis: Are we gonna find your DNA in that backpack? And for what reason?

Randall Richmond: I honestly believe you're not going to find my DNA in that backpack.

Tom Davis: Why's that? Did you ever touch it when you were around her? What would explain it if we found your DNA, touch DNA we call it. Something you've previously may have touched that was in that backpack?

Randall Richmond: I don't ever remember touching anything (sic)... I don't know what backpack you're talking about. I mean she had two or three of them. Each one had different things in it so, one had clothes, one had this, one had business stuff,

Wayne Ivey: So, there's no reason why your DNA should be on anything in that backpack? On that erection cream? On anything like that?

Randall Richmond: No, my DNA should not be on any erection cream. The affair her (sic) and I had was years before. (Torres, 2018, 7:06-8:45)

This was the last recorded interview that Randall Richmond did with the police. The police have been trying to have him come back in for further interviews, but he refuses to.

In July of 2008, a puzzling discovery added another layer to the mystery: Brandy's yellow fire helmet was found floating in the water near Mathers Bridge. This was about a year after the backpack had been located. There was no doubt it was hers; her name and the defiant words, "No Fear," were clearly marked on it. The helmet had traveled a significant distance, found approximately 30 miles south from where Brandy's truck was discovered submerged in the pond. Adding to the confusion, Jeff Hall stated the helmet was usually kept at their West Melbourne welding shop, a place where their kids often played with it. Despite this, police didn't believe the fire helmet was connected to her disappearance. Was this a deliberate act by a suspect, leaving cryptic clues or perhaps taunting investigators? Or was it simply a bizarre and unrelated coincidence?

The case had other frustrating inconsistencies. Remember the tip sheet mentioned earlier? The one where a police officer noted a suspicious vehicle situation involving Brandy's truck, found parked unusually behind a Home Depot? That critical piece of information was inexplicably lost for five years, its existence unknown until it resurfaced one day. The officer, trying to make sense of the situation, later asked Sergeant Pusatere what had become of it. At that point, he had no recollection of the tip sheet at all. If the detectives knew about the tip sheet, they may have been able to ask Randall questions during his interview. Come to find out, there were only two fire captains that worked the night that Brandy disappeared. Randall was adamant with the detectives that he never left the fire station that night. Here is Detective Mike Pusatere talking about Randall's alibi once again:

> One of the difficulties with, quite honestly, with Randall Richmond is moving past him because we have what sounds like credible evidence, he was at the fire department but then when you talk to

the firefighters it's possible, he had left. You have an officer who saw a fire captain truck parked at a gas station near where her truck was seen. There's only two fire captains on duty that night and one of them was alibied for sure by his people and Randall wasn't necessarily completely alibied by his people. So, that's hard to get past. And there was no video in those parking lots at that time that can say yes or no. (Torres, 2018, 15:22-16:01)

Adding another layer to this intriguing situation, retired Detective Sid LaDow investigated this even more. Driven by a strong intuition, Sid felt certain that Randall also met with Brandy that night, and it wasn't just a phone call. This led Sid to a crucial question, how could Randall have possibly left the fire station that night without being seen? Let's hear what Sid discovered about Randall's potential departure from the fire station:

The other one was the vehicle. I stalled out on it for several years. How could he have gotten that thing out of there, that vehicle, without waking everybody up? And then I was talking with another firefighter who said, "that's easy, he didn't take that one, he took the spare in the back." They had a spare back there. I don't know how many supervisors there were at that time but that was a spare vehicle. And that's what he used. And it's a gasoline engine, it didn't make any noise, he purred right out. (Torres, 2018, 16:31-17:09)

This information irks Jeff Hall to no end. He just doesn't understand why nothing is being done regarding this information.

Randall had a portable radio to use as a first responder and listen to radio traffic. Many times, this can be used when on or off duty and can respond if near an emergency. John

Torres made a good point when talking about the radio, here is what he said:

> Well, it appears that Randall turned on his portable radio at 12:30 in the morning. Now, according to Sid's investigation a retired Palm Bay fire captain had "hotwired" a radio in the fire captain's room years earlier. The radio scanned all the police and fire channels. Randall told investigators that he turned on his "pac-set" to see what was going on in the city, but if he never left the fire station that night, there would be no reason to. (Torres, 2018, 19:27-19:57)

Brandy also had a radio; however, it has never been recovered.

Randall never spoke to the police again, but reporters haven't let this case rest. On News 6 WKMG TV Orlando, Randall stated, "Sometimes, I think that she's somewhere hidden in the woods you know, and a, sometimes I think she fell in foul play, wrong hands" (Torres, 2018, 21:13-21:23) Wow, what a comment! Is she in the woods, Randall? I'd sure like to know.

For those wondering, the FBI got involved. They completed their profile and said Brandy was limited with money since she lost her job and Jeff was in prison. They factored in that Brandy's truck, which was one of her prized possessions, had been located in the pond. They determined these factors and said that she couldn't have left. There was also a significant amount of blood in the truck, even after it was submerged in the pond.

Sid LaDow had some interesting things to say about Brandy and an "unnamed" person. Just guess who it might be. Sid wonders if Brandy and Randall drove to the pond like they normally did to meet. Is this where her life ended? Here are Sid's thoughts:

I know from talking with people that Brandy and the unnamed person there were arguing constantly for almost a week, that she was trying to convince him to leave his wife. And he kept saying "no, I'll not leave her." He had a tremendous investment in that house, he and his wife were making excellent money, you got three nice kids, you got a beautiful home. He could not see starting all over again. And he just kept saying no.

I don't know what happened, but it could be that Brandy got...lost her temper. Maybe she hit him a couple of times, could have pulled a gun on him, I don't know what happened. I just don't know what happened in that truck. If he pushed her or grabbed for the gun and hit her, with her head being like it was and the side of her face, it was probably pretty fragile. She could have hit something and broke something loose in her head, because we know the blood came out of her head, logically her nose or her mouth. I have really looked at this thing for hours at a time. Was it an accident? Was it self-defense? Quite frankly, I don't know. (Torres, 2018, 5:25-6:46)

Was there a motive there? It's interesting that the retired detective doesn't want to disclose the "unnamed" person's name, but it's talked about quite often.

Jeff Hall is quite upset about this situation, believing there was ample reason to focus on Randall Richmond. His concerns escalated dramatically when information about another potential vehicle involved in Brandy's disappearance came to light. This revelation caused Jeff to seriously question the police's handling of the case, feeling they were apathetic and had nearly abandoned hope of finding Brandy. There are, as you're aware, many lingering questions about this case. Did the police ever contemplate arresting Randall, perhaps for obstruction, especially given his documented dishonesty? Was professional courtesy a factor? We can't be certain. The central question remains: was the evidence available at that moment sufficient to justify an arrest? Let's hear what Sid LaDow had to say regarding the arrest of Randall:

> That was talked about. During one of the interrogations, they were gonna put him in the slammer because that first night he hadn't seen her, and he hadn't done this and all that and then comes in and halfway squares it away. But I understand one of the city fathers from City Hall over there put the kibosh on the arrest. And they were told "No, don't arrest him." I don't know why, maybe it was "hey, let's build a good case and really get him." But I don't know. I wasn't there then, so. (Torres, 2018, 8:00-8:31)

One thing to consider is the first 48 hours of the murder case; however, that was wasted with Randall's lies about talking to Brandy.

Let's talk about the altercation between Annmarie and Brandy at the seafood festival. Again, here is Wayne Ivey and Randall Richmond in the 2007 FDLE interview:

Wayne Ivey: When Ann (sic) and Brandy got into it at the seafood festival…

Randall Richmond: Well, I was telling him, that wasn't what somebody on the Internet said it was. There were things on the internet that we were reading but that wasn't it, it was not that big, this huge, blown-up drama. But anyway, go ahead with what you were going to say.

Wayne Ivey: Regardless of how big it was or not, I know there was a confrontation.

Randall Richmond: Yeah.

Wayne Ivey: And that confrontation according to some testimony is that Brandy told her, 'Why are you wearing your wedding band? I can have your man at any time' and whether that's true or not these are some of the things that were coming back and some of the things that were obviously fueling this conflict. (Torres, 2018, 9:48-10:31)

The question of motive is central to understanding any mystery, and in Brandy's disappearance, it's particularly compelling. Could the strained relationship between Annmarie and Randall have been the driving force behind her vanishing? As we examine the details, a history of deep-seated tension and conflict emerges. Their bitter text exchanges and their refusal to allow their children to see each other paint a clear picture of an animosity that had been simmering for a considerable time.

Sid LaDow's keen investigation uncovered a significant detail: Annmarie, a nurse, worked the night Brandy disappeared and got off work at eleven that night. This discovery raised intriguing questions: Was it possible she saw her husband's vehicle at the Hess gas station around that time? And if so, did she call him? To gain further insight into the case, Palm Bay Police contacted notable forensic psychologist Richard Walter in 2009. Detective Ernie Diebel met with Walter and requested his review of Brandy's case. Walter subsequently reviewed over 20 hours of interviews. His emailed response to the Palm Bay Police Department on November 30, 2009, is as follows:

In brief, while the investigative effort has eliminated almost every tangential lead, it remains that the primary person of interest has received only nominal attention. That is, as suggested in at least four interviews, Ann (sic) Richmond is the primary suspect that cannot be excluded by motive, method, and opportunity. Furthermore, the situational deceptions presented to the investigators, be it commission and/or omission indicate that Randall Richmond has knowledge and some complicity with the same. (Torres, 2018, 12:09-12:46)

Let's consider Sid LaDow's perspective on where Annmarie went after work. Sid believed Annmarie went straight home, and he likely reasoned this because he knew she was a mother, just like him. He probably understood that, like many parents, her priority after work would be her children. Annmarie had three boys, even though they were in high school, and Sid likely assumed she would want to get home to them, perhaps to ensure they were settled for the night.

Now, this doesn't rule out other possibilities. There's a chance she drove by and saw Randall's fire vehicle on her way home. However, if she did, it's likely she wouldn't have thought much of it, knowing Randall was a firefighter and likely working. Regardless of what she may or may not have seen, given her potential proximity and the circumstances, it's certainly understandable why the police would want to speak with both Randall and Annmarie to get their accounts of that evening.

The search for our beloved firefighter continues, and the community is asking: What more can be done? Despite tireless efforts–utilizing cadaver dogs, distributing flyers, and even raising the reward–there have been no breakthroughs. For anyone who wants to help or has information, Detective Mike Pusatere has a crucial message:

There is nothing new in the case per se. In fact, that's one of the reasons why we're thankful *Florida Today* is doing the "Murder on the Space Coast" and featuring the Brandy Hall, the Brandy Hall case. Because we're hoping that someone who watches this podcast has some information, something they might not think is that important that we haven't looked at or heard of before so we can try to develop some new leads with this case. That's why we've cooperated with the media on this case over the years because we know the public interest in this case as well as the fact that we need the public's assistance in cases like this where it's going on 12 years now. (Torres, 2018, 2:02-2:32)

For nearly two decades, the Brandy Hall case has remained a mystery. Someone, somewhere, holds the key to what happened. Despite the tireless efforts of case investigators over nearly two decades, Brandy is still missing. Yet, just as we might feel the weight of these unresolved years, a new and intriguing development has emerged. John Torres, an accomplished investigative writer and journalist, and his team recently noticed an individual following their podcast about Brandy, using her picture as their profile photo. Here's what John had to say about this discovery:

It all came about when we noticed someone on social media who was following the podcast. The person was using the name Brandy and also using an old photograph of Brandy that we did not recognize. It was clearly her in the picture but not a photo we'd seen before, and we've seen a lot.

So, we decided to try and find another copy of the photo on the internet, and we couldn't. I stored the info away and was going to tell Detective Mike Pusatere about it, but I first wanted to run it by Brandy's mom, Debbie Rogge.

I described the photo to her, and she recognized it immediately. I then mentioned that the particular image being used on social media appeared to have a crease through it and had been exposed to some wear and tear. As soon as I said that to Brandy's mom, there was silence on the other end of the phone.

When she finally spoke, her voice was trembling. She told me that she was shaking. She then sent me a cell phone picture of the exact same photo as the one being used on social media. And I mean exact. Right down to the crease and the markings on it from wear and tear. (Torres, 2018, 1:55-3:09)

There's something about a creased photograph, isn't there? That fold in the center speaks of it being held, tucked away, a tangible piece of someone's life carried close. It gives you goosebumps, doesn't it? To think of the journey this image has taken, and how it arrived in our hands. Brandy's mom, Debbie, shared her thoughts on this very photo with John Torres:

Debbie Rogge: It's a photograph that her dad kept in his wallet and then he put it in his drawer, I guess for safekeeping. He puts all of his things in there and it's, it's just the same picture. It has a special meaning.

John A. Torres: And how we know it's the same photograph is because there's a crease in the photograph because he used to keep it in his wallet, right? Because he used to keep it in his wallet?

Debbie: Right and there was a plastic cover over it. That's probably why the crease is there. (Torres, 2018, 3:10-3:43)

Brandy's mother, Debbie, believes the photograph might hold a deeper meaning, perhaps a message from beyond the grave or a significant sign. She feels strongly that only certain people should view it, particularly given the distinctive crease running through the image. Palm Bay police investigated the photo's authenticity but found no similar image online. The question remains, who possesses this photograph? Debbie discusses the image with John Torres, sharing her concerns and beliefs.

To effectively investigate this case, the detectives need to meticulously examine the timeline leading up to Brandy's death. A search warrant, if necessary, has likely already been executed. Crucially, the detectives must reconstruct the final moments of Brandy's life. What was happening in the minutes before her death? What were her last interactions? This detailed timeline, already discussed, is critical to understanding the sequence of events and identifying potential clues. Brandy and Randall exchanged texts, Randall texting at 10:51 p.m. with a response from Brandy at 10:53 p.m.

- Randall's response text at 10:56 p.m. and again at 10:57 p.m.

- Randall called Brandy at 11:06 p.m. and they spoke for 10 minutes and 46 seconds, ending the call at 11:17 p.m.

Let's examine two crucial time gaps that beg for our attention. First, there's the nine-minute window between 10:57 p.m. and 11:06 p.m.–a brief but perplexing enigma. We're left to ponder what could have transpired during that fleeting moment. Then, a larger puzzle emerges: the 26-minute interval separating Brandy's departure from the fire station and the abrupt end of the phone call. This longer gap deepens the mystery, prompting us to consider the very nature of time and how we account for it. Does this period definitively point to Brandy meeting Randall, as some believe? Or could the answer lie in coincidence, or perhaps something far more unsettling?

Let's introduce the idea of skepticism here. In this situation, we're confronted with two possible explanations for Brandy's actions: she either stopped at the Sunoco gas station, or she returned home before going out again. However, without more concrete evidence, we cannot be certain about either possibility. Consider Jeff's claim that Brandy didn't stop at home. Even if Jeff genuinely believes this, the skeptic in us asks, what is the basis for this knowledge? Without further proof, accepting his statement as an absolute truth remains uncertain. This is where the role of investigation becomes crucial.

Private investigator John Lind is actively trying to reduce this uncertainty by gathering additional information, perhaps through more witness statements or analyzing physical evidence, to build a stronger case for one scenario over the other. He's essentially seeking evidence that can help police move from a state of doubt towards a greater degree of certainty. Even with the most thorough investigation and a wealth of evidence, a fundamental aspect of skepticism reminds us that there will always be some inherent degree of uncertainty or doubt. The police can build a very strong case, but can they ever achieve absolute, unquestionable certainty about past events? Here is what private investigator John Lind had to say regarding his efforts to clarify the situation:

> There's a good possibility that she stopped at home for several reasons. One, she has to drive past the road that leads to her house from where she is at the fire station to make it to where the truck was found or where she was last seen by the police officer. She literally has to drive past it. (Torres, 2018, 4:18-4:35)

John Lind followed up and said the following about Brandy's timeline:

> But it's really important to find the time the gas station, what time she filled up with gas, to put her there because we want to find the distance between Malabar Fire Department and the gas station because it makes a difference if you're stopping at the home

as well as being on the road at the same time as Ann (sic) Richmond. (Torres, 2018, 4:46-5:02)

To gain a clearer understanding of Brandy's movements, John Torres and private investigator Nic Sandberg decided to retrace a possible route she might have taken. Their focus was sharp, the perplexing 9–10-minute gap and the 26 minutes between Brandy leaving the firehouse and her final phone call with Randall. As they drove, their conversation centered on the crucial timeline of Brandy's disappearance.

Their journey began along Malabar Road, the very street where Brandy was last seen driving away from the fire station. They were attempting to reconstruct the events of that night, meticulously considering the interplay of time and location. It was during this drive that John voiced his growing unease, the timeline simply didn't add up. He pointed out a missing period of at least 10 minutes, a window where Brandy might have stopped. However, the narrow, shoulder-less nature of the road made pulling over seem impossible.

As they continued driving, they explored the possibility of Brandy meeting Randall at the Sunoco gas station. They calculated that filling her truck with gas would take about six minutes, placing her arrival there around 11:00 p.m. However, this timeline directly contradicted Randall's claim that Brandy called him at 11:06 p.m. Adding to the inconsistencies, John highlighted a discrepancy in their usual communication. While Randall stated they exchanged numerous texts between 9:30 and 10:45 p.m., the phone records indicated it was uncharacteristic for them not to answer each other's calls during that period.

Remember the "tip" sheet the officer turned in? Nic found out what actually happened that night when the officer found Brandy's truck in the Home Depot parking lot:

> She was already off work, and she was doing due diligence by, she observed that vehicle she saw, the

noting mentally, hey that doesn't seem right that seems out of place. It was a standout to her. So, and even to the point where when she drove out of the parking lot of Walmart, she noticed a green pickup truck with tinted windows and somebody in the vehicle. She wasn't able to call it out because Palm Bay had the channel held. They had an incident somewhere else in the county. So, she was still monitoring the radio and stuff like that and would have loved to call the tag in. (Torres, 2018, 15:21-15:57)

It seems that we have a situation where the officer was performing her duties, even though she was signed off at the time, and she sees two vehicles, Brandy's truck and a Palm Bay Fire Department supervisor's truck. She makes notes about the latter because it seems unusual to her that a fire department supervisor's truck would be parked at a closed Hess Gas Station. Initially, it's said that the officer filled out a "tip sheet" and turned it in, but then it's revealed that this didn't actually happen. Instead, the police officer was summoned to her supervisor's office a few days after Brandy's disappearance because Campbell's patrol car was seen on surveillance footage in the area of the pond where Brandy went missing. The officer was sworn in to make a verbal statement by her supervisor, Sgt. Mike Bandish. Assuming that the statement was recorded (which it wasn't), the officer's assumption about the recording has implications for what she can recall about the event. It seems that the officer genuinely believed she had filled out a report, but it turns out that didn't happen. This blurs the line between what she thought happened and what actually happened.

John Torres discussed his and Nic's findings on their driving experiment. Here is what John said about the timeline experiment:

Now, my little driving experiment with Nic resulted in us learning this: With pretty heavy traffic, stopping at two lights and getting stuck in a left-turn lane that felt like it took forever, we made it to the Sunoco in 7 minutes and 15 seconds. That would put the time at between 10:58 and 10:59. We know Randall calls Brandy at 11:06. So maybe she fuels up for seven minutes, checks her oil, whatever. Maybe she just goes right to the Home Depot parking lot and has the 11-minute conversation there. We are still left wondering about the missing 10 minutes.

But then, Nic and I made the drive again but this time we included a pit stop at the home Brandy and Jeff lived in at the time in Malabar. The theory shared by some is that Brandy went home, maybe she got into an argument with Jeff and then went back out. Now again, for the record, Jeff denies that Brandy came home that night. But here, once again, is private eye John Lind. (Torres, 2018, 17:25-18:23)

Here is what private investigator John Lind had to say about the timeline:

The second thing that leads me to believe that is the interviews, they thought she was going home to say the prayers. We still have to interview a couple of more people but when we interviewed them they did not–being present in a very small room—did not hear her saying prayers with her kids which her mother and even Jeff insisted she would do every night. (Torres, 2018, 18:24-18:46)

What Nic and John Torres discovered about their driving experiment makes so much sense to this case, but still, nothing has been done. According to them, the drive took 15 minutes and 45 seconds to drive from the Malabar Fire

Station to Brandy's home, waiting there for five minutes (Torres, 2018). Did Brandy possibly drive home and get something, knowing that Jeff was maybe asleep? Afterwards they headed to Malabar Road to the Sunoco gas station. This would have put the time at 11:06 p.m., which happened to be the precise time Randall called Brandy and talked for 11 minutes (Torres, 2018).

Let's examine the drug theory in this case. Jeff and Paul Hirsch were arrested and convicted for a significant drug operation. Could this operation have contributed to Brandy's death? Private investigator Nic Sandberg, working pro-bono for Brandy's family, is investigating this possibility:

> I don't think all the law enforcement agencies in this case played well with each other and that's quite common across the United States. But, you know, I've learned several stuff (sic) from the Osceola Sheriff's Office, other interviewees that've had (sic)... and stuff, that you have two, supposedly they downplayed it, low-level marijuana growers, Paul Hirsch and Jeff Hall. They're growing, they're managing, the instrumentation of the effectiveness, a one-million-dollar plant profit that's going on, grow lights, irrigation, you know, that's a lot of maintenance. That's a full-time job. (Torres, 2018, 5:47-6:27)

John Torres wanted to delve deeper into this and spoke to Nic about his thoughts. Here is their conversation:

John: You said his generator was the size of your truck.

Nic: Right. At (sic) $25,000 up to $35,000 generator, diesel generator, with custom tanks on it that was welded.

John: And you have a background in narcotics right? I mean working them, not taking them, right?

John: And you mentioned that a job like that is normally a three-person job?

Nic: You normally got some type of person, either somebody that knows somebody that's in a higher up situational, um cartel, level dealer that's around here moving stuff. Jeff and them didn't have street-level users coming to their house to buy an ounce of pot to smoke on a weekend. When a million-dollar grow profit is going on, you have big bricks. You're not going to be moving that to the street-level user. So, normally you have the growers, you have the people that have the contacts and then you have the transporters. So, I think there were more people involved in that. And from what I can gather, I'm going to follow up on it with the Osceola Sheriff's Office. For the most part, Jeff and Paul seemed overly cooperative. It's me, me, me. I did it. We got it originally from 10 seeds from *High Times* magazine. Come on. Like, you know what I'm saying? (Torres, 2018, 6:28-7:55)

Nic's observations about the grow operation raise some crucial questions. Was someone higher up involved, perhaps someone the retired firefighters knew? Could Randall or Brandy have been part of a larger, unseen network? The claim that they only sold to one person, who has never been identified, is intriguing. This raises the possibility of a more complex operation than previously suspected. Paul Hirsch and Jeff Hall's seemingly straightforward account of the situation is notable, yet it also raises questions. The well-known risk of retaliation for cooperating with cartels, the potential for death, is a significant factor in why those caught often remain silent. However, the detectives in the case don't believe that drugs played a role in Brandy's disappearance. This discrepancy needs careful consideration.

According to John Torres (2018), "Brandy, in at least in one scenario has an argument with a known drug felon who may or may not be involved in her husband's operation" (9:02-9:09). Brandy, a woman who may or may not be involved in her husband's illegal activities, finds herself in an argument with a known drug felon. This encounter raises several questions. John also stated, "She gets to the fire station at 6:30 p.m. and six minutes later she talks with Randall Richmond on the phone for 11 minutes" (9:12-9:18). This is interesting because the two contacted each other that day a total of 87 times (Torres, 2018). According to John Torres (2018) again, he also stated that, "There were 11 phone calls and 76 texts between the two" (9:30-9:33). This is a little dramatic, either they were obsessed with each other, or they were having an argument via text messaging. Unfortunately, those text messages are gone.

Between 6:36 p.m. and 9:38 p.m., there was no contact between Brandy and Randall due to training at the fire station (Torres, 2018). Randall was a fire captain and maybe he was worried about perception, but at 8:44 p.m. he called Jeff to let him know he'd be in court to support him. This call only lasted about a minute, so it may have just been a voicemail or just a quick call. Here is the conversation from the 2007 FDLE interview between Wayne Ivey and Randall Richmond:

Wayne Ivey: I know there was a phone call between you and Jeff about you coming over to testify for him.

Randall Richmond: That was the next day. Wasn't it?

Wayne Ivey: Wasn't there one the night before that you were going to be there for him?

Randall Richmond: Yeah. There was.

Wayne Ivey: Tell me about that.

Randall Richmond: Well, he was worried about his court thing, and I told him that I'd be there. And that's about all I can remember. (Torres, 2018, 12:41-13:13)

After Randall called Jeff, he called his wife, Annmarie, while he was at the Palm Bay Fire Station, which wasn't far from where Brandy was working that night. Afterwords, Randall called Brandy at 9:02 p.m. Maybe this phone call was Randall telling Brandy that he wasn't going to testify on Jeff's behalf.

Brandy's emotional landscape was fraught with uncertainty as Jeff's sentencing loomed. The prospect of being alone, coupled with the unknown future of their marriage, undoubtedly fueled anxiety. The potential consequences of Jeff's imprisonment created a swirling vortex of fear and uncertainty in Brandy's life.

Brandy's financial struggles and extramarital affair with Randall complicate her emotional landscape. Randall's support and affection could be genuine acts of friendship, or part of a more complex dynamic. Was Randall a crutch, offering Brandy solace amidst the uncertainty of Jeff's future? Or was there genuine attraction? The indistinct boundary between friendship and romance raises fundamental questions about human relationships and the potential for emotional manipulation. Was Brandy truly afraid of loneliness, or was something else at play?

At 9:38 p.m., Randall initiated a text exchange with Brandy. Brandy replied at 10:18 p.m., prompting a quick response from Randall at 10:20 p.m. However, Brandy's reply at 10:18 p.m., was followed by a second message from Randall at 10:20 p.m. This triggered a flurry of activity; at 10:43 p.m., Brandy responded, setting off a chain of ten more messages that continued for the next fourteen minutes.

Beneath the surface of Randall's response to Brandy's message lies a deeper question: was it a rote action, or did it reflect genuine engagement, perhaps even anger?

This exchange, in turn, prompted Brandy to announce her departure for the evening, citing feeling unwell. Crucially, the text doesn't reveal whether she communicated her intentions regarding a return to work. Given the shared knowledge among the firefighters about the challenges Brandy was facing, particularly concerning Jeff's situation, her decision to leave is imbued with significant context.

Randall's investment in Brandy wasn't just about money; it was a commitment that touched her emotions and even her sense of self. His financial support allowed her to pursue her passion for operating a skid steer to allow her to complete other side jobs. This was a practical skill that became a source of purpose and independence for her. As they shared experiences and grew closer, their relationship deepened, fostering a sense of mutual understanding and interdependence. This intertwining of their lives raises fascinating questions about the nature of giving and receiving in relationships. When we invest in others, in what ways do we both gain? Does the blurring of boundaries between support and personal growth challenge traditional notions of reciprocity? Was Brandy benefiting from Randall's resources, or was Randall finding fulfillment in supporting her journey? Their relationship evolved over the years, becoming increasingly intimate and intertwined, much like the complexities of a marriage.

On the morning of his sentencing, Jeff waited anxiously for Brandy's arrival, a gnawing uncertainty settling in. Brandy was never late. Her silence—no answered calls, no replies to messages, not even to their friend—only tightened the knot of his concern. At 6:51 a.m., the worry became too much to bear. He dialed her number, hoping to hear her voice, to know where she was. There was no answer. By 7:00 a.m., he was calling a family friend, his mind racing. A minute later, that friend tried Brandy, but the call went straight to voicemail, confirming his worst fears. His next thought, a desperate attempt to cover all bases, was to scribble a note for the house, just in case she somehow arrived there first, letting her know the case was starting earlier than planned.

Randall Richmond finished his shift at the Palm Bay Fire Station at 7:00 a.m. Just four minutes later, at 7:04 a.m., he called his house phone. This was quickly followed by a call from his house phone to the neighbor's. By 7:27 a.m., Randall was on the phone with Jeff, informing him he wouldn't be attending court. Here's what Jeff recounted about that conversation:

> Then Randall called me up and was crying and I said, "What the fuck?" excuse my French, but I said, "What the fuck's wrong with you?" He was crying and crying, and I said Randall calm down I can't understand you. And he said "Well, I can't come to be a character witness." I said that's fine; the judge had already made it clear he's (sic) up his mind. (Torres, 2019, 3:02-3:21)

Now if this is true, Jeff at that time didn't know Brandy was missing. Could Randall be feeling guilty for not going to court for Jeff, or could he be feeling guilty about Brandy?

That's not all, here is the FDLE interview between Randall and then Agent Wayne Ivey:

Wayne Ivey: OK, let me ask you. That morning you call Jeff and what do you tell Jeff?

Randall Richmond: I told Jeff I said listen buddy I know I told you I would be there I said but the position that I'm in, the years that I have in service in the fire department, the things I've accomplished in my career, I can't put that stuff on the line. He said he understood. He said he understood.

Wayne Ivey: Ok, anything else?

Randall Richmond: I believe he asked me have you talked to Brandy this morning. And I said no. He said I've been calling her phone.

Wayne Ivey: What did you do?

Randall Richmond: I said no and then I think he said something else about the case about who was going to be there or who wasn't going to be there.

Wayne Ivey: How did it make you feel when he asked if you had talked to Brandy?

Randall Richmond: I thought well, where in hell did she gone (sic), what has she done?

Wayne Ivey: Did you tell him that?

Randall Richmond: No, I didn't tell him that. She asked me not to tell anybody anything.

Wayne Ivey: So, he asked if you've seen her, and you didn't tell him.

Randall Richmond: Hmm mm

Wayne Ivey: OK.

Randall Richmond: She asked me not to. (Torres, 2019, 4:19-5:46)

A significant discovery emerged: a neighbor was stopped by authorities at either 6:03 a.m. or 6:08 a.m. on the very morning of the murder, just hours before Brandy vanished. This revelation is particularly striking because it might have been overlooked initially. Not only does this police stop raise immediate questions about potential motives, but its connection to a popular reality TV show injects a layer of sensationalism into the investigation. Navigating the wealth of information in this case becomes increasingly challenging, as we must discern what truly matters from what is simply noise. Furthermore, interviews with individuals, some with potentially minor connections to the case, have yielded insights that not only provide new details but also fuel suspicions about possible motives for harming Brandy.

Let's consider a specific instance that highlights the interconnectedness of events. The individual involved in the traffic stop wasn't a stranger; in a surprising twist, it turned out to be Jeff and Brandy's old neighbor from their time in Melbourne. This unexpected connection brings us to the perspective of Private Investigator John Lind, who offered his insights into that encounter:

> Ironically, he works for a company that was directly associated with the same line of work that Brandy, Randall, and those would be involved with, with a well-known construction company that's here in Florida or actually national and has offices here in Florida. And actually, some of the companies where Randall did business have accounts to this day, 30 years later with that company. So, it's very nebulous and murky once you get into it. And ironically, we still have follow-up to do on that, but it led into a crazy situation where we sought out to speak with this individual as a witness and possible neighbor only to be told he hired a criminal defense attorney prior to being able to actually speak to him. Even though he knew we were just there to speak to him as a neighbor and person who knew Brandy. So, these weird roadblocks that keep getting put up and occur make the case even more difficult. (Torres, 2019, 7:43-8:38)

A series of unsettling coincidences connects Brandy's former neighbor, who lived across the street, to her disappearance. Not only does this individual work in the same construction industry, but they also have professional ties with Randall's company. This raises a crucial question: are these simply chance occurrences, or is something far more sinister unfolding? While the probability of such overlaps isn't impossible, it's certainly noteworthy. What truly elevates suspicion, however, is the fact that this same individual was stopped for speeding on the very day Brandy vanished, and then immediately hired a criminal defense attorney when questioned by Nick and John.

At 10:04 a.m., as Jeff awaited his court appearance, Randall's call interrupted him, instantly highlighting the tension between his obligations. On the one hand, he had the clear responsibility of being in court, a commitment he'd already made. On the other, Randall's request presented a legitimate need requiring his immediate attention, could Jeff remove the heavy equipment (a skid steer) from the trailer so Caterpillar could work on it? This is the situation described in the 2007 FDLE interview:

Wayne Ivey: Now, Caterpillar had called you looking for her?

Randall Richmond: Who?

Wayne Ivey: Caterpillar. The equipment people. Because there comes a call later where you're trying to get serviced or something like that.

Randall Richmond: She was supposed to. She had some warranty issues with it, and she was supposed to drop it off to get those warranty issues taken care of. And she hadn't.

Wayne Ivey: And so, what happens with that on that morning? Anything?

Randall Richmond: Um, yeah, I think I made a phone call to Cat and said did Brandy drop the machine off and I think he told me no, and I think I asked Jeff, maybe it was in the same conversation or a different conversation, I'm not sure. Um, where is the machine? Did she drop it off? Maybe I even asked Jeff that? He said, "No, the machine is sitting in the yard on the trailer." And I think I asked him, 'can I go unload the machine off the trailer so Cat can come and get it to fix the warranty issues? Yeah, I think so, to the best of my memory, I think so. (Torres, 2019, 11:38-12:59)

The situation is riddled with questions, particularly concerning Randall's actions. Why, for instance, would he choose a crucial day for Brandy and Jeff to have someone fix the skid steer? It seems counterintuitive; a typical person might have postponed such a task. This detail is significant, and we'll now hear from Nic Sandberg, the private investigator working for Brandy's mother, who sheds light on this very issue:

In an interview with Randall and the police, it's noted that Randall states he goes over to Duncil Lane to remove the skid steer from the trailer where the skid steer is parked, for maintenance to be done with Ring Power supposed to come. I believe the explanation he gave was a problem with the joystick on the skid steer. Confirmation with the interview with Jeff Hall. Jeff Hall, also states that Randall calls him the morning that he's in court asking permission, "hey do you care if I take this off the trailer?" So, it's noted in two different interviews that Randall showed up at Duncil Lane and removed the skid steer from the trailer and to this date I've tried to get information from Ring Power on maintenance and they can't find any maintenance records on the skid steer for those four months. There is a surcharge to go out to a place to actually work on equipment and they said that if the equipment was on a trailer, they normally tell the owner, if there is any way to bring it in, to bring it in.

And you're talking Ring Power from Duncil Lane is only two miles. (Torres, 2019, 13:11-14:23)

Here is what John Lind had to say about the day Randall asked to come over to get the skid steer:

> It's certainly circumstantial but perhaps what's interesting about this is that Randall goes to deal with this equipment the very morning that he was due at court and informed Jeff that he would not be going to court. And at that time, inform Jeff later, a short time later that he was actually going to his house to deal with this piece of equipment that would have been something that is still at Brandy's house that she would have still been currently using for jobs. So, he not only has an appointment in court, but he also has an appointment for the repair on the same day and he's there the very morning she disappears.
>
> Like a lot of things that tend to be circumstantial I think it needs more research before we decide what it means. (Torres, 2019, 14:24-15:09)

Now, if you weren't questioning things before, you certainly should be. Randall's behavior presents a fascinating puzzle, specifically around the philosophy of inaction. We're left pondering the significance of his choice not to act directly in the face of potential consequences. The central conundrum is this, Brandy's equipment needs repair, and Randall, being familiar with her work, chooses to contact someone else, like Jeff, rather than simply reaching out to Brandy herself. A direct call to her phone or Nextel device seems like the most straightforward path.

This passive approach to a seemingly clear problem is truly perplexing. As we've discussed previously, inaction can be incredibly telling in an investigation. It forces us to ask, Is Randall deliberately complicating matters, perhaps with ulterior motives? Or is there something deeper at play? Consider also the peculiar decision to unload the skid steer from the trailer instead of simply taking the entire unit. There was no scheduled repair appointment, which only deepens the mystery surrounding Randall's intentions.

Brandy's livelihood depended on this equipment, so it's reasonable to expect she'd have it repaired immediately. It's unusual that Randall didn't prioritize maintenance, especially given Jeff's court appearance and the whole family's expected presence. Brandy's absence is significant, and it's possible Randall knew she wasn't there. A skid-steer loader, like a Bobcat, is a versatile machine used for tasks such as excavation and digging.

On August 18, 2015, Brandy Hall's family took an unprecedented and deeply moving step, petitioning Brevard Circuit Judge Lisa Davidson to formally declare Brandy's death. This extraordinary request underscores the complex and often blurry line between life and death, highlighting the profound challenges faced by families in such situations.

There's a conception that Brandy's remains are on the very property that she and Jeff rented. The skid steer was taken off the trailer, but it stayed on the property. Here is what John Torres discovered:

> Another factor was that Nic Sandberg researched images on Google Earth and found a depression, an obvious sandy area in the back yard shortly after Brandy went missing that was not there in the weeks before August 17, 2006. Nearly 13 years to the day, on August 16, 2019, the police and private eye brought in two cadaver dogs and some ground penetrating radar to check the back yard. (Torres, 2019, 16:42-17:10)

Here is Palm Bay police SGT Jeff Spears talking about the cadaver dogs and the ground penetrating radar:

So today we're out looking for Brandy Hall. The Palm Bay Police Department is assisting the family and the private investigators with their efforts and what they believe – based on what they know of the case. So today we're out looking, we're checking out some spots. We have some cadaver dogs that have come from across the state to join and help search as well as Y-Comm came out and they're offering their assistance with some ground penetrating radar which is used to help locate anything underground. So, we're out here and ironically tomorrow marks the 13th anniversary since Brandy's disappearance. We're hoping for some good news, we're hoping that we can put closure to this case and locate Brandy. (Torres, 2019, 17:14-18:04)

Unfortunately, Brandy's remains were never located that day.

Brandy Hall's story, a missing firefighter, forces us to confront the complexities of human existence. Her life, marked by a near-fatal ATV accident at age 12, left deep physical and emotional scars. Yet, despite this adversity, Brandy channeled her experiences into a life dedicated to helping others as a firefighter. This dedication, born from a profound desire to serve, raises profound questions about our own existence and the meaning we find in caring for others. Her mother, Debbie, embodies this struggle, living with the raw emotional pain and vulnerability of watching her child face such hardship. How do we reconcile the fragility of human life with the powerful need to support those we love?

Brandy's disappearance highlights the crucial role of detective work and the pursuit of justice. Investigators must meticulously consider all potential scenarios and motivations, while also demonstrating empathy and sensitivity towards the people affected. Ultimately, Brandy's story underscores a timeless truth: courage knows no gender.

Women like Brandy, throughout history, have been on the front lines—literally and figuratively—challenging societal norms and inspiring future generations of female firefighters. Reflecting on her life and disappearance reminds us of the importance of resilience, selfless service, and the profound connections between human beings.

Brandy Hall's story is a powerful reminder of the complexities of human life. Marked by tragedy, resilience, and a profound sense of purpose, her life serves as a poignant example. The ongoing search for answers in her disappearance highlights the crucial importance of empathy, meticulous detective work, and unwavering commitment to justice. Sadly, Brandy's case remains unsolved. If you have any information that could assist detectives, please contact the Palm Bay, Florida Police Department at 321-952-3456.

"Have not I commanded thee? Be strong and of a good courage; be not afraid, neither be thou dismayed: for the LORD thy God is with thee whithersoever thou goest" ~ *Joshua 1:9*

CHAPTER 8

THE TIRE WAS STILL SPINNING

Imagine a chilly evening in Mesa, Arizona, January 2, 1999. The air in this quiet neighborhood was filled with the sound of two sisters, their laughter mingling with the faint, inviting melody of an ice cream truck. Eleven-year-old Mikelle Biggs and her younger sister, swept up in the simple joy of the moment, quickly secured money from their mother and raced out to meet that childhood siren song. As the sun began its descent around 5:50 p.m., casting long shadows, they positioned themselves near the corner of Toltec Street and El Moro Avenue, their anticipation growing with each passing moment. But as the temperature dipped further, Mikelle's younger sister felt the cold and headed back for a warmer coat. When their mother noticed Mikelle wasn't with her, she sent the younger sister back to fetch her. What she found instead was an empty street. Mikelle Biggs had vanished, leaving behind only an unsettling silence and the beginning of a relentless search that would forever mark this community.

The scene that unfolded in the stillness of that late afternoon was hauntingly clear: Mikelle's bicycle lay abandoned on its side, its wheel still spinning with a faint, unsettling momentum, a morbid echo of the joy it had just moments before represented. Nearby, resting in the dirt, were two worn quarters, simple remnants of idle play, their mundane presence made chilling by the context. What was particularly striking was the bicycle's position; not at the corner where they had been waiting, but oddly closer to the house, suggesting a hasty, perhaps panicked, discard. The clock, in this moment, felt like it had stopped. Mikelle had been separated from her sister for no more than ninety seconds, a brief interlude that would tragically stretch into an eternity of unanswered questions and lingering despair. This incredibly short lapse in time became the chilling fulcrum of a mystery that would captivate and torment the community for years to come.

Born on May 31, 1987, Mikelle, a young Caucasian female, possessed striking brown hair and hazel eyes. She vanished without a trace, leaving behind only tantalizing hints of her presence. Those who knew her recognized her by a few unique features: noticeably prominent upper front teeth and a series of moles gracefully dotted along the left side of her neck (The Charley Project, 2013). With pierced ears and hair in a stage of regrowth from a fresh perm, she seemed to be caught in a moment of transition. Each of these details serves as a crucial piece of the puzzle, a silent plea for anyone with information to come forward, as the search for Mikelle continues to echo through time.

Now I understand. When I was on patrol, I issued a citation for child neglect. I'd spotted a four-door sedan idling in the Pizza Hut parking lot, directly in front of the entrance. Several minutes passed with no one emerging, and the gnawing potential of that moment began to outweigh the tempting aroma of pepperoni wafting through the air. I was acutely aware of the ticking clock, the vulnerability of the child left unattended—an easy target for an opportunistic predator. After what felt like seven agonizing minutes, the mother finally returned. Her casual explanation felt like a flimsy attempt to conceal the gravity of her negligence. While it might seem like a minor oversight to some, the reality is an abduction can occur in mere seconds.

The weight of seemingly mundane moments often goes unnoticed until their significance is thrown into sharp relief. I recall a particular day in court, a scene etched in my memory. The judge, leaning forward with a raised eyebrow, inquired about the brief span of time I spent alone with a running vehicle and a child inside that vehicle. My answer, delivered without hesitation, each number a punctuation mark in the room's tension, underscored the gravity of those seconds. The verdict, a jail sentence for the mother, was more than just a punishment; it was a stark reminder of the razor's edge between the ordinary and the life-altering. This incident, seemingly trivial in its initial moments, became a profound lesson in responsibility, its echo lingering long after the gavel fell. It served as a harsh wake-up call for the young mother and left an indelible mark on my own understanding of familial duty, illustrating how, in the realm of law enforcement, even the smallest lapse can spiral into a chilling reminder of the fragility of safety.

This fragility is tragically underscored in cases like the disappearance of Mikelle. In the early evening of her vanishing, Mikelle, a striking 11-year-old, was last seen wearing a distinctive red t-shirt. Illustrated with the name of her elementary school, Lindbergh (occasionally documented as "Lindburg" in official records), this seemingly simple garment, along with her bell-bottom jeans featuring embroidered seams and her white canvas shoes, now serve as poignant markers in a haunting investigation. Though the details remain murky, witnesses suggest she may also have been wearing earrings that day. These seemingly mundane articles of clothing, like the seconds counted in that courtroom, become vital threads in a narrative of a young girl whose vibrant presence abruptly vanished, leaving behind an enduring mystery that haunts the quiet community. They are a stark reminder that even the most ordinary details can become profoundly significant when a life hangs in the balance.

Despite an exhaustive search in the shadow of Mikelle's family's home, authorities found no tangible evidence to illuminate her disappearance. Even the trained search dogs faltered mere feet from where she was last seen, a chilling detail hinting at a grim possibility: Mikelle had likely been taken swiftly, perhaps bundled into a waiting vehicle. Further investigations into the presence of an ice cream truck that fateful day proved inconclusive, and while local vendors were scrutinized, they were all cleared. Similarly, known sex offenders in the vicinity were investigated and dismissed. This persistent lack of evidence surrounding Mikelle's vanishing leaves a haunting void and underscores the unsettling mystery that envelops her fate.

In the disappearance of Mikelle, investigators have encountered a myriad of false leads that have only deepened the mystery surrounding her case. On January 9, a frantic search led police to a site just outside Mesa, where the earth had been disturbed as if a grave had been hastily concealed (The Charley Project, 2013). However, this grim expectation yielded nothing but disappointment, as the excavation uncovered only empty soil.

Facing the challenge of unlocking memories, authorities made a desperate attempt by using hypnosis on two witnesses, hoping to uncover crucial details (The Charley Project, 2013). However, this unorthodox method yielded no results, only deepening the mystery. Compounding the uncertainty, a copper-colored Jeep was reportedly spotted near Mikelle's home when she vanished (The Charley Project, 2013). Investigators located and questioned the driver, but he was determined to be just a bystander and not a suspect, offering no useful information about that fateful day. As the search continues, these inconclusive leads only add to the obscurity surrounding Mikelle's case, highlighting the heartbreaking complexity of an unresolved story.

In the quiet neighborhoods where childhood laughter once echoed, investigators conducted thorough searches of residences with the owners' consent. Despite this extensive effort, these searches yielded no clues to unravel the mystery. Only one homeowner, cloaked in an air of silence, denied the request for a search, though he remains firmly outside the circle of suspicion. Adding another layer of complexity, on March 10, 1999, an alarming report surfaced: a man allegedly attempted to abduct two young girls, aged ten and eleven, while they played in a schoolyard (The Charley Project, 2013). Authorities swiftly connected this incident to Mikelle's case, raising hopes for a breakthrough. However, the shadows of fear soon lifted when the supposed abduction was ultimately exposed as a fabrication. Consequently, the truth of that fateful day remained frustratingly out of reach, leaving behind only whispers and unanswered questions.

Amidst the ongoing enigma of Mikelle's disappearance, investigators have unveiled haunting sketches depicting two individuals who may hold keys to the mystery (The Charley Project, 2013). While these images are now part of the case summary, authorities have chosen not to widely circulate them due to their uncertainty about any true ties these men may have to Mikelle's fate. This absence of clarity leaves a lingering question mark, as the community clings to hope and seeks answers from the shadows of these drawn faces.

In the unsettling shadows of the Mikelle Biggs case, one name lingers with the weight of suspicion: Dee Blalock. Residing merely two blocks away from the Biggs household in 1999, Blalock's troubling past, marked by a series of convictions for sex offenses across three states, had already branded him as a registered sex offender (The Charley Project, 2013). This proximity, coupled with the alarming trajectory of his criminal history, immediately made him a figure of interest. By 2001, he had escalated his depravity, facing conviction for the brutal rape of a neighbor and attempted murder (The Charley Project, 2013). Consequently, he now endures a fifteen-and-a-half-year sentence within the stark confines of an Arizona prison (The Charley Project, 2013). While the search for Mikelle continues to haunt the community, her father believes he knows the face of the man who stole his daughter's future, raising unsettling questions about justice, accountability, and the shadows that linger over unresolved tragedies.

In the dim light of a cold case room, a faded photograph of Blalock hangs, a silent witness to the unsolved mystery of Mikelle's disappearance. The shadows of suspicion initially fell upon him, though his wife fiercely asserted his innocence, insistently declaring he was safely in their home garage throughout that fateful night (The Charley Project, 2013). Yet, grief-stricken and desperate for answers, Mikelle's parents eventually confronted Blalock in his sterile prison cell, seeking the truth that had eluded them for so long (The Charley Project, 2013). With an unsettling calm, he denied any involvement, insisting he knew nothing of their daughter's fate (The Charley Project, 2013). This chilling claim left them grappling with the haunting uncertainty tied to his words, a stark reminder that in a case steeped in shadows, the search for truth often leaves many questions unanswered.

Mikelle's family lives under the long shadow of loss, navigating the turbulent waters of grief and unanswered questions. Five years after her tragic disappearance, they gathered with heavy hearts to honor her memory. An empty casket, a poignant symbol of both lingering hope and profound despair, was laid to rest (The Charley Project, 2013). For years, whispers of foul play have haunted their thoughts, a chilling belief that Mikelle was taken from them far too soon, her light extinguished shortly after she vanished. Despite the weight of suspicion and their relentless quest for truth, no charges have ever been filed, leaving the case suspended in the realm of unresolved mysteries. They continue to grapple with the painful silence surrounding the circumstances of her fate.

Mikelle was a vibrant and promising young girl, celebrated for her intelligence and artistic talent. At the time of her mysterious disappearance, she was an honor student actively involved in her school's student council and captivating audiences with her clarinet performances. With dreams of becoming an animator, her creativity illuminated every aspect of her life. Deeply connected to her family, she shared a special bond with her younger sisters and brother, often bringing joy and support into their lives. Her favorite color, purple, reflected her unique personality and zest for life. Despite exhaustive searches and investigations, the trail has gone cold, leaving her family and community desperately seeking answers. With few leads and growing questions, Mikelle's case remains unresolved, a sad reminder of the void her absence has left behind.

Top of Form

Mikelle Biggs was the eldest of the four Biggs children, a role that carried both the weight of responsibility and the deep bonds of family loyalty. Growing up in a lively household, she was known for her nurturing nature and fierce protectiveness of her younger siblings. Often regarded as the "golden child," Mikelle's dreams shone as brightly as the desert sun, making her a source of hope and pride for her family. However, everything changed on a tragic day in 1999, when she mysteriously vanished without a trace. Her vibrant presence was suddenly extinguished, leaving her loved ones in a state of endless longing and unanswered questions. What was once a bright, lively spirit has now become a haunting mystery—her laughter a distant memory, her fate forever shrouded in uncertainty.

Following Mikelle's disappearance, an enormous search operation was launched, turning the usually peaceful neighborhood into a hive of frantic activity. Police meticulously examined every trash container, digging through refuse with careful precision in hopes of finding any clue about the missing girl. Officers also visited homes, knocking on doors and questioning neighbors, determined to gather any information. Yet, despite their efforts, witnesses remained silent; no one recalled seeing anything unusual that day.

Amidst this chaos, detectives worked closely with Kimber, Mikelle's sister, retracing their steps on that haunting January 2nd. Could those fleeting 90 seconds hold the key to solving the mystery of Mikelle's fate? It seemed that time was both a relentless pursuer and a fragile, fleeting ally in this heartbreaking investigation.

The search for Mikelle Biggs grew more intense, unraveling layers of mystery and deception within her tightly knit family. As investigators delved deeper, their attention shifted to a startling first suspect: Darien Biggs, Mikelle's own father (Sarkar, 2021). Initially, Darien claimed he was at work when he learned of his daughter's disappearance through a frantic phone call from his wife. However, a crucial discrepancy soon emerged, his alibi was false. Instead of being at his workplace, he was found at a friend's house. This revelation cast suspicion on Darien and complicated the investigation. As more details surfaced, it became clear that beneath the façade of a concerned parent lay a darker truth: he had confided in his wife about an affair (Sarkar, 2021). This development left investigators grappling with the unsettling possibility that the very person who was supposed to protect Mikelle might have been entangled in a web of lies, lies that could hold the key to her whereabouts and what truly happened to her.

In the shadowy recesses of a case that had long remained unresolved, the narrative took an unexpected turn. Despite voluntarily taking a lie detector test, Darien's results were inconclusive; detectives observed that his emotional distress might have influenced the outcome, leaving lingering doubts about his innocence (Sarkar, 2021). After a painstaking year of surveillance and investigation, he was ultimately cleared as a suspect, his involvement fading into the rearview mirror of the case. However, the focus soon shifted to another figure: neighbor Dee Blalock, a man with a disturbing history of violence and sexual offenses, including allegations of child molestation (Sarkar, 2021). Blalock re-emerged in the investigation after being apprehended for the brutal assault and rape of local resident Susan Quinnett (Sarkar, 2021). This development prompted investigators to wonder, could this man hold the crucial piece needed to unravel the chilling mystery that had shaken their once-quiet community?

Forever changed and burdened by a revelation that could alter everything, Susan saw a potential connection between her assailant, Blalock, and the chilling fate that had befallen Mikelle (Sarkar, 2021). This unsettling insight was shared with Tracy Biggs, sparking a flicker of hope amid the despair. In a bold and desperate move, Susan offered to drop the assault charges against Blalock if he would confess to any possible involvement in Mikelle's disappearance (Sarkar, 2021). Driven by hope and desperation, the Biggs parents poured their hearts into a series of letters to Blalock, who was then-confined in Arizona's maximum-security prison (Sarkar, 2021). They eventually met him face to face, eager to uncover the truth that seemed just within reach. However, in a disconcerting turn, Blalock firmly denied any connection to Mikelle's disappearance, insisting on his innocence. His denial left an unsettling void, and the case remained cold and unresolved, shrouded in mystery (Sarkar, 2021).

In 2004, as the sun cast long shadows over a community forever changed, the Biggs family gathered in quiet mourning to mark the fifth anniversary of Mikelle's disappearance. At the front of the room stood an empty, stark white casket, adorned with delicate purple flowers, the color Mikelle loved most (Sarkar, 2021). This somber tribute was more than a memorial; it was a heartbreaking act of closure for a family haunted by unanswered questions. Each petal symbolized their lingering sorrow, a silent testament to the hope that had gradually faded over five long years. Meanwhile, the Mesa Police Department documented the search for Mikelle as one of their most costly and exhaustive investigations (Sarkar, 2021). It served as a sobering reminder that, despite their extensive efforts and resources, the truth remained elusive, hidden in the shadows of what once was, and what might never be known.

In 2018, a flicker of renewed hope ignited within the Biggs family when a seemingly innocent dollar bill was discovered in Wisconsin, bearing a cryptic message: "My name is Mikel Biggs kidnapped from Mesa Az I'm Alive" (Sarkar, 2021, para. 12). This tantalizing clue sent shockwaves through the investigation team, still tirelessly searching for Mikelle Biggs, who had vanished without a trace more than two decades earlier. However, as meticulous detectives examined the note, their optimism waned. The misspelling of Mikelle's name, coupled with similarities to a suspicious note from 2009 and handwriting analysis, led them to dismiss the message as either a cruel hoax or a juvenile prank (Sarkar, 2021). After more than twenty years, Mikelle's disappearance remains an unsolved mystery, lingering like an echo of unfulfilled hope in the shadows of time.

Over two decades have passed, yet the haunting mystery of Mikelle Biggs's disappearance endures, casting an unrelenting pall over the community that still clings to hope. Despite the years that have gone by, time seems to stand still on that fateful day, where the boundary between the known and the unknown becomes blurred. Echoes of unanswered questions resonate through the lives of those left behind, and the case, layered with uncertainty, remains dormant, waiting for a spark that might reignite the investigation and finally bring to light the long-shrouded truth.

Recalling the day Mikelle disappeared, Kimber, her younger sister, wandered toward the end of the road, the familiar path now shrouded in unsettling uncertainty. As she ambled forward, an ordinary sight emerged from the haze, a scene that would soon become extraordinary. "I started to walk towards the end of the road when I saw something, and it took a minute for it to come into focus," Kimber remembered (Castillo, 2024, para. 6). Then, the chilling truth struck her, "That's when I realized my bike was in the road with the tire still spinning" (Castillo, 2024, para. 6). In that haunting moment, everything around her seemed to freeze, and Kimber knew her sister was gone.

In the hushed stillness of early evening, Kimber's world was turned upside down. According to Mickeala Castillo (2024), Kimber recalled, "I just remember within hours there were police cars. The road was blocked off. There were news cameras. There were helicopters, search parties with posters already going up" (para. 9). Picture this: within mere hours of the incident, a chorus of sirens sliced through the quiet, signaling the arrival of police vehicles that swept through the neighborhood like ominous messengers of dread. The familiar road, once a simple path of daily life, was now barricaded and cordoned off, hiding its secrets from prying eyes and whispers of fear. News crews hurried to set up their cameras, capturing every unfolding moment as they probed into the depths of uncertainty. Above, helicopters hovered like ominous vultures, their searchlights piercing the night sky, while ground teams scoured the area, clutching posters bearing haunting images and desperate pleas for Mikelle's safe return. The atmosphere was thick with urgency, hope and fear collided as the community rallied against the shadows of a mystery that had ensnared them all.

Amidst the shadows of the investigation, police uncovered a chilling persona lurking behind Darien's stoic exterior. Kimber described him as an "angry zombie," vividly illustrating a man who seemed detached yet seethed with unresolved rage (Sarkar, 2021). During intense questioning about his daughter's mysterious disappearance, Darien's fury erupted unexpectedly. He violently overturned a table in the interrogation room, a stark outward display of his inner turmoil (Sarkar, 2021). This unpredictable behavior raised red flags, prompting investigators to probe deeper into the couple's connections. As the case progressed, Tracy and Darien began exchanging letters with a second suspect, Dee Blalock. Their correspondence flowed at nearly regular intervals, weaving a complex web of relationships that raised a crucial question: what truths lay hidden within their words, and could they hold the key to unraveling the mystery surrounding Mikelle's fate?

Just a few seconds shattered Kimber's world, transforming her life in ways she could scarcely comprehend. Deep inside, she clings to the haunting belief that the man who took her sister from their lives, Dee Blalock, a convicted sex offender and child molester, still lurks just next door, his ominous presence casting a shadow over their neighborhood (Sarkar, 2021). Despite his conviction, Kimber's relentless quest for justice remains painfully incomplete, her yearning for answers wrapped in uncertainty. The anger that flared when suspicion initially fell upon her own father for Mikelle's disappearance still simmers beneath the surface, a stark reminder of the dark shadows that continue to weave through their lives. Driven by an insatiable need for closure, Kimber immerses herself in the digital world, her voice echoing through her personal Facebook page and a dedicated memorial site for Mikelle. There, she continues to honor her sister's memory and seek the truth that has eluded them for far too long (Sarkar, 2021).

In the months following the creation of the Facebook page dedicated to Mikelle Biggs, a noticeable shift took hold within the community. Kimber, a waitress in Mesa juggling her part-time job while navigating the tumultuous waters of grief and hope, found herself overwhelmed by responses. "People started coming forward, not only with support but also with information and potential leads," Kimber recalled, a flicker of determination shining in her eyes (Sarkar, 2021, para. 7). This surge of engagement prompted her to rebrand the page; what had begun as a memorial titled "Remember Mikelle Biggs" evolved into a rallying cry under the banner of "Justice for Mikelle Biggs" (Sarkar, 2021, para. 7). As Kimber desperately sought answers amid her heartbreak, her Facebook profile offered a glimpse into her life, she was a dedicated mother to her son, Tayven, and appeared to be in a relationship, sharing the responsibilities of parenting. Yet, beneath the surface of her daily life lay the lingering questions about a case that had haunted their community for years.

The passage of time has not faded Kimber's memory of her sister, Mikelle, who remains forever etched in her mind. "Her hair was all golden in the sun, and she was happy and having a good time, and that's the last image I have of her," Kimber recalled (Paredez, 2024, para. 3). This vivid memory, while tinged with sadness, captures a moment of pure joy, a lasting snapshot of happier days amid the shadows of uncertainty. Despite the heavy weight of loss that still bears down on her, a flicker of hope remains intertwined with her memories, a reminder that love endures, even in the face of unanswered questions and unsolved mysteries.

Kimber stated, "I came in through the back door and as soon as I walked in, my mom said, 'nope, go tell Mikelle she has to come in" (Paredez, 2024, para. 5).

The investigation into Mikelle's disappearance began in a scene marked by haunting emptiness, two quiet quarters lying in the dirt and the bike she had been riding, serving as unsettling symbols of her sudden absence (Paredez, 2024). As law enforcement meticulously examined the details, the community rallied together, launching their own grassroots efforts to find her. Flyers were distributed, and search parties combed the surrounding areas, fueled by a deep sense of urgency and collective solidarity (Paredez, 2024). Amidst this chaos, Mikelle's family struggled to grasp the reality unfolding before them, clinging to hope despite the unbearable uncertainty of her sudden disappearance. Each passing hour intensified their sorrow, while the desperate search for answers grew more urgent with every moment.

In a recent interview with the newly assigned detective handling the longstanding cold case, reporters uncovered a significant shift in the investigation's direction. The detective revealed that he is now focusing on critical evidence linking the crime to a convicted sexual predator, a name that had quietly lingered in the background from the very beginning (Paredez, 2024). This renewed focus suggests that the key to solving Mikelle's case may have been right under their nose all along. As the detective navigates the shadows cast by past convictions, he works to unravel the intricate web of the case and uncover the truth that has remained hidden for years.

ABC15 reporter Ashley Paredez (2024) asked, "Is that person still a person of interest?" (Paredez, 2024, para. 13). In response, Mesa PD detective Paul Sipe stated, "I would say he is the person of interest" (Paredez, 2024, para. 14). It was confirmed that Dee Blalock is the primary person of interest; however, he has never been formally charged in connection with the incident. Despite this confirmation, the fact remains that Dee Blalock has yet to face any charges related to Mikelle's disappearance, even as he remains the focal point of ongoing investigations and community concern.

Detective Sipe's comments took on a somber tone as he reflected on the profound human implications of the case. He stated, "What I'd like to say to the investigative lead that we have is, that he has children of his own and knowing that and imagining what he would feel like if his children were missing for 25 years" (Paredez, 2024, para. 18). This stark reminder of the human cost of unresolved questions hangs heavily, resonating through the passage of time as the search for justice grows colder with each passing year. In the shadows of this cold case, memories linger, and the prospect of closure remains a distant hope, leaving both the affected families and the community struggling with the unsettling reality of loss and enduring uncertainty.

As the sun sets over Mesa, casting long shadows that flicker between memories of laughter and loss, the story of Mikelle Biggs remains a poignant reminder of life's fragility and the resilience born from sorrow. Despite the heartache and unanswered questions that have marked the search for answers, the unwavering spirit of the community continues to shine brightly. Each flyer fluttering on a telephone pole and each whispered prayer among neighbors serve as enduring testaments to the love for a girl who once pedaled her bicycle down these very streets. In the face of uncertainty, the Biggs family remains steadfast, cherishing Mikelle's memory and holding onto hope that someday, the truth will emerge, and justice will be fulfilled. Until that day, they carry her spirit with them, committed not only to keeping her story alive but also to ensuring that no other family endures the ache of an empty chair at the dinner table.

If anyone has any information on the disappearance of Mikelle Diane Biggs, please contact the Mesa Police Department at 480-644-2211.

"The Lord watch between me and thee, when we are absent one from another." ~ Genesis 31:49

CHAPTER 9

THE DISAPPEARING CYCLIST

In the quiet morning hours of a seemingly ordinary day, a young cyclist vanished, casting a shadow over the peaceful landscape and reminding us of life's fragile and unpredictable nature. This unsettling disappearance compels us to confront the delicate balance between existence and the capricious hand of fate. The haunting possibility that a vibrant life could be cut short urges us to recognize that everyone's story is a tapestry woven from choices, choices whose ripples extend far beyond the individual, shaping the interconnected web of human experience. As we delve deeper into this cold case, we uncover the profound links between our decisions, the unpredictable twists of destiny, and the ethical weight carried by every action. With each clue unearthed, we walk a tightrope between emotional engagement and rational detachment, meticulously assembling the fragments of a life lost while contemplating the myriad paths that led to this moment of crisis.

September 20, 1988, was meant to be a typical day for Tara Calico, a young girl with a spirit for adventure and a love for the outdoors. She left her home on Brugg Street in Belen, New Mexico, at 9:30 a.m., riding her mother's bright neon pink Huffy Mountain bike after her own had a flat tire. Her destination was a solo ride along Highway 47, a simple, familiar journey that symbolized her growing independence and a moment to feel the wind in her brown hair. But as the hours passed, something went terribly wrong. The day that was supposed to be ordinary suddenly turned into a mystery that would haunt a community for decades.

The last confirmed sighting of Tara was at 11:45 a.m., about two miles from her home. Her bike, with its distinctive yellow control cables and sidewalls, was nowhere to be found. Search parties scoured the surrounding desert, desperately looking for any sign of Tara, but she seemed to have vanished into thin air. The community's mind raced with questions: What truly happened to Tara Calico? Was she a victim of circumstance, perhaps lost in the vast, unforgiving desert? Or was there something more sinister at play lurking beneath the surface of this mysterious disappearance?

Tara Leigh Calico was born on February 28, 1969. At the time of her disappearance, she was 19 years old. She stood approximately 5 feet 7 inches tall and weighed around 120 pounds. The last known sighting placed her wearing a distinctive outfit: a white T-shirt emblazoned with the phrase "1st National Bank of Belen," paired with white shorts featuring green stripes. Her attire was completed with white ankle socks and her signature turquoise and white Avia sneakers (The Charley Project, 2020). She also wore jewelry, including a gold butterfly ring set with a diamond insert, a gold amethyst ring, and half-inch gold hoop earrings, adding to her unique and recognizable appearance.

Tara was obviously known to ride her mother's neon pink Huffy Mountain bicycle with the notable yellow control cables and sidewalls, and she was also associated with a dilapidated 1953 Ford pickup truck, described as either dirty white or light gray and topped with a handmade white shell (The Charley Project, 2020). Distinguishing features included brown hair and striking green eyes. She bore a significant scar on the back of her right shoulder and another scar on her calf, complemented by a dime-sized brown birthmark located on one of her legs. Additionally, she had a lazy eye and a cowlick on her right temple (The Charley Project, 2020). Her dental history included braces, and her ears are pierced, making her recognizable in public settings (The Charley Project, 2020). Each detail provided can serve as a clue in piecing together the events surrounding her disappearance and continue to haunt investigators as they seek answers in this enduring cold case.

As we delve into this cold case, we will examine the known facts, consider the possible motivations behind Tara Calico's actions, and reflect on the "what ifs" that continue to haunt this enduring mystery. What compelled Calico to ride out into the unknown? Was she searching for something beyond a simple bike ride? And what secrets might be hidden within the vast desert landscape that could hold the key to unraveling this enigma? The disappearance of Tara remains one of the most perplexing unsolved mysteries in recent history. Through our investigation, we aim to shed new light on this baffling case and bring clarity to a story that has puzzled many for decades.

As we know, Tara was an avid cyclist, faithfully navigating her familiar 36-mile route with unwavering dedication. During her daily ride, several witnesses reported seeing a dirty white or light gray 1953 Ford pickup truck, equipped with a distinctive handmade white shell, closely trailing her bike (The Charley Project, 2020). The connection between the truck and Tara's disappearance remains unclear, and it appears she was unaware of its presence. Alarmingly, her mother's bicycle has never been recovered, a chilling detail that deepens the mystery of her absence. The circumstances surrounding Tara's vanishing suggest the possibility of foul play, leaving her family and authorities desperately searching for answers and clarity in this perplexing case.

So, who was Tara, and what was her life like? Tara Calico was known for her competence and independence, traits that shaped her daily routine. She was meticulous about creating lists to organize her days and often prioritized her commitments with great precision. An avid runner, she placed a strong emphasis on maintaining her schedule, demonstrating maturity beyond her years. On the day of her disappearance, her concern for punctuality was evident; she instructed her mother, Patty Doel, to come and find her if she had not returned home by 12:00 p.m., reflecting her keen awareness of time and the importance she placed on it, qualities that set her apart from many other 19-year-olds. Little did she know that would be the last time she would be heard from, leaving a chilling void in the timeline of her otherwise orderly life.

On the day of her disappearance, Tara had a busy schedule planned. She had arranged to play tennis with her boyfriend at 12:30 p.m. and attend a class at 4:00 p.m. At the time, she was a promising sophomore at the University of New Mexico at Valencia, having recently graduated from Belen High School. With a high grade point average and aspirations of becoming a psychiatrist or psychologist, Tara was a focused and dedicated student. She also balanced her academic pursuits with a job at a local bank. Yet, in a troubling twist, she inexplicably vanished that day, leaving behind her sneakers, tennis equipment, schoolbooks, and purse, clues that now remain cold, unanswered, and haunting the mystery of her last day.

At precisely 12:05 p.m. on the day Tara disappeared, Patty Doel set out to search for her daughter, her concern growing with each passing minute. When her familiar bike route yielded no sign of Tara, her anxiety intensified, and she quickly contacted law enforcement, eager to find her daughter and uncover what had happened.

The following day, fate took a chilling turn. Just three miles from Tara's home and on the opposite side of the highway, Patty stumbled upon a cassette tape, a haunting symbol of Tara's presence and a crucial clue. The Boston tape had been discarded, suggesting she had made a sudden departure, perhaps in haste to escape or during a struggle. This grim discovery deepened the mystery surrounding Tara's disappearance, leaving investigators and her mother with more questions than answers, intensifying the sense that something far more sinister was at play.

Discovering evidence the next day can be a complex process, especially if the area wasn't properly cordoned off from the public—a crucial step known as "securing the scene." Investigations are like assembling a giant puzzle; over time, the pieces eventually come together to reveal the full picture. The cassette tape found by Tara's mother marked one of those vital pieces. It serves as physical evidence that Tara had been near that location recently. Its presence raises important questions about her activities on the day she disappeared. Being found three miles from her home and on the opposite side of the highway suggests she may have traveled away from her usual routines. This could imply that Tara was either intentionally leaving or had encountered a situation that forced her to alter her course, adding layers of complexity to the mystery surrounding her disappearance.

The manner in which the tape was found, abandoned and out of place, could suggest a sense of urgency or even a struggle. If Tara dropped it while riding her bike, it raises questions about what might have caused her to leave it behind. Tara was intelligent and resourceful; perhaps she intentionally dropped the cassette, hoping someone would find it and trace her route. Law enforcement could use the tape as a key piece of evidence, potentially containing fingerprints, DNA, or other forensic traces that might offer new insights or lead to suspects. However, it's important to note that DNA technology at the time was not as advanced or widespread as it is today, limiting the information that could be gleaned from such evidence in 1988.

In a chilling turn of events, another crucial piece of evidence surfaced later; part of Tara's distinctive Sony Walkman was found lying desolate nineteen miles east of Highway 47, near the isolated John F. Kennedy Campground (The Charley Project, 2020). Investigators, including Tara's mother, speculated that Tara may have intentionally discarded these items as a desperate attempt to mark her trail, a silent plea for help woven into the fabric of her disappearance. Surrounding the area of the cassette tape, investigators uncovered faint bike tracks intertwined with troubling impressions, scuffs, skid marks, and signs of a struggle; that hinted something violent or sudden had occurred. These clues suggested that whatever transpired here was far from ordinary. This discovery once again raised countless questions, Where was Tara Calico, and what circumstances had led her to this seemingly forgotten place?

For decades, a sinister mystery has persisted, one that intertwines the fate of a missing woman with a chilling Polaroid photograph discovered in a parking lot in Port St. Joe, Florida, on June 15, 1989, nine months after her disappearance. The haunting image sparked widespread speculation that the unidentified woman captured within the frame might be none other than Tara Calico. Adding to the eerie intrigue, witnesses reported a white Toyota cargo van lingering near the location where the photo was found, casting suspicion on its owner and deepening the enigma. As the years have passed, the connection between the van, the photograph, and Tara's case has become increasingly tangled, like threads of time, cementing its place among the most perplexing unsolved mysteries in recent history.

The photograph discovered by a passerby sent chills through investigators. It depicted a teenage girl and a young boy lying on disheveled sheets, their mouths sealed with duct tape and their limbs bound, a haunting and disturbing image. The woman who found the photo was shaken but determined; she relayed to police that, just moments before her arrival, a white Toyota van had been parked nearby. The driver, described as a mustached man in his thirties, had left no trace and disappeared into the night. Authorities quickly set up a roadblock in hopes of intercepting the vehicle, but their efforts proved futile, deepening the mystery surrounding the chilling image and raising numerous questions about the fate of the bound children and the identity of the abductors.

This particular Polaroid garnered national attention when it was featured on *America's Most Wanted*. When Patty Doel first saw the grainy photograph, a wave of doubt washed over her. The image was dim and shadowy, obscured by the passage of time and neglect, leaving much to uncertainty. Yet, with each lingering glance, familiar contours began to emerge from the haze; a fleeting recognition ignited deep within her memory. Was her mind playing tricks on her, fueled by hope and longing for Tara? As seconds stretched into minutes, the shadows gradually sharpened into undeniable clarity, transforming what was once a whisper of familiarity into a chorus of certainty.

A mother's familiarity with her children can be likened to a deep, instinctive knowledge that goes beyond mere observation. This bond is cultivated over time through countless moments of interaction, listening to their laughter, noticing the subtle nuances of their moods, and understanding their unspoken needs. A mother often becomes attuned to the slightest shifts in her child's behavior, able to detect a smile that doesn't quite reach the eyes or a sudden withdrawal that hints at underlying struggles. Consider how a mother might know her child well enough to predict their reactions in various situations. This intuitive understanding is not solely the result of observation; it is enriched by shared experiences, moments of joy, sorrow, and everyday life, that create a profound connection and a sense of knowing that is almost instinctual.

In the photograph, a subtle, discolored streak was visible on the female's thigh, a scar eerily reminiscent of the one Tara had sustained from a childhood car accident. The resemblance was chilling, intertwining their fates in an unsettling way. Beside her, almost as if deliberately placed, lay a well-thumbed paperback, its dog-eared pages a testament to frequent reading. The cover bore the name V.C. Andrews, a beloved author of Tara's. These connections were undeniable, adding yet another layer of complexity to an already perplexing cold case that longed for resolution. Were those involved playing with the public, with Tara's family? The torment felt real, no longer just a haunting thought, but a tangible, painful reality.

A faded Polaroid still held the power to ignite a flicker of hope in Patty's heart. Staring back at her was a girl whose appearance, especially after the passage of time and the removal of makeup, bore a striking resemblance to Tara. Driven by unwavering conviction, Patty believed she was looking at her missing daughter. However, the authorities remained skeptical. Experts from the Los Alamos National Laboratory expressed doubts about the identification, and the FBI, entangled in layers of uncertainty, struggled to offer definitive conclusions. Yet, across the Atlantic, a glimmer of hope emerged when Scotland Yard took an interest. After careful examination, they boldly asserted that the girl in the photograph was indeed Tara Calico.

It was determined that the photograph must have been printed recently, as the film used in the Polaroid was not available before that time. Officials at Polaroid confirmed a disturbing detail: the film employed in the snapshot was not accessible to the public until after May 1989. This raised another pressing question, who was the boy in the photograph with the girl? An anguished family of a nine-year-old named Michael Henley emerged. They sought to identify the young boy depicted in the Polaroid as their son, Michael, who had vanished without a trace in New Mexico during a hunting trip with his father in April 1988. What began as a hopeful search soon turned into a painful wait, as both families struggled with the chilling uncertainty that hung over them like a dense fog, leaving them to wonder if the answers they desperately sought would ever surface. For these families, the photograph represented a potential beacon of hope, even if it did not ultimately confirm that the girl and boy were Tara and Michael.

In the shadows of the Zuni Mountains, a tragic chapter came to a somber close, marking the end of a haunting mystery. In 1990, the skeletal remains of Michael Henley were discovered just miles from the campsite where his laughter once echoed through the crisp mountain air. Despite the peaceful appearance of the landscape, it concealed profound sorrow. Evidence indicated that Michael had succumbed to exposure, his life had been extinguished long before any enigmatic Polaroid could shed light on his disappearance. Amid the labyrinth of unresolved losses and unanswered questions, only one family was left with the painful truth, grief forever entwined with the mountains that bore witness to a young life lost far too soon.

The girl depicted in the haunting Polaroid is believed to have been spotted near the windswept shores of Port St. Joe shortly before the photograph's unsettling discovery. Witnesses recall observing a troubling scene, the young girl was seen walking under the watchful gaze of several unidentified adult Caucasian males, whose demeanor suggested a disturbing level of control as they appeared to issue her verbal commands. This raises a chilling question, could this have been a case of human trafficking, or was it simply a situation of parental guidance?

The vibrant life of Tara Calico was abruptly cut short, leaving behind a chilling mystery that has haunted her loved ones and investigators for decades. Over time, eyewitness accounts reveal that on the day of her disappearance, two teenage boys reportedly confronted her. Their initial jovial demeanor quickly shifted to reckless behavior as they followed and harassed her. In a moment of chaos, their truck collided with her, a fateful accident that spiraled into an even darker narrative. As investigators piece together fragments of this tragic encounter, a sinister possibility emerges, overwhelmed by panic and fear of the consequences, the boys may have taken her from the scene and silenced her to prevent her from alerting authorities. The shadows of complicity grow deeper, as allegations surface suggesting that others may have conspired to cover up the crime, weaving a web of deceit that complicates the quest for justice in a case still shrouded in uncertainty.

As investigators sift through the remnants of the past, it is important to note that the information currently available has yet to be substantiated, and no suspects have been publicly identified. Nonetheless, authorities are compelled to believe that Tara's remains may likely lie within the same vicinity from which she vanished. This lingering uncertainty raises a haunting question: what truly transpired on that fateful day? The search for answers endures, as the echoes of her disappearance continue to resonate within the community, demanding closure and justice. In 1998, a final verdict was issued in the courtroom: the judge declared Tara Leigh Calico deceased, marking her death as a tragic homicide.

For fifteen years, Tara's mother and stepfather remained in the very house where she had vanished, a stagnant relic filled with memories and unanswered questions that hung heavily in the air. Eventually, the weight of the past became too overwhelming, prompting them to seek refuge in Florida, marking the end of an era steeped in sorrow. The passage of time continued to claim lives: Tara's mother passed away in 2006, and her biological father succumbed to his own tragic fate in 2002. Despite their losses, remnants of the family still linger, with her stepfather's surviving relatives and siblings left to grapple with the lingering questions. As the years go by, the case of Tara Calico remains shrouded in mystery, a haunting puzzle waiting to be solved amid the silence that still surrounds her disappearance.

As the shadows of uncertainty continue to cast over the case of Tara Leigh Calico, the silence surrounding her 36-year disappearance remains deafening. Anyone who possesses even the slightest fragment of information regarding Tara's fate is urged to come forward. Please direct your insights to the Valencia County Sheriff's Department at 505-865-9604 or contact the FBI in New Mexico at 505-224-2000. In an effort to break through the enduring mystery, the FBI has announced a reward of $20,000 for any credible leads that could shed light on Tara's whereabouts. Every detail matters, a whisper of the truth could potentially unravel years of unanswered questions and bring peace to those still seeking justice for Tara.

"Heal me, Lord, and I will be healed; save me and I will be saved." ~ Jeremiah 17:14

PART III

FINALLY, SOME ANSWERS

CHAPTER 10

SHE WAS JUST A GIRL

Debbie Lynn Randall was a freckled girl with a smile that touched everyone she met. It was said that Debbie liked to collect leftover laundry soap from the laundromat and bring it home, perhaps her way of helping her family. Even at a young age, she was already showing nurturing qualities. Growing up, she enjoyed typical girlhood activities: playing with Barbie dolls, spending time with friends, and, of course, cheerleading. The Suds and Duds laundromat became her favorite meeting place with friends, where they would play with dolls and enjoy each other's company. Having grown up near the laundromat, since her parents did their laundry there, Debbie considered it a safe and familiar place.

On the evening of January 13, 1972, Robert Hooker, Debbie's stepfather, was doing laundry at the laundromat, accompanied by Debbie. A short time later, Robert left the laundromat, confident that Debbie would follow shortly behind. About thirty minutes after he departed, Debbie was seen trailing behind with laundry detergent in her hand. She had every intention of returning home, but beneath the surface of normalcy, an ominous shadow of doom lurked. In an instant, she vanished without a trace, never to return home. Her sudden disappearance sent ripples of concern through the community, shattering the tranquility of that night.

According to the Marietta Police Department, some witnesses reported seeing a dark pickup truck driving along the street around the time Debbie vanished. The police stated that the truck stopped in front of the Hooker home before backing into a secluded area nearby. Later, investigators recovered the detergent bottle Debbie carried on her way home that evening. Once the community learned of her disappearance, they united as if they were part of her family, exemplifying the spirit of togetherness that a community should have. Volunteers searched tirelessly everywhere they could, through the woods, vacant buildings, homes, and any place a child might hide or wish to hide.

On January 29, 1972, students from Southern Polytechnic University assisted in the search near Powers Ferry Road and Windy Hill Road, where Houston's Restaurant now stands. Their efforts led to the discovery of Debbie's motionless body in a remote wooded area. Her lifeless form was found 17 days after her disappearance, concealed within a secluded location that seemed to whisper secrets of a heinous crime. The individual who found her chose not to disturb her body and kept a respectable distance. As investigators examined the remnants of her tragic fate, each detail fueled an urgent quest for justice, unraveling the dark story of a life cut short and the elusive shadows of the perpetrator still at large. It was later determined that Debbie had been brutally raped, strangled, and left for dead. Unfortunately, DNA technology wasn't widely available in the 1970s, making it even more challenging to identify her attacker.

Despite exhaustive investigations that meticulously cleared family members of suspicion and scrutinized a wide range of potential suspects, from known serial killers to seasoned rapists and other felons, the detectives found themselves entangled in a complex web of dead ends. The years passed from the turbulent 1970s into the uncertain mid-1990s, a period when the promise of DNA testing was still a distant hope on the horizon. As each lead faded, the case gradually slipped into obscurity, becoming another haunting chapter in the archives of unsolved mysteries.

Debbie's remains were ultimately discovered in the woods. Imagine the headline: "Georgia Girl Brutally Murdered." The habitat was teeming with animals and insects, complicating the investigation. Detectives noted the possibility of a drag mark, suggesting she may have been moved or carried. Her body was believed to be nude or partially nude at the scene; however, she was later redressed, and her coat was found with her. According to Detective Morris Nix, he remarked on the discovery of her remains, offering insight into the challenging circumstances surrounding her tragic end:

> I thought. I was thinking in my head and this before I ever saw any photograph of which there was only a handful, I thought we were going to find a nude or partially nude body. We didn't. She had on a coat, it was zipped all the way up, which I always thought was a little strange. There was some damage, facial damage, probably from wild animals. I was trying to (sic), which will also answer some questions for me. There was a rag in her vaginal area, and I'm thinking, why did that happen? Well, looking back on it, I think that she was bleeding so profusely,

he did not want her bleeding in the vehicle, so he puts the rag in there, puts her underwear back on her, takes her to this location, which I think was not planned. I think he pulled out a Dixie Cap and stone. She's bleeding. He stopped and thinks she's about to mess my truck up, gets her out, walk right down, and leaves her body. I have always wondered, and my prayer is that she was deceased at this point, but I've also wondered if maybe he pulls out and realized she's not dead. (McCollum, 2023, 16:44-18:03)

The Dixie cup, or the white Navy sailor's cap, is more than just a piece of headgear—it is a symbol of tradition and resilience within the U.S. Navy. By piecing together clues, understanding the history and symbolism of such an item can shed light on hidden connections and lead investigators closer to uncovering the truth. According to the January 31, 1972, issue of the *Reading Eagle*, authorities harbored high hopes of capturing the "kidnap-killer" and indicated that clues had been left behind in the wooded area where Debbie's body was discovered. A reward of $10,000 was announced to encourage tips leading to the suspect's arrest, but ultimately, no one claimed the reward money. Police Captain C.W. Elliot stated that an autopsy revealed Debbie, just nine years old, had been sexually assaulted and strangled. The captain also emphasized that she was apparently killed within four hours of her abduction, underscoring the brutality and swift violence of the crime.

The quiet, unassuming stretch of Windy Hill Road had long gained a sinister reputation as the final resting place for several lost souls who crossed paths with an elusive killer. As the sun dipped below the horizon, casting shadows over the overgrown brush, whispers of fear lingered in the air. Deep within the woods, the haunting question remained: once the horrors were unleashed and darkness receded, where did the killer vanish to? Did he slip back into the folds of the ordinary world, or was he still lurking nearby, watching and waiting for his next victim? The search for answers pressed on as detectives tirelessly pieced together a mystery that refused to be buried.

An eyewitness had reported seeing the killer's black truck and noted spilled detergent at the scene when Debbie was taken. It was also described that Debbie appeared to be fighting with the truck's driver, most likely struggling for her life. Was Debbie unconscious from a blow, or was she simply scared and hiding deep within the floorboard of the truck? What would a 9-year-old do in such a terrifying situation? I can imagine her crouched down, arms wrapped around her knees, terrified and wondering where she was being taken. The cold case detective speculated that perhaps she was threatened into silence, afraid to speak, or resist.

Detectives searched tirelessly for evidence and interviewed family members, but they found nothing conclusive. They also spoke with individuals of interest, including serial killers, rapists, felons, and anyone who fit their profile, yet no solid leads emerged. So, what happens when there is no identified suspect? The detectives did everything they could, dedicating their hearts to the case, even as it remained unresolved.

Over the years, numerous stories have been told in hopes of uncovering answers. Local media covered the case extensively, and podcasts dedicated episodes to her story. With cold cases, that's often where they stay, dormant until new evidence surfaces. This is where the community can step in and lend a hand. Media outlets, true crime shows, news broadcasts, and podcasts all serve to keep her memory alive. Someone out there is listening, holding onto the hope that the person responsible will be brought to justice. The retelling of her story, the whispers across podcasts, and the dedication of true crime enthusiasts symbolize the enduring human desire for closure. Through these media, we are reminded that even in our darkest moments, hope persists.

Her memory lives on, and her story remains unforgotten, inspiring continued pursuit of justice and peace.

The Cobb County Cold Case Unit never gave up. The case made such a lasting impact that even retired detectives vowed to continue searching for Debbie's killer. A central question persisted: was the perpetrator someone the family knew, or was he a complete stranger? As technology advanced, so did their ability to solve the case. It wasn't until February 2016 that authorities obtained a DNA profile, also known as a DNA fingerprint or genetic fingerprinting. This process involves analyzing an individual's unique DNA characteristics to identify or exclude suspects. Today, DNA profiling is a vital tool in criminal investigations, but in 1972, little was understood about DNA. It wasn't until 1984 that genetic fingerprinting was discovered by Sir Alec Jeffreys, a British geneticist at the University of Leicester, England. This breakthrough revolutionized forensic science and brought new hope to cold cases like Debbie's.

In the Marietta Police Department's archives, a haunting mystery remained unsolved for decades. During the initial investigation, detectives meticulously examined the scene, recovering a single hair strand and a piece of cloth that initially seemed inconsequential. The forensic advancements of October 2001 offered a glimmer of hope, as an FBI analysis successfully eliminated numerous potential suspects, but progress in the case came to a halt.

Fast forward to May 2015, when renewed and determined investigators revisited the evidence with fresh eyes. The cloth, once considered an afterthought, was sent for updated forensic analysis. This effort yielded a tantalizing clue, a partial DNA profile linked to an unidentified white male. This breakthrough was significant because it allowed authorities to narrow down the suspect list, ruling out Hispanics, Asians, and African Americans, reducing the potential pool of around 100 names and bringing new hope for solving the long-standing case.

The arrival of COVID-19 brought unprecedented challenges to police departments, especially within their cold case units. The pandemic created numerous obstacles for law enforcement agencies in managing and processing evidence, such as DNA, in unsolved cases, those crimes that have remained unresolved for years. One of the most significant impacts was on resource allocation. As the pandemic unfolded, many agencies had to redirect personnel and funding away from cold case investigations to focus on immediate public health and safety concerns related to COVID-19. This shift meant that valuable time, effort, and specialized expertise were diverted from efforts to solve long-standing crimes, further complicating the pursuit of justice for victims like Debbie.

The pandemic also significantly impacted the operational capacity of law enforcement, especially regarding field investigations. Lockdowns and social distancing measures made it much more difficult for investigators to conduct in-person interviews and interact with witnesses or informants—crucial components of cold case investigations. Additionally, many forensic laboratories faced disruptions due to COVID-19, either because of scaled-back operations or being overwhelmed with evidence from ongoing investigations. This backlog delayed the processing of DNA and other forensic evidence, further hindering progress in cold cases.

The pandemic also posed challenges to community engagement, which is often essential in solving long-standing cases. With traditional public events and outreach programs suspended or limited, law enforcement agencies found it harder to build trust with the community, gather tips, and solicit information related to unresolved crimes. Consequently, even when leads were identified or evidence uncovered, the wheels of justice slowed, and resolutions were often delayed. The intersection of a public health crisis and law enforcement efforts underscores how social issues are interconnected, demonstrating how crises like COVID-19 can have far-reaching effects on crime, justice, and community safety. It serves as a poignant reminder of the complexities and challenges faced by law enforcement in their relentless pursuit of justice for victims and their families.

The cold case unit, along with Detective Morris Nix, made every effort to speak with anyone who knew Debbie, though most of those individuals had already passed away. With additional funding secured for advanced DNA testing in 2019, the scrap of fabric was re-examined in 2022. This re-analysis marked a pivotal turning point in the investigation. One word encapsulates the breakthrough: technology.

> Detective Nix spoke to the DA, Ron Alder, at the time and here is what he said happened: Hey, we've narrowed this down. I believe, he said, to two places, two possible families, and I knew in my core. I said, this is the beginning. This is the beginning of the end. A little more time rocks along. He called me one day and says, we know who his daughter is. I knew then we got him. A little more time goes along. I'm thinking about two weeks, and I cannot sleep. I cannot you know, I'm just dressing. He called me back and says his name is William Rose, and I'm going to it's a little bit embarrassing to admit this, but I kind of went down in my basement, in my corner and I had my moment. I think it all just came out. It was a culmination of a lot of people doing a lot of work. Without that DNA, this case would not have been solved because William Rose, as we found out later, had committed suicide approximately two years after he did the crime. And over the years I couldn't understand. I was trying to think, now, who does this kind of crime? One time? Why isn't he in CODIS? (McCollum, 2023, 31:50-33:12)

It's a system so precise that it can unravel the threads of a decades-old mystery in an instant. CODIS, the Combined DNA Index System, stands as the silent guardian of justice, quietly storing the genetic blueprints of the nation's most elusive suspects. Within its digital vault lie the DNA profiles of the guilty, the unknown, and the vanished. It is here that detectives often find their most crucial clue, a genetic thread that links a crime scene to a suspect's very identity. By comparing DNA samples from the darkest corners of the past with profiles from convicted offenders, missing persons, and unidentified remains, CODIS illuminates the path to justice, leading investigators to the doorstep of the guilty and providing long-overdue answers for the victims' families.

Detective Nix's heart was heavy when Debbie's brother called to inform him that their mother had passed from leukemia in 2018. Debbie's mother had sought closure before her passing, and in a way, she found it, reconciliation with Debbie on the other side. Debbie's father passed away in 2022, both unaware that Debbie's case was finally nearing resolution. After 51 years, this cold case finally offered the family some measure of closure.

In pursuit of answers, officials enlisted DNA Labs International for an exhaustive examination. Their efforts bore fruit: they uncovered relatives of the unknown suspect, whose familial connections provided critical DNA samples for comparison. As the genetic threads converged, investigators identified a name that had been previously lost, William Rose. At the time of his death in 1974, he was 24 years old. Detectives had learned that he had taken his own life. Through advanced genetics and DNA analysis, investigators successfully exhumed William Rose's remains, providing the final piece of the puzzle and conclusively establishing that he was, in fact, Debbie's killer.

The decision to exhume a body is often viewed as a last resort, a desperate effort to uncover the truth buried with the deceased. In William Rose's case, new leads compelled investigators to seek a court order for exhumation, a process governed by strict legal protocols and ethical considerations. Once approval was granted, law enforcement approached William Rose's family with sensitivity, recognizing the delicate nature of the inquiry. The forensic teams arrived at the cemetery, equipped not only with tools for excavation but also with the care needed to handle the fragile remnants of a life once lived. As shovels pierced the earth, unearthing the secrets of the past, each layer of soil was carefully removed with reverence, honoring the memory of the individual while seeking justice.

Although William Rose was a killer, he was still a person with a spirit and a life. The remains were carefully excavated and placed on a sterile surface, providing forensic scientists with the opportunity to analyze them, whether through physical evidence, tissue samples, or the stories etched into bone. Once their work was complete, the remains were respectfully re-interred, and the grave restored. Yet, with this renewed effort, the hope for justice was rekindled, breathing new life into an investigation that had long been considered a forgotten tragedy. DNA was recovered, and William Rose, once a shadow in the case, had now emerged into the light, casting a chilling pall over a case that had nearly faded into silence. The tangled threads of the past remained, but with each discovery came the possibility of closure for those still yearning for answers.

Melvin, Debbie's brother, was present at the news conference when the community was assured that Debbie's killer had been identified. He wished his mother could be there to see this moment and said, "I know she's in heaven now, and it's finally over. We just want to say thank you to everyone for what you've done to make this day come to pass" (Chasan, 2023, para. 11). At the press conference, District Attorney Flynn D. Broady Jr. stated:

The answer we are providing today cannot bring her back. We cannot extract justice from the perpetrator, but I know he must answer to a higher power, and I hope it will provide some relief and answer the question that has lingered for more than 50 years, young life and bright smile ended 51 years ago, gone too soon. (Harris, 2023, para. 5)

Morris Nix said it perfectly, "Technology does not get old, it does not retire, it does not get sick. And it doesn't quit. Technology was seeking William Rose, and it found him in the grave" (Harris, 2023, para. 8).

In the end, the haunting case of Debbie Lynn Randall stands as a poignant reminder of childhood's fragile nature and the shadows that can linger long after innocence is shattered. Her gravestone, engraved with "Deborah Lynn Randall, August 21, 1962, to January 13, 1972," serves as a somber marker for a story that began with a brutal crime and remained etched in the hearts of a grieving family and a community united in their search for answers. After 51 long years, that story has finally reached a somber conclusion. The relentless pursuit of justice, bolstered by advances in DNA technology, led to the identification of William Rose, a man whose actions robbed a family of their beloved daughter.

Though he cannot be punished for his heinous crime, uncovering his identity offers a crucial measure of closure for those left behind. As Debbie's brother Melvin emotionally expressed, "It's finally over," providing a bittersweet comfort to a family that carried the weight of uncertainty for decades. While no amount of closure can bring back a lost child or fully heal the wounds of tragedy, the unwavering dedication of law enforcement and the power of modern forensic science have illuminated a path toward peace. Debbie's story, now forever etched into the collective memory, serves as a beacon of hope for families still grappling with unsolved mysteries, reminding us that even in darkness, the truth has a way of emerging, shedding light on the shadows that may haunt us.

"Peace, I leave with you; my peace I give to you. Not as the world gives do I give to you. Let not your hearts be troubled, neither let them be afraid." ~ John 14:27

CHAPTER 11

TRUST YOUR GUT

In the quiet suburbs of Rochester, New York, a life began on October 7, 1991. Brittanee Drexel was born to young parents: John Kahyaoglu, of Turkish heritage, and Dawn, a teenager navigating the challenges of motherhood. Their unwed relationship was brief, and shortly after Brittanee's birth, Dawn chose a new path by marrying Chad Drexel, who would officially adopt her as his own. Chad's background in military service marked his role in the family as they settled into a modest home in the sleepy town of Chili, New York, a community of about 29,000 residents. Unbeknownst to them, the innocence of Brittanee's early years would soon be overshadowed by a mysterious disappearance, an event that would haunt the community and baffle investigators for years to come.

Brittanee's world was one marked by mystery and resilience. Born with persistent hyperplastic primary vitreous clouding her right eye, her early years were characterized by a series of surgeries aimed at restoring some level of vision (Newlands, 2014). Despite these efforts, her eye remained shrouded in darkness, a continual reminder of the struggle she faced from birth. To conceal the unsettling tendency of her eye to drift into abnormal angles, she wore contact lenses that gave her a striking and distinctive appearance, serving as an outward mask to hide the complexities behind her gaze (Newlands, 2014). Each lens was more than a corrective tool; it was a symbol of her strength, framing a life caught between the worlds of sight and shadow.

In April 2009, a seemingly innocent request from Brittanee to her mother set the stage for a mystery that would haunt her family and the community for years to come. Eager to join her friends on a spring break trip to Myrtle Beach, South Carolina, Brittanee's enthusiasm met with a firm denial from her mother (Newlands, 2014). With no familiar faces among the other teenagers and no responsible adults to supervise the trip, her mother's instinctive unease intensified (Newlands, 2014). She couldn't shake a chilling premonition that something ominous lurked just beyond the horizon, a warning of a harrowing chapter yet to unfold in the annals of cold cases.

Tensions between mother and daughter had been escalating for days, a silent war of unspoken words simmering beneath the surface. On April 22, amid mounting friction, Brittanee approached her mother with what appeared to be an innocent request: permission to spend a day or two at a friend's house to find some peace (Baker, 2016). Exhausted by the conflict, Dawn consented, unaware that this decision would be the last time she would see her daughter. That very day, Brittanee slipped away, boarding a vehicle bound for South

Carolina with other students, leaving behind a world of discontent and a mother with unanswered questions (Baker, 2016). The circumstances of that day would soon become a pivotal piece of a case that would haunt both her family and investigators, raising unsettling questions about intent and the unraveling of familial bonds.

Three days after arriving at the hotel in Myrtle Beach, the calm of the trip suddenly shattered. Brittanee made a call to her mother, casually mentioning she was at the beach. Those simple words would later carry a heavy weight, as her mother, comforted by the familiarity of the location, assumed Brittanee was at a familiar stretch of Lake Ontario's shoreline, a plausible assumption given the unseasonably warm 80-degree weather that enveloped Rochester that day. Unaware, her mother did not realize that this seemingly innocent phone call would become one of the last confirmed moments of Brittanee's whereabouts, casting a dark shadow over what was to come, a chilling disappearance that would leave investigators grasping for answers amid the sultry coastal haze of Myrtle Beach.

Meanwhile, Gates Chili High School in New York was left to grapple with the sudden disappearance of Brittanee, a talented junior and a rising star on the soccer field (Baker, 2016). With aspirations of pursuing a career in nursing or cosmetology, Brittanee had taken a bold risk by traveling to the beach town without her parents' knowledge or approval (Baker, 2016). What began as a youthful act of rebellion quickly spiraled into a haunting mystery that would torment her family and community, leaving questions about her whereabouts unanswered and creating a void on the soccer field that could never be filled. According to KC Baker (2016), Brittanee's mother said the following:

I didn't know she was going. The day she left she was angry with me because she asked me if she could go and I told her no. I said, 'There's no adults going and I have no idea who these kids are, and I don't feel comfortable with it.'

I told her I just felt something was going to happen to her. I just felt it. (Baker, 2016, paras. 25-26)

On the night of April 25, 2009, the peaceful atmosphere of Myrtle Beach was shattered by the mysterious disappearance of 17-year-old Brittanee Drexel from Chili. Filled with the carefree spirit of spring break, Brittanee left her hotel and headed to a nearby establishment. It was there, amid laughter and revelry, that she sent her final text to her boyfriend, a simple message indicating her intention to return to her accommodation, the Bar Harbor, a motor inn (Baker, 2016). This brief communication marked the last confirmed sighting of the vibrant young woman, casting a haunting shadow over a case that would torment her loved ones and investigators alike. Her disappearance that night sparked a relentless search, transforming her story into a perplexing cold case filled with unanswered questions and lingering fears.

At approximately 8:45 p.m., the last known sighting of Brittanee was captured by hotel surveillance cameras. Dressed in a black and white tank top, lightweight shorts, and flip-flops, she exited the building, seemingly unaware that this would be the final moment of her life, a life leaving behind unanswered questions and a trail of concern (Baker, 2016). As the footage flickered on the screen, the stark reality set in what happened in the moments that followed remains a haunting mystery, shrouded in darkness and uncertainty. Where is Brittanee Drexel?

Years have gone by, and Brittanee's parents were still waiting for answers. Brittanee's father, Chad Drexel, never gave up looking for her. Chad stated, "As a father, I have a sense of duty to protect my children, but in this case, I can't. Brittanee is my heart. She was my right hand" (Baker, 2016, para. 3).

During a somber Wednesday press conference on June 8, 2016, FBI Special Agent in Charge David Thomas announced a significant development in the long-standing case of Brittanee Drexel, who vanished on April 25, 2009. Investigators have assembled evidence indicating that Brittanee was abducted near the Blue Water Resort, her last known location, before being transported approximately 60 miles south to a remote rural area. This region includes parts near McClellanville, South Carolina, as well as North Charleston and South Georgetown (Baker, 2016). As the investigation advanced, these new details deepened the mystery surrounding her disappearance, reigniting questions about what truly transpired that day. During the press conference, Special Agent Thomas stated, "We believe she was killed after that," underscoring the gravity of the case (Baker, 2016, para. 11).

According to Baker (2016), Special Agent Thomas stated, "Other people came in contact with her, saw her, know that she was here, so we know there is information in the community" (para. 13). Authorities also reported that the last known signal from Brittanee's cellphone was detected the day after her mysterious disappearance, near the desolate banks of the South Santee River, a stretch of land located between McClellanville and Georgetown (Baker, 2016). This critical piece of evidence suggests a connection to her final known location, yet it only deepens the mystery surrounding her case, leaving investigators and loved ones grappling with unanswered questions as potential leads grow colder and colder.

Following the press conference, the FBI issued a renewed plea for assistance from the public, urging anyone with knowledge about Brittanee Drexel's disappearance to come forward. They appealed to those who might hold the key to unraveling the mystery surrounding her fate, emphasizing the importance of every piece of information. As time continued to pass, unanswered questions loomed large, waiting for the right voice to break the silence and bring the truth to light once and for all. In an effort to motivate tips, the FBI announced a $25,000 reward for any information that could lead to an arrest and conviction in this case, which is now believed to involve foul play. Special Agent Thomas underscored the urgency, stating, "Somebody does have information" (Baker, 2016, para. 16).

From the moment Chad received the devastating news that his daughter was missing, he launched into a relentless search fueled by desperation and love. Night after night, day after day, he walked the streets, distributing hundreds of fliers featuring Brittanee's hopeful face. He poured his resources into hiring private investigators, trusting that someone out there held the answers behind her sudden disappearance.

"I did everything I could to try to find her," Chad reflects, his grief palpable, as he reveals the depth of his bond with Brittanee, his adopted daughter and the only child he ever truly called his own (Baker, 2016, para. 19). "I'm the only father she has ever known," he states firmly, each word laden with a sorrowful determination (Baker, 2016, para. 19). "We were very close" (Baker, 2016, para. 19). Yet despite his tireless efforts, each passing day only intensified the haunting uncertainty, what happened to Brittanee Drexel?

Brittanee, affectionately dubbed "a spitfire" and a "tomboy" by Chad, was a multifaceted young woman who balanced her love for makeup and fashion with an adventurous spirit (Baker, 2016, para. 20). The two shared many moments of camaraderie; Chad took it upon himself to teach her essential life skills, from changing a tire to fostering self-reliance (Baker, 2016). Chad recalls the fateful Tuesday when the FBI delivered the devastating news that their daughter had likely been murdered. "I was shaking. My adrenaline was going. I was sweating profusely," he said (Baker, 2016, para. 21). In that moment, a storm of emotions overtook him. He felt a deep, seething anger rising within, and he admits, "I was livid and holding back with every bit of my might not to go and find the killer or killers who did it" (Baker, 2016, para. 20). The relentless desire for justice burned fiercely in his heart, fueling his determination to confront the harsh reality, he was committed to seeing those responsible brought to justice.

One aspect that haunts Chad continuously is the thoughts and emotions of Brittanee in the days leading up to her tragic disappearance (Baker, 2016). Imprisoned against her will, she faced a harrowing reality that remains obscured from those left behind. "That's the scariest thing in the world and what had me nerved up by the time I got to the meeting with investigators," he reveals, his voice heavy with anguish. "She was not able to leave wherever she was," (Baker, 2016, para. 22). This emotional reflection not only captures the terror of her situation but also underscores the desperation felt by those seeking answers in a case that continues to guard its secrets.

In the ongoing investigation of this chilling cold case, the FBI issued a $25,000 reward for any information that might lead to the arrest and conviction of those responsible for the heinous crime. Driven by grief and hope, Dawn Drexel, Brittanee's mother, made a heartfelt plea to the public. She implores anyone with even the smallest detail that could shed light on this tragedy to come forward, emphasizing the crucial role that community involvement can play in bringing her daughter's killer to justice. As the search for answers persists, the stakes remain high, and the hope for resolution endures.

This case remained a haunting reminder of the unresolved anguish lingering in the hearts of those left behind. Dawn, her voice trembling with sorrow, tearfully confessed, "After seven long years of waiting and praying for the return of my daughter, we know she is not coming home alive" (Smith, 2016, para. 7). This heart-wrenching statement encapsulates the profound sense of loss and desperation experienced by families of missing persons, where hope diminishes over time but the relentless quest for closure endures. As investigators continue to revisit old leads, the weight of Dawn's grief underscores the importance of remembrance and the ongoing pursuit of truth in a case that refuses to fade into oblivion.

Dawn continued to implore anyone with information to come forward and help unravel the mystery surrounding her daughter's tragic fate. Her heartfelt plea resonated deeply with many, as she sought justice for Brittanee and her family, hoping that someone, somewhere, might hold the key to capturing her elusive killer. Despite the passage of years, her case remained unsolved, serving as a stark reminder to the community that even the smallest detail could be the breakthrough needed to crack open a cold case that has lingered in shadows for far too long.

In a chilling development, the investigation into the 2009 disappearance of 17-year-old Brittanee Drexel has taken a significant step forward. FBI agent Gerrick Munoz released the first comprehensive account of the case, stemming from a startling confession by an inmate currently serving a 25-year sentence for voluntary manslaughter. The inmate, Taquan Brown of Walterboro, disclosed crucial details in a jailhouse confession, claiming he witnessed the tragic events unfold shortly after Brittanee was abducted. According to his testimony, Brown entered a so-called "stash house" in McClellanville along with other men, where he was confronted with a harrowing scene: Timothy Da'Shaun Taylor, then just 16 years old, allegedly in the act of sexually abusing Brittanee Drexel. This disturbing revelation has renewed hope for justice and closure in a case that has long haunted authorities and the community.

In the chilling narrative recounted by the FBI agent, Brown described a sequence of events that took place within the confines of an ordinary-looking house. As he moved through the rooms, he saw a disturbing scene involving a girl, Brittanee, and Da'Shaun Taylor. The situation escalated when Brown went to the backyard to exchange money with Shaun Taylor, Da'Shaun's father. During this exchange, Brittanee attempted to escape but was violently subdued and dragged back inside after being "pistol-whipped." Ominous gunshots followed, leading Brown to believe Shaun Taylor had fired at her. The grim climax of this ordeal was marked by the chilling image of Brittanee's body being wrapped up and removed from the scene, leaving behind a web of unanswered questions and a haunting mystery that remains unsolved.

When questioned about the remains, the FBI agent testified that Brittanee Drexel's body has not been recovered. However, he stated that "several witnesses have told us Miss Drexel's body was placed in a pit, or gator pit, to have her body disposed of. Eaten by the gators" (Pardue & Smith, 2016, para. 12). Agent Munoz detailed the extensive efforts of investigators who searched multiple alligator ponds in their search for crucial evidence, but all efforts have so far been fruitless. He noted that local reports indicate the region contains as many as 40 such ponds, which complicates the search significantly (Pardue & Smith, 2016). Additionally, investigators have thoroughly examined a suspected stash house, hoping to uncover leads that might shed light on this perplexing case (Pardue & Smith, 2016).

Chilling revelations emerged from a Georgetown County jailhouse confession that supported several key pieces of evidence. According to a fellow inmate, Da'Shaun Taylor allegedly picked up 17-year-old Brittanee Drexel in Myrtle Beach shortly after she left the Blue Water Hotel on April 25, 2009. Brittanee had defied her parents by traveling from Rochester, New York, to enjoy spring break on the sun-kissed shores of the Grand Strand, only to vanish without a trace.

The Georgetown inmate provided a horrifying account of what allegedly transpired next, claiming that Taylor introduced Brittanee to a circle of friends and engaged in heinous acts of human trafficking, coercing her into disturbing activities. As media attention intensified and awareness of Brittanee's disappearance grew, panic reportedly spread among her abductors. The inmate recounted that, faced with the increasing risk of being caught, Brittanee's life was tragically ended, and her body was disposed of in a grim manner, an unsettling testament to the dark realities surrounding her case.

During a recent bond hearing concerning the controversial case of Da'Shaun Taylor, the FBI agent's testimony raised questions about the integrity of the charges against him. Taylor's attorney argued that the prosecution had employed coercive tactics aimed at compelling his client to confess and cooperate with authorities. This assertion paints a troubling picture of potential misconduct or manipulation within the legal process, highlighting the ethical dilemmas and complexities surrounding the case. As the details continue to emerge, such claims could have significant implications for the pursuit of justice and the way evidence is gathered and used in court.

Taylor's attorney contended that there was insufficient "hard" evidence to justify a conviction. Federal prosecutors charged the 25-year-old with interfering with interstate commerce by threat or violence, related to a robbery at a Mount Pleasant McDonald's in 2011. As the getaway driver, Taylor played a key role in the crime, during which two accomplices threatened staff members and left the store manager injured with two non-life-threatening gunshot wounds.

After confessing and cooperating with law enforcement, Taylor received a sentence of probation, which he successfully completed. In contrast, his accomplices faced harsher penalties: the gunman was sentenced to 25 years in prison, while the second robber received a six-year sentence, suspended after serving just 10 months. This case illustrates a complex web of decisions, consequences, and the ongoing pursuit of justice, highlighting the varying levels of accountability in criminal acts.

Within the intricate landscape of American law, federal prosecutors have the authority to pursue parallel charges when both federal and state laws are violated. This legal strategy became especially prominent during the civil rights movement, when federal authorities often pursued charges for rights violations against individuals who had been acquitted or not charged under state law. The case against Taylor exemplifies this intersection of jurisdictions, as federal charges rely on nearly identical evidence that led to his confession regarding the McDonald's robbery—a crime for which he has already served his state sentence. However, the stakes are significantly higher now: the federal charges, which include the use of a deadly weapon, could lead to a life sentence, casting a long shadow over Taylor's past and future.

During Taylor's bond hearing, Assistant U.S. Attorney Winston Holliday acknowledged the complexities surrounding the case, admitting that crucial evidence had yet to be uncovered. This revelation piqued curiosity and speculation among those following the proceedings, as it underscored the lingering questions and unresolved aspects of the investigation. With each passing moment, the courtroom became a stage for the unfolding narrative, highlighting the delicate balance between the pursuit of justice and the mysteries that often accompany cold cases. Taylor's fate had now depended not only on the evidence already presented but also on the sobering reality that, at times, the truth can remain elusive, hidden in uncertainty even within the sanctity of the justice system.

In the dim light of a forgotten room, dust of years settled heavily on an evidence box, each item as a silent witness to the tragedy that had unfolded long ago. The Drexel family waited, their hearts heavy with unanswered questions, their hopes flickering like a dying flame. Yet beneath the layers of neglect and silence, a breakthrough was sparked, perhaps by a determined investigator's intuition, advances in forensic technology, or a sense of remorse. This moment ignited a renewed sense of hope, bridging the gap between sorrow and resolution. As the pieces of the long-unsolved puzzle began to fit together, the story of that cold case was on the verge of being rewritten, not as an unresolved mystery, but as a testament to the relentless pursuit of truth and justice. What had once been an enigma was now moving toward illumination, revealing the faces and voices that had long been yearning to be heard.

In early May 2022, the cold case surrounding Brittanee Drexel's disappearance took a significant turn when Raymond Moody, a 62-year-old registered sex offender, voluntarily turned himself in to the Georgetown County Sheriff's Office, facing an obstruction of justice charge. Moody had been a person of interest since 2012, when he first came under scrutiny in connection with Drexel's vanishing.

Under police questioning, Raymond Moody confessed to the crime and disclosed the location where he claimed Brittanee Drexel's remains could be found. He led investigators to a site in Georgetown County, approximately 35 miles (56 kilometers) down the coast from where she was last seen, revealing that her cellphone had been detected in Moody's vehicle the night she vanished while walking alone along the scenic Myrtle Beach waterfront. Brittanee's remains were subsequently recovered from that location (Collins, 2022). This breakthrough not only provides crucial insight into the circumstances surrounding her disappearance but also highlights the advancing capabilities of forensic technology in solving long-standing mysteries.

Steph Watts, an investigative journalist and guest on the podcast *Zone 7*, shared Brittanee's story as she understood it from FBI documents and information obtained from Raymond Moody. Here is an account of what transpired on the day Brittanee Drexel was abducted and ultimately murdered:

Angel Vause exited the Explorer to talk to Brittanee to kind of soften her up a little bit, maybe trust us. Vause succeeded and led Brittanee back to the car. They used a ruse that they were tourists from out of town and learned that Brittanee was also a tourist. Brittanee told them the name of a hotel and they offered to drop her off. However, as they drove north on the boulevard her hotel (sic) towards her hotel, talking casually, Moody turned off the boulevard, acting like he was lost. Brittanee did not say anything.

At that point, Moody drove across King's Highway and then stopped, claiming he was lost and needed to change drivers. This was part of the abduction plan, and Moody quickly initiated the next step. When they walked around the car to get outside, Moody (sic) into the back seat to restrain Brittanee. The back door was locked from the outside. Moody insisted (sic) entering the passenger side front door, and before Vause put the vehicle into reverse, Moody dove through the seat and immediately physically restrained Brittanee with his arms and hands. He told her not to panic because he kidnapped girls, demanded a five thousand dollars ransom from the city Chamber of Commerce, then returned the girls safely. Moody told Brittanee that the city usually paid the ransom without question because they didn't want negative media attention. Moody recalls handcuffing Brittanee at that point either in the car at the Pole Yard Landing and stayed with her in the backseat. Brittanee did not say much during her transport. (McCollum, 2025, 25:47-27:10)

Angel Vause was Moody's long-term partner for nearly 15 years. Brittanee's reaction—or notably, her lack of response—raises important questions about agency and the psychological impact of fear and surprise in high-stress situations. Why didn't she speak up or attempt to resist when her surroundings changed so dramatically? This prompts deeper discussion about human behavior in moments of extreme stress. We all know the phrase "fight or flight," and it's rooted in real biological responses that occur under threat. From an investigative perspective, I would ask: what motivates someone like Moody to commit such acts? Is it desperation, a desire for thrill-seeking, or perhaps other underlying factors? This leads us into criminological theories that examine the various influences contributing to criminal behavior, whether sociopathic traits, environmental factors, or personal histories. I have always taught my students that individuals are often a product of their environment.

Again, Angel Vause had every opportunity to let Brittanee go, but she never did. She was the one who convinced Brittanee to get into the vehicle. As Steph Watts summarized it:

> Mr. Moody has a ritual before he performs his hideous sexual acts, and one of them is that he needs to take a shower. So, he returned to his hotel, which was seven miles away, to get as graphic as this is, (sic) drugs and sex toys, shower and return. So, there's Angel Vause, okay, picture this Cheryl, sitting in a campsite, and then like I've been out there. I mean it's I mean I wouldn't stay there in a tent with Brittanee Drexel, okay, And I said to Mike, what I want to know is what they talked about during that time. She had all that time to let her go, to release her, and she didn't. This act, this hideous act committed against Brittanee Drexel, was Angel Vause's fantasy. Let me elaborate a little bit on that. Angel Vause knew that Raymond Moody had a fantasy of abducting and raping young girls. Angel, in her desperate attempt to maintain her presence with Moody, texted him one

day and said, I also want to abduct and rape a young girl. I want to do it with you, And Raymond said, that's all you need to say. So, you know, how does one monster meet another monster? (McCullum, 2025, 28:26-29:45)

Raymond Moody remained shrouded in the shadows of a dark and troubling past. In 1983, the courts convicted him of a series of horrific crimes, including violent sexual offenses and the abduction of young girls, crimes that eerily mirrored the tragic case of Brittanee Drexel. A predator cloaked in the guise of a man; Moody was sentenced to an imposing 40 years behind bars. However, the justice system granted him an unsettling reprieve: he was released on parole after serving just 20 years, in 2004. Returning to the quiet streets of South Carolina, it was only three years later, upon the conclusion of his parole in 2007, that a darker transformation began to unfold within him, raising haunting questions about the potential for recidivism in individuals who have once unleashed their darkness upon innocent lives. What motives lurked behind his eyes as he re-entered society? The specter of his past loomed large, foreshadowing an ominous narrative that was about to unravel. Raymond Moody's path intersected with Angel Vause, setting the stage for the tragic events that would follow.

Raymond Moody serves as a chilling reminder of how quickly the past can resurface. Just months after his parole expired, Moody was re-apprehended in 2008 for the disturbing crime of indecent exposure. Evidence suggests that the possibility of rehabilitation for Moody may be nothing more than an elusive hope. The grim question remains: how many victims did he truly leave in his wake? Investigators speculate that the FBI may uncover a trail of further victims, silent echoes of transgressions he has yet to disclose. In the complex tapestry of criminal behavior, one cannot help but wonder how the specters of our past actions can lie in wait, ready to strike at the most inopportune moments.

Within the dimly lit confines of prison, Raymond formed an unlikely bond with a fellow inmate named Ernie Merchant. Their relationship, one that the hardened walls of their shared isolation could only describe as "jailhouse husbands," blossomed amid the stark reality of incarceration. Raymond, known for his nurturing nature, tended to Ernie's needs with a loyalty born of shared hardship. Ernie, serving time for drug trafficking, a crime born not of addiction but of unfortunate choices, was a man caught in the crosshairs of circumstance. When he was finally released in 2000, escaping the haunting presence of prison life., the lingering question was: what would become of the bond forged in confinement, and how would the shadows of their past intertwine with the paths of their futures?

The separation between these two men loomed large. Unlike Raymond, whose life continued to spiral into chaos during their years behind bars, Ernie had embraced a new path upon his release. He reconstructed his life, transforming it into a success story as a sought-after hairdresser. Yet, the world outside had changed drastically during their confinement; a veil of technology had descended, rendering the prison landscape starkly different; no cellphones, no tablets, no internet to bridge the chasm of silence. Among inmates, discussions of their charges were fraught with risk; revealing such secrets could be tantamount to a death sentence in that unforgiving realm. Throughout their shared imprisonment, Raymond had kept his own truth hidden from Ernie, burdened by a secret he carried alone. It wasn't until Ernie stepped into freedom that the chilling revelation surfaced, leaving him horrified and questioning everything he thought he knew about his former friend. The shadows of their past would forever haunt him; woven into the fabric of the life he had worked so hard to build.

Ernie, a seasoned inmate, had extended a lifeline to Raymond during their time behind bars, promising that once they were released, they would support each other in rebuilding their lives. With a firm belief in redemption, Ernie took it upon himself to guide Raymond toward a brighter future, convinced that if he could turn his life around, his friend could too. After their release, the duo forged a new existence side by side: Raymond found his calling as a cabinet maker, while Ernie built a successful career as a hairdresser. However, in 2007, the fragile stability of their lives was disrupted when Raymond crossed paths with Angel Vause. Despite Ernie's cautions urging Raymond to proceed carefully, the introduction of Angel would soon unravel the fabric of their newfound stability, leading them down a path no one could have anticipated.

In a calculated move, "Detective" Ernie intensified his investigation, focusing intently on Raymond as the key to unlocking the tangled web of secrets surrounding Brittanee's tragic death. His goal was clear: to extract a confession from Raymond's tightly sealed lips and to unravel the mysterious connections linking Angel Vause to the crime. As Ernie carefully probed for the truth, whispers of a larger, more sinister narrative began to surface, suggesting a trail of other heinous crimes that Raymond may have committed but never been brought to justice for. Ernie's findings were quickly relayed to the FBI, and the atmosphere was thick with anticipation: the long-held silence was about to be broken, and shocking revelations were finally poised to come to light.

The FBI conducted an intensive excavation at the site Raymond Moody indicated, a remote area off a gated private drive near Georgetown. Over the course of three days, their efforts paid off on May 11, 2022, when human remains were uncovered approximately four feet underground. Subsequent analysis confirmed the remains to be those of Brittanee

Drexel through DNA and dental records on May 15, 2022, finally bringing resolution to a decade-long mystery.

According to Jeffrey Collins of the *Associated Press*, "Moody said he then strangled Drexel because he realized he would go back to prison as a convicted sex offender, having previously been convicted of raping an 8-year-old girl in California" (Collins, 2022, para. 5). No one wishes to confront the grim reality of such horror, least of all a mother who should cradle her child in love, not grief. Yet, the harrowing details of Brittanee's last moments have come to light: she was subjected to unspeakable violence, brutally raped, and then strangled in a desperate fight for her life. The attacker went further, plunging an icepick into her heart, a final act of cruelty, before casting her almost lifeless body into the depths of the river, where her innocence was forever submerged.

The arrest warrant revealed that Brittanee had been strangled and was buried by the morning of April 26, 2009. This distressing information was publicly disclosed on May 16, 2022, by the Georgetown County Sheriff's Office in collaboration with the Drexel family, coinciding with the announcement of Moody's arrest. Charged with murder, kidnapping, and first-degree criminal sexual misconduct, each alleged to have occurred on the day of Brittanee's disappearance, Moody faced severe legal consequences. On October 19, 2022, he pleaded guilty to all charges, resulting in a life sentence plus two additional consecutive 30-year terms. In court, Raymond Moody confronted his own darkness, stating, "I was a monster. I was a monster then and I was a monster when I took Brittanee Drexel's life" (Collins, 2022, para. 6).

The echo of the gavel in the courtroom on February 13, 2025, marked a chilling punctuation to a case that had simmered for years. Angel Vause, a name whispered in connection with Brittanee Drexel's murder, had haunted the coastal South for over a decade, and at last, she faced justice. Sentenced to a lengthy 18-year term, the 57-year-old woman, the girlfriend of the man convicted of Brittanee's murder, saw the consequences of her choices catch up with her. Her crime? Not the horrific act itself, but the web of lies she spun to obscure the truth and shield those involved. It served as a stark reminder that in the pursuit of justice, even those on the periphery can become ensnared by the long arm of the law, ultimately betrayed by their silence.

As the courtroom doors slammed shut on the case, the echoes of justice, or perhaps a semblance of it, lingered. Assistant U.S. Attorney Winston Holliday, his tie loosened, faced a swarm of reporters. The harsh glare of flashbulbs illuminated the fatigue etched onto his face as he offered a carefully crafted statement, a final summation for the cameras.

> One would be, obviously, the family. As you could probably tell, a lot of pain, a lot of emotion with the family, but that has motivated them to stay with the case from 2009. And then also the persistence and perseverance of the FBI. This is one of the most extraordinary efforts I've ever seen from the FBI. Ray Moody would not be in prison if not for the FBI. (Thompson et al., 2025, para.7)

After months of meticulous preparation and a trial that uncovered the darkest corners of human depravity, Assistant U.S. Attorney Winston Holliday finally regarded the verdict with a measured sense of satisfaction. He stated, "You know, she's a 57-year-old woman, 18 plus 57 is 75. It's a long time, so it's a significant sentence. That gives her a long time to think about it" (Thompson et al., 2025, para. 9).

Angel Vause stood in front of the court, a figure caught between remorse and justification. "I am not a monster," she implored, her voice trembling with a mix of conviction and despair. "I am not a horrible person; I am a victim, victimized by the very substances that have ensnared my life, drugs and alcohol." I can imagine her eyes cast downward as she turned her gaze toward the Drexel family, offering a direct, heartfelt apology for the irreparable loss of their beloved daughter, an act seemingly overshadowed by the weight of her actions.

Judge Richard Gergel listened intently, his expression solemn as he articulated the gravity of her involvement, labeling her as a key facilitator in a tragedy that would forever alter the lives of those left to grapple with its aftermath. As the gavel fell, sealing Vause's fate to serve time until she reaches the age of 75, the courtroom was engulfed in an unsettling silence, echoes of regret mingled with the harsh reality of accountability, leaving the path to redemption shrouded in shadows.

As we examine the unsettling details of the Drexel case, one fact stands out clearly: Judge Gergel emphasized that Vause's involvement was far from incidental. It's difficult to ignore the possibility that, had Vause not lured the unsuspecting 17-year-old into their car, this entire nightmare might have been averted (Thompson et al., 2025). Vause did not merely play a passive role; she actively participated in the kidnapping, abandoning Drexel to face her grim fate alone. Her decision to seize Drexel's phone effectively sealed her fate, cutting off any chance of escape or outside help. It's crucial to consider what might have happened if Vause had made different choices, if she had answered the frantic calls or dialed 911 (Thompson et al., 2025). With her inaction, she possessed the power to disrupt Moody's heinous plans, yet instead, she stood by as a bystander, watching a tragedy unfold. This raises a heavy and haunting question: how many other lives could have been saved if Vause had recognized the urgency of the situation and taken action to intervene?

In the shadowy depths of this enduring mystery, investigators have reached an impasse, relying heavily on the account of the man at the center of it all, Raymond

Moody. An unsettling question looms over the case, Did Brittanee willingly enter Moody's SUV, or was she forced into it? With time slipping away since the 17-year-old's disappearance, the prosecutor's findings only deepen the eerie atmosphere surrounding the case. Details about what truly happened to her, whether she was strangled, abused, or suffered in some unimaginable way, remain frustratingly elusive. Each passing year seems to erode the fragile thread of truth that could potentially unravel this cold case, leaving behind a haunting emptiness for those who loved Brittanee and yearn for justice.

For Brittanee's mother, grief is intertwined with a fierce resolve. She wears her daughter's ashes in a necklace, a constant reminder of her profound loss. In an emotional confrontation with Moody, Dawn Drexel did not hold back, labeling him a "serial child predator" and emphasizing the brutality of his actions, especially knowing he has three daughters of his own. The story takes a poignant turn as Dawn shares how brave Brittanee was in her final moments. She fought back against her attacker, leaving scratches on Moody's head, neck, and face in a desperate effort to survive. "I hope you suffer in prison for the rest of your useless life," Dawn declared, a statement infused with deep sorrow, yet also a testament to her unwavering strength and boundless love for a daughter who deserved so much more.

In the haunting aftermath of a 13-year-long mystery, the tragic story of Brittanee Drexel has finally reached a semblance of resolution, though it is tinged with profound sorrow and lingering unanswered questions. For those who knew her, Brittanee was more than just a name; she was a vibrant teenager with dreams as bright as her smile. Her heartbreaking journey, from her joyful laughter to the grim discovery of her remains, reveals a dark narrative that starkly underscores the fragility of youth and the unimaginable depths of human cruelty.

Raymond Moody's eventual confession and the painstaking excavation of Brittanee's remains are pivotal moments that resonate deeply with her family and the community. These revelations, while offering a measure of justice, also evoke unsettling reflections on the tragic events that led to her untimely death. As her loved one's grapple with the chilling details of her abduction and murder, the long-awaited closure feels bittersweet, like turning a page in a heartbreaking novel they had hoped would end on a happier note.

In their hearts, they carry the weight of memories filled with love and potential that were extinguished far too soon. Each piece of the puzzle revealed by Moody adds another layer to their grief yet also reinforces a collective resolve to honor Brittanee's spirit. Her story stands as a testament to the enduring love of those left behind and serves as a call for the community to remain vigilant and compassionate, offering hope for others still grappling with the pain of unresolved loss.

Though the quest for truth amid the shadows of tragedy may bring some closure for Brittanee Drexel, it also ignites a relentless commitment to honor her memory and advocate for all those who remain lost in silence. The fight for justice does not end here; it transforms into a powerful reminder of the love that endures beyond loss, urging us all to carry forward the light of those we have loved and lost.

"Daughter, your faith has healed you. Go in peace and be freed from your suffering." ~ Mark 5:34

CHAPTER 12

JUSTICE DELAYED, BUT NOT DENIED

This is the tragic story of Teresa Lee Scalf, a journey marked by a pursuit of justice. Teresa was a dedicated healthcare professional with a passion for guiding her family into the medical field, aiming to nurture a tradition of healing and compassion. Behind the image of a selfless caregiver, her dedication to mentoring family members into the medical profession was more than mere coincidence; it reflected a deep sense of purpose rooted in her commitment to alleviating suffering. Teresa was also a loving mother, leaving behind a heartbroken eight-year-old son. Just a year and a half after the untimely death of her 23-year-old brother, who lost his life in a tragic diving accident, Teresa herself became a victim (Luperon, 2023).

Remembering family members after they leave this earth, especially suddenly, is a deep human experience. According to Betty Scalf, Teresa's mother, Teresa was a do-gooder who would befriend those with no one. She shared, "When Teresa was about 14 years old, she brought a man she didn't know to the house because he needed food" (Edwards, 2003, para. 16). Teresa's sister, Lynn Scalf, also recalled her sister's compassionate nature, saying she was "always rescuing stray animals and stray people. She was a deeply caring person. She was very sweet and very, very well-liked" (Edwards, 2003, paras. 17–18).

On October 27, 1986, tragedy struck Lakeland, Florida, when 29-year-old Teresa Lee Scalf became the victim of a heinous, sexually motivated assault that ultimately cost her life. The details of this brutal attack paint a harrowing picture. Teresa was discovered in her home, the scene marred by violence, with evidence of a desperate struggle, her hands bearing significant defensive wounds. These wounds testified to her valiant fight for survival against an assailant whose identity would remain unknown, casting a long shadow over the lives of those left behind and leaving law enforcement with a cold case that haunted the community for three decades.

Betty Scalf, Teresa's mother, grew increasingly alarmed when her daughter failed to show up for work at the hospital. Using a credit card, Betty broke into Teresa's home in Lakeland, Florida, and was confronted with an unimaginable sight, her daughter's lifeless body. Tragically, it was Betty who made this devastating discovery, a moment that would forever haunt both the family and the community. At the time, in 1986, the widespread use of a universal 911 emergency system was still a distant reality. Desperately searching her daughter's home for help, Betty finally found a small magnet affixed to the refrigerator, bearing the tiny number of the local police department. The chilling circumstances of that grim day remain etched in the memories of those seeking justice for Teresa.

The experience of a mother discovering her daughter stabbed to death in her own home would be an unimaginably traumatic ordeal, one that could trigger a whirlwind of intense emotions and thoughts. Initially, she might be overwhelmed by shock and disbelief, struggling to accept the horrifying reality before her. This could be followed by profound grief, an ache that pierces the soul, leaving her to grapple with the loss of her daughter, the shattered dreams she had for her future, and the love that spanned a lifetime. Anguish would likely intertwine with feelings of guilt, as she might question what she could have done differently to protect her child.

Fear and anger could also surface as she confronts the violence that has forever changed her family. Alongside sorrow, a desperate need for answers and justice might emerge, fueling frustration with a system that feels incomprehensible in the face of such loss. Ultimately, this heart-wrenching experience could profoundly reshape her understanding of safety, trust, and life's fragility, forcing her to reevaluate her identity and her role as a mother in a world that suddenly feels far more perilous. Betty will never forget that fateful day she lost her daughter.

By the end of 1976, the fledgling 9-1-1 emergency service was beginning to gain traction, serving just 17% of the United States population (NENA The 911 Association, n.d.). However, like a snowball rolling downhill, its growth accelerated rapidly. By 1979, an impressive 26% of Americans had access to this life-saving service, and nine states had enacted legislation to ensure its widespread implementation (NENA The 911 Association, n.d.). The pace was extraordinary, with approximately 70 new systems being established each year, marking a seismic shift in how people responded to emergencies. By 1987, the service covered nearly 50% of the U.S. population, a testament to its transformative impact (NENA The 911 Association, n.d.).

Initial estimates suggested that Teresa was killed around 3:30 p.m., but by the time Betty arrived at the scene later that evening, the relentless rain had washed away much of the evidence, as Betty recounted (Raven, n.d.). Nearly all traces of forensic evidence had been erased, complicating any investigation. Teresa's neck had been brutally severed, almost to the point of beheading, with the attacker seemingly targeting a specific, precise angle. The once vibrant young woman now stared into eternity, her tragic death leaving profound repercussions that would resonate through her family and community.

A crucial piece of evidence from the crime scene raised more questions than answers. Blood found at the scene did not match Teresa's DNA, marking a pivotal moment in the investigation. This discovery set in motion a meticulous inquiry that would remain unresolved for over 30 years, until advances in forensic technology finally offered new hope. A small vial of blood, seemingly insignificant, was submitted to the Combined DNA Index System (CODIS), a vast database containing DNA profiles of convicted offenders, unsolved crime scene evidence, and missing persons at the local, state, and national levels. But could this tiny sample hold the key to finally bringing justice for Teresa?

In the quiet gloom of the evidence room, hope flickered within the boxes filled with cases that had yet to find resolution. Banker boxes held countless unsolved mysteries, cases that investigators had poured hours into, tirelessly searching for answers. Their minds raced with the possibility that the perpetrator might have been apprehended by another agency or caught in a different crime, leaving behind DNA that could, perhaps, hold the key to unlocking the truth. Each unresolved case was but a thread in the intricate tapestry of justice; somewhere out there, the vital piece of evidence might be waiting to be discovered, poised to finally bring closure to a haunting story of loss and unanswered questions.

For decades, the DNA sample lay dormant, entangled in the cobwebs of somewhat forgotten evidence, a silent witness to a crime desperately awaiting resolution. Each passing year added another layer of dust to the evidence box, while advances in forensic science shimmered tantalizingly just beyond reach. The fragmented strands of genetic material, once a promising lead, gradually became a ghostly reminder of lives that were forever changed. Despite the relentless march of time, no match emerged from the depths of databases or through familial connections, leaving the haunting echo of an unknown suspect and an unresolved fate to linger in the shadows of Teresa's cold case.

In 2022, amid the lingering shadows of an unresolved murder, the Polk County Sheriff's Office took a pivotal step by enlisting the expertise of Othram, Inc., a cutting-edge genetic genealogy laboratory. This innovative partnership breathed new life into Teresa's case, employing advanced DNA analysis to trace the blood left at the crime scene. Through meticulous examination of genetic data, Othram uncovered a glimmer of hope, identifying a network of distant relatives connected to the unknown suspect. As investigators delved deeper, focused interviews with these relatives gradually illuminated a more concrete lead. Their efforts ultimately pointed to Donald Douglas, a 33-year-old whose home stood directly behind Teresa's at the time of her tragic death.

The landscape of cold case investigations began to shift notably in 2018, as breakthroughs in genetic genealogy gained prominence. Unsolved murders, missing persons, and decades-old questions were on the verge of a second chance at justice, thanks to this groundbreaking technique. Born from the intersection of genetics, genealogy, and forensic science, genetic genealogy became the key to unlocking the past. Imagine a complex puzzle with a million pieces, each piece representing a DNA sample collected from a crime scene, an arrestee, or a genealogy database. For years, this data had remained dormant, waiting for a breakthrough. Then came the power of genetic genealogy: by comparing crime scene DNA to public profiles and ancestral databases, investigators could trace the suspect's family tree, mapping a digital lineage that led them closer to justice.

Genetic genealogy began gaining prominence with the case of the Buckskin Girl, a cold case from 1981 whose identity remained a mystery for decades. While it wasn't the very first case to involve genetic genealogy, it marked the beginning of a new era. Using this technique, investigators were able to identify her as Marcia King, opening the floodgates for its application in solving other complex cases. The breakthrough was exemplified in 2018, when investigators used genetic genealogy to identify Joseph James DeAngelo as the Golden State Killer, a serial rapist and murderer responsible for crimes across California between 1976 and 1986. This case represented a major milestone in forensic science, helping to popularize genetic genealogy as a powerful investigative tool. With each new case, the pieces of the puzzle gradually fell into place, shedding light on the past and bringing closure to many families. It's worth noting that genetic genealogy has since been used to solve numerous other cold cases, and it continues to be a vital component in modern investigations. However, each case is unique, and the technique is often employed alongside other investigative methods to ensure thorough and accurate results.

In a twist of fate, Donald Douglas had previously been questioned by detectives during a routine canvassing in 1986. However, without concrete evidence at the time, he slipped through their grasp, allowing the case to remain in ambiguity for decades. According to Alberto Luperon (2023) from *Law & Crime*, Polk County Sheriff Grady Judd stated, "He had the right answers" when investigators questioned

Douglas during that canvass, and he showed no obvious injuries that might have raised suspicion (para. 7).

An obscure event from the distant past ultimately proved to be the key in unraveling the DNA mystery. In 1949, a distant relative of Douglas gave birth to a child out of wedlock, which later rekindled familial connections that would eventually narrow the investigation. Sheriff Judd explained in a press conference, "Douglas' third cousin, someone he probably did not even know, had a child out of wedlock. It was through that distant relation that investigators zeroed in on him" (Luperon, 2023, para. 9). This seemingly minor detail from decades ago became the crucial link that helped uncover the truth.

In 2008, Douglas passed away from natural causes at the age of 54, leaving behind only memories and unanswered questions. As investigators continued their search for answers, they turned their focus to Douglas's son, an unlikely suspect at first glance. However, a crucial DNA sample, willingly provided by the son, ultimately shattered the case wide open. When the results were disclosed, the young man was left shaken and mortified (Luperon, 2023).

A closer examination of the evidence unveiled an astonishing truth: Douglas, a 54-year-old man with no known arrests or criminal history, was not the person he appeared to be. In reality, he was a killer, his crimes long left unresolved and unrecorded in the justice system. How could this seemingly ordinary man conceal such an extraordinary secret? What circumstances or choices led him down this dark and hidden path?

Determining a criminal's motivation can be complex and often requires analyzing a range of psychological, social, and situational factors. In the case of Donald Douglas, while we may not have direct insight into his personal thoughts or feelings, we can consider several common motivations observed in criminal behavior. One prominent factor is the desire for power and control. Many violent offenders are driven by a need to dominate, intimidate, or instill fear in their victims. If Douglas felt powerless in other areas of his life, engaging in acts of violence could have been a way for him to reclaim a sense of authority and control. Ultimately, we may never fully know his true motivations, but understanding these patterns can offer important insights into criminal behavior.

Anger and resentment are also important factors to consider when examining Douglas's behavior. Personal grievances or accumulated rage can sometimes drive individuals to act violently. Douglas may have harbored unresolved issues or deep-seated hostility—possibly even towards Teresa, who, according to reports, did not want his attention. Additionally, impulse and rage can play a significant role in criminal acts. Some crimes are committed in the heat of the moment, overwhelmed by intense emotions such as anger, jealousy, or fear. It's possible that Douglas's actions were impulsive rather than carefully planned, driven by a sudden emotional outburst rather than a calculated decision. Ultimately, we may never know his true motivations or the full story behind his actions.

If Douglas exhibited antisocial behavior or had a history of mental health issues, these could contribute to a lack of empathy and an increased propensity for violence. In this case, his motivations might stem from deeper psychological problems rather than specific grievances, but once again, we will never know. There is also the crime of opportunity. Sometimes criminal acts occur because the perpetrator sees an opportunity and takes it. Much like an unlocked car door with a laptop lying on the back seat. If Douglas had been in a particular location and found Teresa vulnerable, he may have acted without substantial motivation beyond the opportunity presented. He was Teresa's neighbor and may have known her routine, making a crime of opportunity more likely.

Finally, the last piece to analyze is Douglas's previous life experiences. We know he didn't have a criminal record or criminal history. Depending on Douglas's background and life experiences, there may be a contextual backdrop influencing his motivations. Past trauma, juvenile criminal history, or interactions with society and peers could have contributed to shaping his outlook and potential motivations for committing such a crime like sexual assault and murder. Ultimately, exploring the motivations behind criminal behavior is challenging and often varies from case to case. It is also important to remember that understanding motivation does not excuse the actions taken; rather, it can provide insights into the complexities of human behavior and the factors that may lead to criminality. We will never know.

Sheriff Grady Judd suggested it may have been a sexual rejection. During a press conference, Lynn Scalf, Teresa's sister, said the following:

> Teresa had told us about some creepy neighbor that had showed up at her house with what looked like he had yanked a flower out of the ground and slapped it into a pot, and he was sort of stalkerish. She had told us about him, but she never described him. (Luperon, 2023, para. 12)

Teresa's mother, Betty Scalf, said, "All I want to say is, I'm 84 years old. I lived to see this done. I think that's why I lived so long" (Luperon, 2023, para. 13). Betty clung tenaciously to the flickering ember of hope, her unwavering faith resting in the hands of Polk County's Sheriff's Office and their band of investigators. Betty's resolve became a beacon in the murky depths of uncertainty. With each passing day, she wondered if the skillful detectives, armed with a relentless pursuit of truth, could finally unravel the threads of her daughter's murder, rekindling the flame of justice that had long since dimmed in the hearts of those left behind.

It's ok to be angry as a victim's family member. Teresa's sister said it perfectly:

> We don't have closure for grief. There will never be closure when you have something this violent against a decent human being. It's not human. It's not humane. So, for that, we will have no closure, but we have closure of questioning constantly because when it's a deliberate act, you question everybody, her best friend, her ex-boyfriend, the cousins, anyone she's run into in the last five years. (Luperon, 2023, para. 2).

I've mentioned it before, there's no such thing as closure when there's a criminal act so violent. As a mother, Betty found her daughter's lifeless body. Her intuition knew something was wrong. In the press conference, Sheriff Grady Judd said the following to the community:

> We are extremely grateful for the assistance from Othram, Inc., who provided us with multiple investigative leads and ultimately the missing genetic evidence needed to bring this investigation to a successful conclusion. With their help, our detectives were able to negotiate through a family tree that led to the identity of Teresa Scalf's killer. I want to thank Mr. Douglas' son, who was cooperative and willing to assist our detectives. Thanks to Othram, Inc., our detectives' hard work, and Mr. Douglas' cooperation, we were able to help bring long-awaited closure to Teresa Scalf's devastated family. (Bruchey, 2023, para. 11).

At the news conference, Teresa's sister, Pam Shade, shared that Teresa was a dedicated trauma nurse at a Lakeland hospital, and was a passionate advocate for pursuing careers in the medical field, inspiring her family to follow in her footsteps (Wright, 2023). Pam also stated, "I've been a nurse for 38 years now. My brother is a trauma nurse, my sister works in mental health, my mother worked at the hospital for 25 years, all due to her. It was all due to her" (Wright, 2023, para. 23).

The struggle for answers that once seemed elusive culminates in a striking revelation. Teresa Lee Scalf, the vibrant healthcare professional and loving mother, whose life was brutally extinguished on that fateful October day in 1986, finally afforded the recognition she deserves a face to the shadow that hovered over her memory for far too long. The relentless pursuit of truth, buried beneath layers of time and evolving forensic science, has ultimately unveiled the identity of her assailant, Donald Douglas, the very neighbor who once evaded scrutiny and disappeared from the memories of those left distraught in the wake of the violence.

In the decades that followed Teresa's horrific death, a mother's heartbreak reverberated through a community, yet the commitment to seek justice was unwavering. With sheer persistence, the case, long cloaked in despair, re-emerged through the innovations of genetic genealogy, which illuminated the path toward closure amid heartache. The transformation of unresolved pain into a defined narrative is both cathartic and haunting; it raises profound questions about the hidden darkness that can reside within the ordinary facades of our neighbors and challenges us to confront the reality that some mysteries, although solved, leave indelible scars.

As we reflect on Teresa's story, we come face-to-face with the delicate nature of grief intertwined with justice. Tightly woven into this narrative is not only the sorrow of loss but an enduring testament to the resilience of a family fighting to reclaim the light snuffed out far too soon. In the emotional words of Teresa's mother, Betty, who has witnessed this journey to its reluctant conclusion, we are reminded that the emotional turbulence of violent crime often leaves victims' families without closure, even as answers emerge.

The relentless inquiry into this case urges us to honor Teresa's legacy, not merely with the solving of a crime, but through a reinvigoration of our shared commitment to protect the vulnerable and hold accountable those who'd flout the sanctity of life. While the shadows of injustice continue to haunt the echoes of past violence, the light of investigation shines a little brighter today, signifying not just the end of a quest for truth, but a renewably steadfast resolve among communities to shield against the darkness that, unchecked, can extinguish the brightest of lives. This is yet another hallway lengthened by loss but now, perhaps, illuminated with a promise: that justice, though late, has a way of bringing light to the darkest corners of humanity.

"I will seek the lost, and I will bring back the strayed, and I will bind up the injured, and I will strengthen the weak, and the fat and the strong I will destroy. I will feed them in justice." ~ Ezekiel 34:16

CHAPTER 13

HOLDING SECRETS

This is a particularly haunting cold case; one I'll never forget. It's almost beyond belief that someone could carry such a dark secret: killing two people in two different states and hiding it for years. In fact, the killer might have taken that secret to the grave if he could have. The pressing question is, are there more victims out there? The circumstances of this case might lead you to believe there are, especially after learning about the second murder. I must say, it was truly an honor to work alongside the cold case detectives, the Commonwealth Attorneys, and the dedicated police department that ultimately brought justice to this case.

Kathleen O'Brien Doyle was born on April 8, 1955, in Pennsylvania. She grew up in a military family, being the daughter of a naval officer, which likely influenced her own path in life. This background may also explain why she married a naval aviator; her connection to the military was a significant part of her life. After marrying Lt. Stephon Doyle, just nine months into their marriage, Kathleen had to learn what it meant to be the spouse of a Navy man. Soon, her husband was scheduled to deploy to sea aboard the USS Eisenhower, leaving Kathleen alone at their home in Norfolk, Virginia. During this time, she cared for their orange tabby cat, Ike, most likely named after the USS Eisenhower, which was affectionately nicknamed "Ike."

Let's take a closer look at Kathleen's life in the days leading up to the tragic event. On September 9, 1980, Kathleen was alone at home, as her Navy husband was deployed in the Indian Ocean, fulfilling his military duties. That day, she had a close friend over, someone she trusted and confided in, sharing conversations, gossip, and comfort. For many women in similar situations, having a friend visit is a natural way to cope with the loneliness that comes with being a newlywed military spouse. These visits often serve as a support system, helping them pass the time and feel less isolated.

When a service member is deployed, it can feel as if the world around them pauses, everyone's focus is on the mission. But for the spouse, life continues, often filled with a mix of emotions, loneliness, worry, and the need for connection. While Kathleen might have been somewhat accustomed to this, perhaps due to her upbringing in a military family, being a spouse brings its own unique challenges. On that particular day, she may have simply been feeling lonely or eager to catch up with her dear friend, Vivienne Mahoney. Whatever her reasons, that visit marked an ordinary moment in an otherwise unsettling time.

On the evening of September 9th, around 7:30 p.m., Vivienne arrived at Kathleen's Norfolk home. The two friends spent the evening together, sharing a glass of wine and catching up. As they talked, Kathleen might have looked out her window toward the Miles Methodist Church next door, perhaps hoping her husband would return safely from his deployment. Being married to a Navy pilot, thoughts about his safety and well-being were probably a constant part of her mind. Their conversation lasted about two hours, and they ended their visit around 9:00 or 9:30 p.m., leaving Kathleen to continue her evening, unaware of the events that would soon unfold.

Weather and lighting conditions are often important clues in criminal investigations, helping to establish timelines and possible opportunities. On September 9th, the sunset was around 7:21 p.m., and the temperature that evening was approximately 78 degrees. When Vivienne left Kathleen's home, the temperature had dropped slightly to about 74 degrees. Given the cooler evening, it's possible that Kathleen might have had some windows open to enjoy the fresh air and the peaceful sounds of the night.

Throughout that week, nighttime temperatures generally ranged between 43 and 63 degrees, with the lowest being 62 degrees on the 9th and daytime highs reaching up to 85 degrees. During this time of year, fall is just beginning to show itself, with trees starting to display vibrant orange, yellow, and red leaves, beautiful but fleeting. Perhaps Kathleen was gazing out her window, lost in thought, maybe daydreaming about her husband or simply appreciating the changing season.

The following day, September 10th, saw a slight drop in temperature, with a high of 79 degrees and an average low of 58 degrees. Little did Vivienne know that she would never forget the events that unfolded next, an incident that would forever change the course of Kathleen's life and the investigation into her death.

Kathleen was a college graduate with a degree in journalism, which suggests she was skilled at expressing herself through writing. While her husband was deployed, she turned to her journal as a way to cope with the distance and the challenges of being a military spouse. Journaling can be a powerful tool for processing emotions, reflecting on one's past, and even maintaining a sense of connection to loved ones who are far away.

According to Findagrave.com (2018), Kathleen wrote, "I will most likely write so that anyone looking over my shoulder would neither raise an eyebrow nor really raise too much interest" (para. 1). This indicates that she was cautious about her words, perhaps wanting to keep her thoughts private or protected. The same source mentions that "Kathleen was writing about her past in order to understand herself and where she fits into the future" (para. 1). This introspective purpose is something many people relate to; I've done the same in my journals, feeling nervous about revealing too much but also seeking clarity and self-understanding.

So, what was Kathleen's reason for journaling? Was it simply a way to cope, or was she searching for something deeper, a sense of identity, reassurance, or understanding in her life? And could her writings hold secrets or clues that might shed light on her state of mind during that time? These questions make her journal not just a collection of personal thoughts, but potentially an important piece of the puzzle in understanding who Kathleen was and what she was experiencing before her tragic death.

The next day, Vivienne tried to reach Kathleen by phone, calling her multiple times, but there was no answer. Naturally, this would have started to raise concerns. What might have been going through Vivienne's mind? She knew Kathleen well, and her repeated calls going unanswered could have been a sign that something was wrong. Perhaps Vivienne wondered if Kathleen was just busy, or if she was feeling unwell. But given their friendship and the fact that Kathleen wasn't answering, concern likely began to grow.

Should Vivienne have been worried? Was this behavior typical for Kathleen? If Kathleen was generally reliable and active in returning calls, then the silence could have been a red flag. On the other hand, back then, caller ID didn't exist until the mid- to late-1980s, roughly between 1984 and 1989, depending on the location and provider. Without caller ID, it was harder to know who was calling or if the phone was even working properly, which might have added to her uncertainty.

Later that evening, Vivienne decided to call Kathleen one last time. Still no answer. Recognizing that it was late and that she had already made several attempts, she decided to let it go for the night. But deep down, she likely felt that this silence was unusual and perhaps even unsettling. She probably wondered what was wrong, why wasn't Kathleen answering her calls? Had the wine she had shared earlier upset her stomach? Did she accidentally upset her during their visit? Or maybe Kathleen was busy with family or had company over, especially considering her husband was out at sea fighting for the country.

As a close friend, I can imagine the thoughts racing through Vivienne's mind that night. The worries about her friend's well-being, the uncertainty, and the growing sense that something might be very wrong. It's heartbreaking to think she never would have imagined that her dear friend Kathleen could have been murdered, especially living next door to a church, a place that symbolizes peace and community. Little did Vivienne know that quiet night would soon be shattered by events that would forever change her life and the course of the investigation.

The next day, September 11th, Vivienne and her husband James tried calling Kathleen once more. Still no answer. As they sat there, likely feeling a mixture of concern and helplessness, Vivienne would have been thinking about her friend's silence all night. Did Kathleen simply not answer because she was tired, overwhelmed, or perhaps unwell? Or was her absence more serious? The uncertainty must have weighed heavily on her mind. Whether she managed to get some sleep or stayed awake worrying, the lingering fear was undeniable.

Eventually, out of concern and a desire to reassure herself, Vivienne and James decided to go to Kathleen's home. Maybe seeing Kathleen in person would put her mind at ease and confirm that she was safe. As they drove there, the atmosphere inside the car might have been tense. Perhaps Vivienne shared her worries with James, telling him how strange it was that Kathleen hadn't answered her calls all night. Or maybe she remained quiet, overwhelmed by anxiety, and instead turned to prayer or silent reflection during the drive.

There may have been no words spoken at all as they traveled, just the hum of the car, their thoughts racing, and perhaps a shared moment of prayer or hope that Kathleen was okay. Little did they know their trip would soon lead to a shocking discovery that would forever alter their lives.

James and Vivienne arrived at Kathleen's home shortly before noon. James parked the car, and Vivienne stepped out, her mind racing with a mixture of worry and uncertainty. What was she feeling at that moment? Probably a deep sense of unease, her thoughts swirling with questions. Was Kathleen okay? Had something happened during the night? Or was it something more serious at play?

Meanwhile, James might have felt more confused yet equally concerned. They both knew Kathleen as a reliable, friendly person who always kept her home in order. The sight of her house, white with brick accents around the porch, looked familiar, but the overgrown shrubs on either side of the porch suggested neglect, which was unlike Kathleen.

Vivienne approached the front door and noticed a few odd details: the outdoor lights were still on, the mailbox had mail, and two newspapers lay on the ground outside. That accumulation of mail and newspapers was a common sign to police that someone might be missing or in trouble. It suggested Kathleen hadn't been out or checking her mail recently, which added to the suspicion. The screen door was unlocked, another unusual detail, especially for someone who usually kept her home secure.

Curious and increasingly concerned, Vivienne looked through the tiny windows in the door. Through the glass, she saw the two wine glasses from her visit on September 9th, an unsettling reminder that Kathleen had been there just days earlier. The scene was out of the ordinary and made her heart race. She knew this wasn't typical of Kathleen's routine.

Realizing the situation was serious, Vivienne decided to knock on the front door. Her concern was now mingled with fear, something was definitely wrong. She was about to find out what lay behind that door, and the truth would soon come to light.

Vivienne knocked or perhaps banged loudly on the front door, and it swung open slightly, revealing a scene that would forever change her life. As she stepped inside, her mind was flooded with disbelief and dread. The house was eerily silent, exactly as it had been when she and Kathleen parted ways just days earlier. But now, something felt terribly wrong. Her eyes instinctively searched the room, and her heart sank as she saw Kathleen lying motionless on the floor in the bedroom.

In that instant, Vivienne's thoughts raced; shock, fear, confusion. She hurriedly ran out of the house, her voice trembling as she yelled for her husband, James. "James! Kathleen's on the bedroom floor, I think she's dead!" Her words were filled with panic, disbelief, and a desperate hope that she was wrong.

James, hearing the alarm in Vivienne's voice, sprinted into the house and rushed to the bedroom. What he saw was horrifying, the room was in disarray. The mattress had been moved, and signs of a struggle were evident, torn bedding, disturbed furniture, and a scene that screamed violence. The brutal reality was clear, Kathleen had been attacked.

James immediately told Vivienne to call the police. She hurried to the kitchen, but the phone wasn't working properly. Her heart pounded as she struggled to get through, but the line was dead. Unknown to her, the dispatcher could hear the frantic voices from inside the house, but they couldn't hear her. Frantic and desperate, James managed to make a call from the neighbor's house, alerting authorities to the tragedy unfolding inside Kathleen's home.

On September 11, 1980, just over a week after her first journal entry, Kathleen O'Brien Doyle, a young woman of only 25, was found brutally raped and murdered in her quiet Norfolk home. She had only recently celebrated her marriage and was just beginning her life. Her death shocked the community and marked the beginning of a harrowing investigation into a heinous crime that would haunt everyone involved.

When the Norfolk Police arrived at the scene, their initial assessment was that there was no sign of forced entry or a struggle at the doors and windows. They carefully examined the exterior of the house, checking the frames, locks, and glass, finding everything to be intact and undamaged. This suggested that whoever committed the crime might have known Kathleen or entered through means other than breaking in, such as from an unlocked door or window.

As the officers moved inside, the scene inside the bedroom revealed a different story. There was clear evidence of a violent and bloody altercation, disturbed furniture, blood spatters, and signs of a fierce struggle. It was evident that Kathleen had fought hard to defend herself. Then, the grim discovery, the body of Kathleen O'Brien Doyle, lying there in her own room.

Detectives quickly assessed the scene and determined that Kathleen's body had likely been there for approximately 48 hours before James and Vivienne found her. This estimation was based on the state of her body, decomposition signs, and other forensic indicators. Interestingly, the detectives noted that this didn't seem to be a robbery or burglary. Despite the violent assault, items of value remained untouched, money left on the dresser, jewelry, and other personal belongings that were not disturbed. This suggested that the attacker's motive was not theft but perhaps something more personal or malicious.

This scene raised many questions: Who could have entered so quietly and left without taking anything? Why was Kathleen targeted? The investigation was only beginning, but the evidence started to paint a picture of a crime driven by intent beyond simple theft, a brutal assault that left a young woman dead in her own home.

James's account of discovering Kathleen was detailed and grim. He described finding her on the bedroom floor, with her hands bound by cords wrapped around her. His immediate attempt to check her pulse showed his concern and desire to confirm her condition. Noticing dried blood and the possibility that she had been killed earlier indicated that the crime had taken some time to unfold.

Blood evidence can tell a lot about the timing of a crime. When blood pools or drips, it begins to dry from the outside edges inward. The bright red color of fresh blood, rich in hemoglobin, gradually turns brown or black as it oxidizes, thanks to iron, a key component in blood. This process, called oxidation, occurs when blood is exposed to air, transforming the color and texture of dried blood over time. Dried blood becomes flaky and darker, often accompanied by a distinctive musty smell caused by the breakdown of blood cells and the oxidation process.

This smell, combined with the appearance of dried blood, can help forensic investigators estimate how long ago the injury or death occurred. In Kathleen's case, the presence of dried blood and the condition of her body suggested her death had likely happened several hours prior to discovery, possibly around 48 hours earlier, aligning with the police's initial estimate.

All these details, her bound hands, the dried blood, the scene's disarray, paint a picture of a violent attack that was both personal and brutal. The investigation would now focus on understanding who was capable of such violence and what their motive might have been, as every piece of evidence added another layer to this tragic and complex case.

The moment Kathleen O'Brien Doyle was officially pronounced deceased at approximately 12:00 p.m., on September 11, 1980, it marked a heartbreaking and shocking day for everyone involved, particularly for Vivienne and James, who had just discovered their friend in such a tragic state. Vivienne's mind was undoubtedly flooded with the "what ifs," questions about whether she could have done something differently, whether she might have arrived earlier, or if there was anything she missed. These thoughts are natural and often persistent in the aftermath of a traumatic discovery, even if they may not change the reality of what happened.

When Kathleen was found, her body was on the floor, naked, with her hands behind her and bound. She was also gagged, and a cord was wrapped around her neck, indicating a brutal and carefully executed assault. The presence of sharp force trauma, such as a stab wound to her left chest, pointed to a violent and personal attack. This detail, combined with the methodical nature of the crime, taking time, leaving evidence of torture, reminded many of the infamous BTK Killer, who also took his time with victims, binding and torturing before killing.

The scene raised unsettling questions: Was the killer a serial murderer, someone with experience and a pattern of carefully planned crimes? Did they know how to commit the "perfect murder," leaving little evidence behind? The killer's apparent calmness and methodical approach suggested a level of confidence and knowledge in executing such violence.

As the investigation continued, authorities would seek to determine whether this was an isolated incident or part of a pattern. The meticulous nature of the crime scene hinted at a dangerous individual, possibly a serial offender, who believed they could get away with their crimes. The questions of motive, identity, and whether this attacker had a history of similar crimes would become central to solving the case. The path to uncovering the truth was just beginning, but the brutality of Kathleen's murder underscored the terrifying reality of what had happened in this quiet neighborhood.

The Deputy Chief Medical Examiner, Faruk Presswalla, made his way to the murder scene. One thing he observed about Kathleen's body was that the death had occurred a substantial period before the victim was discovered. He noted that the victim's body was in full rigor mortis and cold to the touch. Rigor mortis is when the body becomes stiff following death. The muscles in the body are loose and limp and will begin to stiffen a couple of hours after death. This was another tell-tale sign the murder may have happened the night Vivienne was over.

The next piece of evidence that Dr. Presswalla noted was the dried, matted, whitish substance in the genital area, which could potentially be semen. Here, we have a naked deceased female, with her hands bound behind her back, lying on the floor with a gag in her mouth and an electrical cord around her neck. The evidence here is tremendous. I wish they had known then what they know now about DNA, but we'll get there; it just takes time. The ME ordered the deceased victim's body to go to the Office of the Chief Medical Examiner's Office for a full autopsy. All deaths, as in this death, should go to the ME's Office for a full autopsy if the death is suspicious.

The detectives from the Norfolk Police Department began their investigation the moment they arrived on scene. Detectives begin triaging the witnesses and conduct a canvass of the neighborhood. A canvass is when the detectives and police officers go door to door to ask neighbors if they saw or heard anything prior to the incident that occurred. While the detectives canvassed the area, the forensic investigators began processing the scene. Forensic investigators process the crime scene by documenting, collecting, and preserving evidence. Unfortunately, the canvass resulted in no witnesses to what had happened.

With evidence collection, processing a residence for fingerprints was a priority. During this time, DNA really wasn't spoken of too much and the forensic investigators did what they needed to do, dust the house for prints and collect any evidence related to the homicide. This was customary to do in the 1980s. Unfortunately, the fingerprints found in the residence were a wash. The only fingerprints found in the residence were identified belonging to Kathleen and Vivienne. There were no unidentified fingerprints located in the Doyle residence.

The diagram of the crime scene was documented by the forensic investigators who responded to the scene. This can be a tedious but important job while processing any scene. The residence is drawn in the diagram with all evidence. This is important in case there needs to be a reconstruction of the crime scene. This doesn't always happen, but when it does happen, it's used to determine the sequence of events that happened during and after the crime was committed. This allows for a longer interpretation of the evidence and the patterns left on the scene, like blood stains and physical evidence.

Detectives remembered that James and Vivienne stated that they had trouble calling 911 so they went to examine the white push-button telephone on a table in the kitchen near the pantry. The detectives were smart and unscrewed the mouthpiece of the phone, which became one of the pieces of evidence in this case. The internal mouthpiece, or receiver, to the telephone had been removed. Let's remember, cell phones weren't really a thing, and most people had the classic push-button landline phones or the rotary phones (the one with the dial) in their homes. Also, these types of landline phones had cords connected to the base of the phone. Cordless phones came later. Now, having a corded phone with mouthpieces that can be removed would have prevented someone from calling another number. Seems premeditated, doesn't it? I'm pretty sure this is why James Mahoney had to go next door to call 911 when he discovered Kathleen's body.

The forensic investigators also noted that the bedroom light was left on. The question is, did Kathleen turn it on, or did the killer? Was Kathleen asleep in her bed when the killer broke into her home? So far, we know that the outdoor light was still on, so the killer broke in during the night. We also know that the mail and newspapers were piled up. Another piece of evidence collected was a green bed spread. The green bed spread was dark with colorful flowers and birds, which was later sent to the Bureau of Forensic Science, which is now the Department of Forensic Science, for forensic examination.

When forensic investigators respond to an indoor scene, like a homicide, one of the first things they do is an initial walkthrough. This is important because they can locate evidence, and a possible point of entry or exit can be established. In this case, the forensic investigators determined that there was no forced entry into the home. It was reported that all the windows in the residence were closed; however, the police noted that there was a total of nine windows that were unlocked. The question is, what window did the killer use to enter the residence?

To answer that question, it was one of the rear windows. There was a piece of wood leaning against the house under the spare bedroom window in the rear of Kathleen's residence, which was near the utility meter. This means the killer used the wood and, quite possibly, the utility meter to gain entry through the spare bedroom window. Yes, a wanna be Spiderman. Later, we will discuss what the odds were with this dare-devil entry.

Another important piece to understand is that the storm window was also raised to gain access. The attention to detail by the investigators on this scene remained important. Without a suspect yet, time was of the essence. The investigators looked everywhere, but they still couldn't locate the knife that was used to stab Kathleen. They also couldn't locate the amplifier in the mouthpiece of the telephone. What they did find was the rolling pin from the kitchen in the bedroom near Kathleen. Does this mean the killer had an intention to kill or harm someone if they were home? Kathleen's body was badly injured with obvious signs of trauma. The detectives on the scene had observed the rolling pin on the floor next to Kathleen's body. She had blunt force trauma to the rear of her head, perhaps from the rolling pin from the kitchen. Let's find out what the autopsy report revealed about Kathleen's injuries and how she died.

The Autopsy Report

The next day, September 12, 1980, the autopsy of Kathleen O'Brien Doyle was performed by Dr. Presswalla. His findings were documented later, on September 15, 1980. Dr. Presswalla concluded the following in the autopsy report:

> Death resulted from homicidal causes; the decedent showed evidence of sexual abuse with punching and blunt force injuries to the face and mouth, kicking to the stomach, being tied up, gagged, and strangled with an electrical cord and stabbed in the back, with a separate stab in the front which failed to penetrate due to the blade impaling on the rib, which was fractured.

As with any sexual assault case, swabs were also taken during autopsy from the vaginal area and cervix, which indicated that spermatozoa were present. According to the autopsy report, the formal cause of death was "Mechanical asphyxia by strangulation and stab wounds with internal hemorrhage." Mechanical asphyxia is the use of the electrical cord being used for strangulation around Kathleen's neck. When a person is strangled, the individual can develop seizures, loss of consciousness, impaired breathing, defecation and urine, and then death. Other forms of mechanical asphyxia can encompass smothering, choking, positional asphyxia, and traumatic asphyxia. The different mechanisms can include ligature strangulation, hanging, and manual strangulation. In the case of Kathleen, the cord was the ligature.

When a person is strangled, it can take only 152 seconds before death. In the first five to ten seconds the person loses consciousness. By the time fifteen seconds passes, the person loses bladder control and then urination occurs. After thirty seconds, the loss of bowel control occurs and the person defecates. Between one to three minutes, death can occur. When forensic investigators work at a crime scene where there is a strangulation death, one of the tell-tale signs is petechiae. Petechiae are noticeable in the whites of the eyes and appear as little red dots. It can appear on the eyelid as well. Other obvious signs could be on the neck if there's a ligature left behind or marks of a ligature. If there isn't a death in strangulation, the person strangled may end up dying from carotid artery dissection or respiratory complications. Blood clots could travel to the brain and a brain embolization can occur.

Dr. Presswalla put in the autopsy report that the manner of death was homicide. What is interesting is that the manner of death often gets lay people confused with murder and homicide. Homicide is the killing of one person by another person, which is how the medical examiner rules the manner of death. Homicide is the legal term used to refer to the killing of another; however, murder is the crime that was committed. So, not to be confused, murder is what the suspect is charged with, and homicide is the manner of death deemed by the medical examiner.

The medical examiner was detailed when he wrote the autopsy report, as it should be. There are a few things mentioned in the report that are disturbing, and knowing another human can do this to another human is sickening. To begin, the first two words of the autopsy report are "Nude body." Some jurisdictions remove clothing before the deceased is taken to the medical examiner's office; however, Norfolk leaves the clothing on the deceased, and the detective will pick up the clothing and other items found on the body or in the clothes.

Let's go back to the rear bedroom window where the assailant entered the residence. This next piece of evidence would make you think this was a thought-out plan once the killer entered. Did he see Kathleen sleeping in her room and get himself prepared for what he was going to do next? Was Kathleen sound asleep from the wine and company she had had earlier?

According to the autopsy report, Kathleen's hands were tied behind her back, and her wrists had a Venetian blind type of cord wrapped around them. The detectives had determined that the rope was a four-strand rope. This rope was military grade and not available to the public. It was later discovered that the wrists had been tied post-mortem since there was no bruising. The other disturbing piece of evidence found was Kathleen's mouth was gagged with green leotards tied tightly behind her, and her tongue had been pushed backward into her mouth. There was also bruising and several lacerations in her upper lip that matched her teeth impressions. According to the medical examiner, "this was due to a forceable blow to the mouth."

The autopsy report stated the obvious medical terminology referencing the injuries, and it is worded from head to toe, documenting all injuries found on Kathleen's body. Kathleen's neck had an electrical cord that was cut and tied tightly around her neck. It was tied three times and then tied into a granny knot. Although there was no bruising, there were indention marks on the neck. Below the ligature, on the right side of her neck, there was a superficial cut, meaning it was a cut on the surface of her skin. Above the ligature to the left was a red/brown abrasion. On the right zygoma was a circular brown area, where the medical examiner noted that it looked like an abrasion/burn. This burn-type mark could be from the rubbing of the skin with the cord or from the floor like a "rug burn;" however, it could have also been from a cigar or cigarette burn. For those nonmedical individuals, the zygoma is the bony arch area of the cheek, also known as our cheekbone. There were other smaller injuries, like on Kathleen's lips, that were similar.

On the right side of the parietal area of the scalp, which is the upper area above the ear and center of the head, there was a contused laceration. Lacerations are caused by blunt force trauma. When the skin is hit, it eventually breaks open. This particular laceration had jagged edges; however, there was no fracture under this laceration. The medical examiner also noted and suggested that a round or oval object was used as a weapon for this injury. As mentioned earlier about checking for petechiae, the medical examiner noticed petechiae over the right upper eyelid and in the palpebral conjunctiva, which is a thin, clear membrane that protects and covers the inside of the eyelid and the white of the eye.

Let's take a moment and think about the injuries Kathleen's body has suffered so far. Do you think these injuries happened fast and abruptly, or do you feel like the killer took his time brutally abusing Kathleen's body? Think about the type of force that was used to subdue Kathleen before she succumbed to her injuries. The injuries listed on the head area were the main ones I thought were important to talk about.

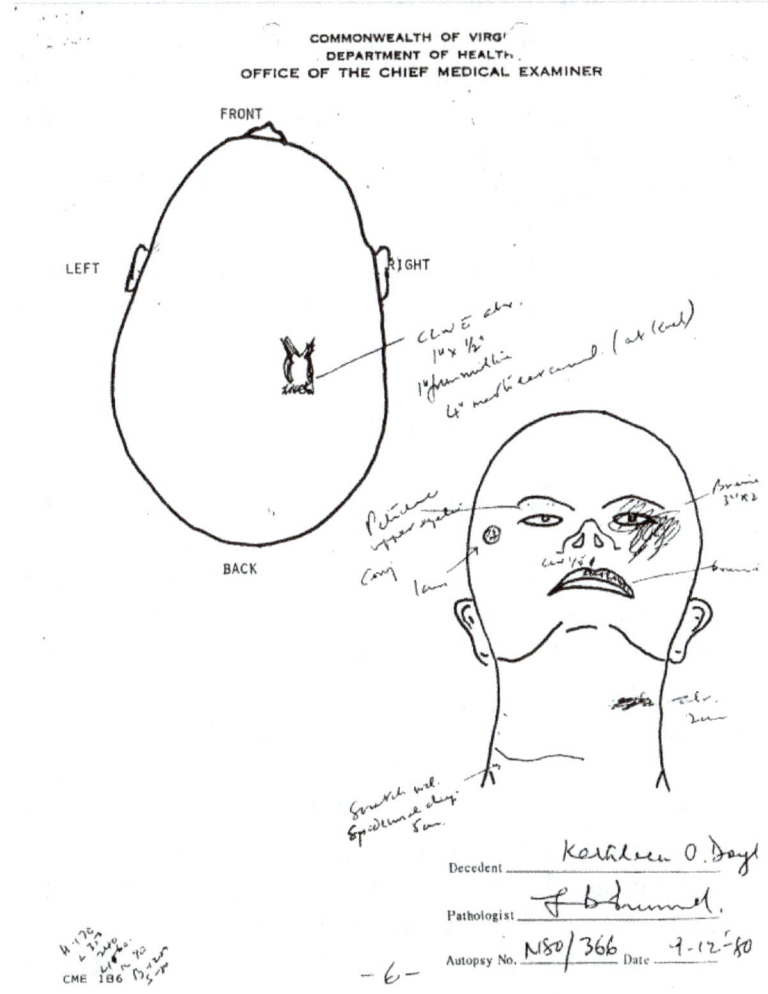

Moving down to the chest area, more distinctively, the upper breast area. There were a set of three oval bruises. Look at your fist for a moment. Look at the three knuckles that stick out. Yes, you have it! The medical examiner noted that the three oval bruises were consistent with knuckle and finger imprints from a fist blow. On the right mid-abdomen, there was a curve-like abrasion. According to the medical examiner, this abrasion resembled the toe print of a shoe. The lower left chest area had a stab wound with tailing. This means that an edged weapon was used, and towards the ending area of the cut, it becomes shallow. This really depends on the amount of force used and the positioning of the killer and victim. There was another stab wound on Kathleen's left lower back; this wound penetrated from the back to the front, piercing her heart, most likely caused her death. Her left lung had partially collapsed. There was a fracture on her fifth rib from the knife wound that had been wedged into the rib. According to the medical examiner, this wound matched the corresponding stab wound on the front of her. Her 8th rib on her left side was also nicked by a knife.

On the left arm, there was a small "irregular" stab, according to the autopsy report. This stab may have been a laceration. There was also a circular abrasion on the back of the left arm. Kathleen's wedding ring remained on her left ring finger. Now, here is where it gets more disturbing. There was matting of pubic hair with whitish material located near the entrance of the vagina. There was also whitish material near the anal opening.

Kathleen's blood alcohol content was 0.04% grams. The blood alcohol content, known as BAC, is how much alcohol is in the blood. This is the most precise way to measure intoxication. This is calculated per 100 mL of blood. On the night of her death, her meal consisted of beans, greens, peppers, and cabbage. Let us not forget she also had wine with her dear friend, Vivienne. When a person has a BAC level of 0.02%, the individual will start to experience muscle relaxation, increased body warmth, and loss of judgment. At 0.05%, a person can experience a lowered reaction time, impaired judgment, heightened mood, and a loss of motor control. Let's remember that Kathleen was most likely sleeping when the intruder came into her home. Also, some time had passed since she and Vivienne drank wine together. This means that some of the alcohol had already burned off.

The burn-off rate is about 0.016% per hour, and during this burn-off, the body metabolizes or breaks down alcohol and later removes it from the blood.

Here is a recap of most of the injuries listed by the medical examiner:

Mechanical Asphyxia

The electric cord that was tightly wrapped around Kathleen's neck. The leotards were tightly tied together and pushed into Kathleen's mouth, which caused her tongue to be pushed back. Petechiae was present in her upper right eyelid, showing there was strangulation.

Blunt Force Trauma Injuries

There was bruising on Kathleen's face on the left side of her cheekbone. There were signs of having been punched in the mouth, showing crushing of the upper lip. The cluster of bruises on the abdomen where the medical examiner believed it to be a fist. Also on her mid-abdomen was a shoe-toe imprint from being stomped on. The back of her skull was fractured.

Sharp Force Trauma Injuries

Kathleen had two knife wounds on her body. One wound was a stab wound on her left lower chest, and the second was a stab wound on her left lower back. This is where she ultimately ended up with a fractured rib.

The postmortem lab examination revealed that Kathleen did, in fact, have spermatozoa that were identified in the vaginal area. This was obviously collected by cervical swabs. The matted whitish material was also observed in the pubic hair. According to the autopsy report, the matted whitish material found was indeed positive for semen. This will ultimately help in the future of this case. The case summary by Dr. Faruk B. Presswalla stated:

Death resulted from homicidal causes; the decedent showed evidence of sexual abuse with punching and blunt force injuries to the face and mouth, kicking in the stomach, being tied up, gagged and strangled with an electrical cord and stabbed in the back, with a separate stab in the front which failed to penetrate due to blade impalement on the rib, which was fractured.

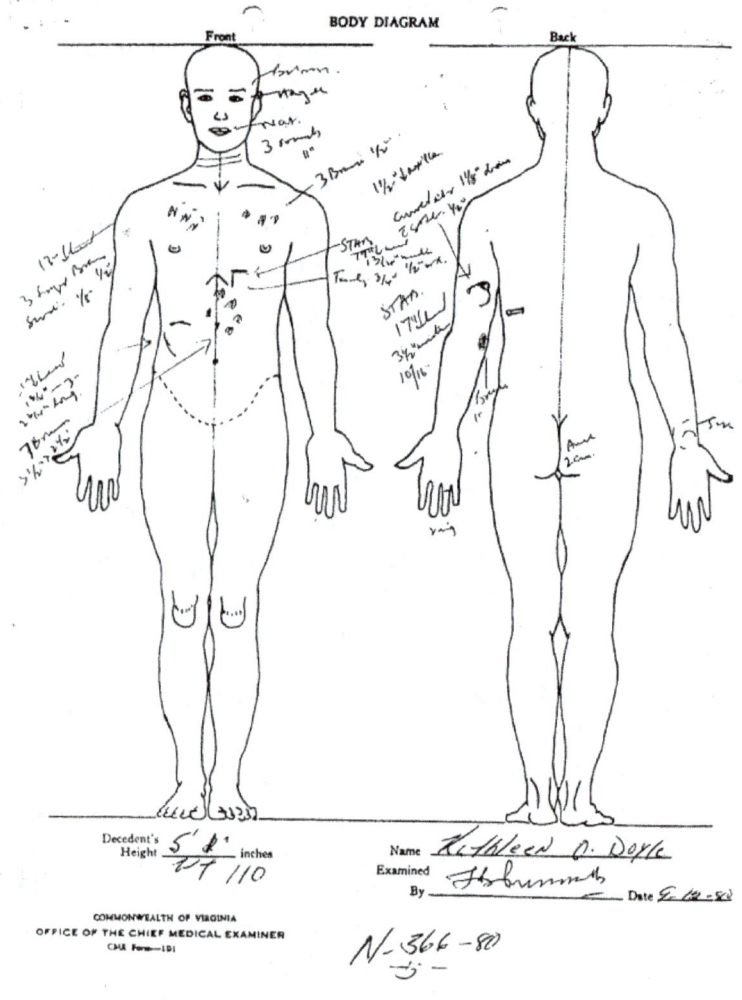

The Investigation

This is where the pressure began: the investigation. The questions really were, who and why? The detectives knew time was of the essence, and the more time that passed, the colder the investigation would turn. The crime scene was an important start to this case. There were no answers, just evidence at the crime scene. What we know so far from the crime scene is that the telephone amplifier was missing and the mouthpiece was screwed back on. The rolling pin was found in the bedroom near Kathleen's body. Near Kathleen's nude body was lying on the bedspread on the floor and her pajama shirt that was inside out, there was also her hair attached to the shirt. Her blue jeans were also on the floor.

One of the first places the detectives looked was the build-up of the newspapers from the last two days before the discovery of Kathleen's body. The two newspapers that were left at Kathleen's front door were from September 10, 1980, and September 11, 1980. Let's not forget September 11, 1980, when Vivienne and her husband discovered Kathleen deceased on her bedroom floor. Detectives interviewed the paperboy who delivered the newspapers to the Doyle's residence. The paperboy spoke with police and told them he had tried to collect the newspaper dues and knocked on the door; however, there was no response. Collecting money for the newspapers was customary for the 1980s; this was before the internet and all those debit cards we use today. People paid cash or by check for their papers most likely.

The detectives continued to look at the evidence that the forensic investigators collected. The police decided to complete a search warrant for the phone calls made at the residence. The detectives discovered that on September 9, 1980, at 9:32 p.m., Kathleen made a long-distance call trying to contact a friend who lived in Connecticut; however, he did not answer so she left a message. The police also discovered that Kathleen's mother had tried to call her at 11:00 p.m., but Kathleen never answered.

As with any investigation like this, detectives started to interview the family and everyone in her everyday life. This meant everyone, including Kathleen's ex-boyfriends. If they couldn't find a suspect, they could certainly rule people out. This wasn't a fast and easy task. It took a few months to interview all of Kathleen's known family members, friends, neighbors, co-workers, and any people known to Kathleen. The detectives were thorough and interviewed Kathleen's husband and his U.S. Navy contacts he had. There were concerns that the killer was someone Kathleen had known through the association of her husband's career since the military rope was left at the scene. Unfortunately, there were no leads from any of these interviews. The detectives were back to square one.

Detectives interviewed everyone they could think of. They interviewed another pilot that stayed behind and didn't go on the deployment Kathleen's husband was on. The detectives also looked into a neighbor that had recently left the military and was attending Old Dominion University. The detectives in the case completed interviews and polygraphs on both individuals. Interestingly enough, both individuals had deceptions indicated during the polygraphs.

The neighborhood lived in fear and remained vigilant, knowing there was a murderer out there somewhere. There were still no suspects seven months later and the detectives knew that time was of the essence. With each passing moment, memories started to fade, witnesses' recollections became less reliable, and evidence may end up compromised or lost. These detectives knew that the initial hours after the homicide are when witnesses' statements are the most accurate and when the trail is fresh.

By this time, the first 48 to 72 hours are long gone. It has been a few months since Kathleen was found deceased. The case is turning cold, with no leads for the detectives. Is this case still on the detective's desk, or is it in their file drawer waiting for a miracle? The first 48 hours are often called the "golden hours" and are crucial in homicide investigations. The detectives gathered evidence from the crime scene, examining every area and piece for clues. The forensic investigators meticulously collected possible DNA samples and any other potential piece of evidence that could lead to the killer's identity, but still, there were no leads.

For a moment, let's dissect what the "golden hours" really entail. We know that the "first 48" is vital because it is often believed to be the most crucial period in solving a homicide case, especially this case. We start with the freshness of evidence. This immediately follows a crime; evidence and witness testimonies are generally more accurate and reliable. As time passes, memories fade, evidence degrades, and potential leads become more challenging to track. Let's not forget that this homicide was in 1980, and the technology was nowhere near today. Therefore, the first 48 hours offer a precious opportunity to gather information before it becomes less reliable to the case.

Now, we move on to the witnesses and possible suspects. During the initial hours after the homicide, witnesses and potential suspects are often nearby or may still be in the vicinity; however, this isn't always the case. This increases the chances of finding individuals with valuable information or connections to the crime. As time passes, these individuals might disperse or become less accessible, making it harder for investigators to interview or trace them down. By the detectives acting immediately, they can secure the crime scene, collect evidence, and employ a focused plan of action, also known as a POA. Any delay can allow potential evidence to be tampered with or contaminated, making the investigation more challenging for the detectives to find a suspect or once it goes to court.

Detectives need to build momentum. This means finding and advancing leads. The first 48 hours most certainly set the pace for any homicide investigation; therefore, enabling law enforcement to establish a foundation of facts, identify leads, and connect the dots can lead to potential breakthroughs in the investigation. This can make a significant difference in the resolution of the case. It is worth noting that the "first 48" does not deem a case unsolvable beyond the 48 hours. It does emphasize the immediate response to the homicide due to the advantages that were mentioned. The detectives will continue to work diligently beyond the first 48 hours, but the possibility of quick breakthroughs will eventually decrease.

In Kathleen's case, one breakthrough came on March 18, 1981, from the Bureau of Forensic Science. A certificate of analysis was issued for the presence of spermatozoa from the vaginal smears, cervical smears, and stains that were recovered from the autopsy. This was great news for the detectives, but unfortunately, there were still no other leads the detectives could pursue. The detectives kept investigating, knowing it was incredibly disheartening that there were no other leads, especially after the certificate of analysis. The progress towards solving the homicide was again stalled, and justice for Kathleen remained elusive. The lack of leads was particularly frustrating for the family and friends of Kathleen, who were seeking closure and accountability for the tragedy that occurred back in September of 1980.

Family and friends may experience psychological and emotional distress during a homicide investigation. During the investigation, the family may experience uncertainty and fear. This is especially true in this case because the Doyle's house was broken into and Kathleen was brutally murdered. There were no leads, so the family may constantly be grappling with questions like: Who committed the crime? Are they still a threat to our family? Will justice ever be served? These uncertainties can generate significant emotional distress and anxiety.

We must acknowledge the grief and loss the family and friends endured. The family goes through a tremendous sense of loss when a loved one is murdered. They must somehow navigate the painful grieving process of mourning, not only for the physical loss but also for the abrupt end to a future that was supposed to be shared experiences and relationships. Grief will manifest differently for everyone. Some may experience feelings of sadness, anger, guilt, and even denial. Since everyone experiences grief differently, it may even impact relationships. Homicide investigations can strain the relationships that the family has built throughout the years, like marriages and births. Every member of the family may have similar or different ways of coping and ways of grieving, leading to potential tension and conflict within the family. Additionally, the increased attention on the investigation can create external pressures and expectations, causing strains within the family.

The families of homicide victims often have a strong desire for justice to be served, as they should. They may closely follow the legal processes, like attending court hearings and actively participating in solving the case. The process can be exhausting and emotionally draining and may result in disappointment if the outcome does not align with their expectations. The victim's family must relive everything from that tragic day to include photos of the crime scene and the autopsy. I know about cases resulting in disappointment. It happens way too often, and nothing can be done. There is that thing called double jeopardy, which is a concept primarily associated with the legal system, but it also has philosophical implications. It is where an individual cannot be tried for the same crime twice after they have been acquitted (found not guilty) or convicted (found guilty) and have completed their punishment or sentence. The laws were always made to help the defendant, so if they were convicted, they were guilty. Yes, there are still innocent people in jail.

My very first homicide case was just that. It fell apart because the witnesses "did not remember" or refused to testify. It still disturbs me to this day because the murdered victim crawled himself to the back of a church, where he died in the wet grass. It also disturbs me that a life was taken, and no one wants to testify on behalf of the victim. Luckily, Kathleen's case was nothing like that. The detectives never quit and just waited for a lead to come into their hands, knowing technology was getting better as time passed.

As the detectives were hopeful, another lead fell into their hands in November of 1984. The Norfolk Police detectives found out that there were serial killers in custody at the Williamson County Jail in Texas who were confessing to hundreds of murders. Those serial killers were Henry Lee Lucas and Ottis Toole. Ultimately, the detectives had requested and received arrest warrants for Henry Lee Lucas and Ottis Toole for the murder and rape of Kathleen Doyle. This caused a chain reaction in Virginia because other Virginia police departments got word and went to Texas to interview the confessing serial killers. All the Virginia detectives knew that Henry Lee Lucas and Ottis Toole were confessing to dozens of murders across the United States, so they wanted that chance to talk to them.

During the interview with Henry Lucas, the Norfolk Police detectives inquired if Henry Lee was ever in Norfolk. Of course, he said he was and was passing through "off and on." The Norfolk detectives had to pull out a map and show Henry Lee Norfolk having him identify what area he was in. Disturbing enough, Henry Lee Lucas pointed to Chesapeake Boulevard, which wasn't that far from the Doyle residence. Talk about chills going down your spine! It's interesting watching the interview because there's a pot of coffee on the interrogation table. A hot pot of coffee between the detective and the suspect at the time, Henry Lee Lucas. Let's not forget smoking was allowed back then too and Henry Lee held one in between his fingers.

Now detectives are hopeful and decide to show Henry Lee photos of the Doyle residence. The photo of the house was given to Henry Lee. The white house with brick around the porch and a chimney. The front of the house looks like an isosceles triangle with three ground windows and a circular window under the peak. The shrubs in the front of the house were overgrown and seemed out of control. Henry Lee took the photo and wiped his arm across his forehead and said, "I don't remember that house" (*Interrogation Raw*, 2023, 9:15). That was eerie. The detectives now ask Henry Lee if it would help if he saw the inside of the house. The detectives wanted to try everything because if he was the suspect, they didn't want to let him go.

The detectives showed Henry Lee the photo of the living room. Henry Lee held the photo and said, "I remember a house like that, that I stabbed a woman in" (*Interrogation Raw*, 2023, 9:39). Cold Case Detective, Jon Smith, made a point to say that four years had gone by and the detectives did not have any leads. During the interview on *Interrogation Raw* with Detective Smith, he points out that the detectives thought that they really had the killer in their case. Detectives continued their questioning with Henry Lee, hoping to find the answers they needed. They asked him what Kathleen looked like. He gave some details as to what she looked like and the detectives continued with questions, some asking what happened in the bedroom.

In the interview, Henry Lee stated, "That's one that I had taken. Went up to the door and asked for some water, and she invited me in" (*Interrogation Raw*, 2023, 10:57). This was interesting because after he made that statement, he went on and said, "After I was in the house, well, I got to messing around with her and took her on into the bedroom. Sexually assaulted her, Killer her" (*Interrogation Raw*, 2023, 11:08). Such a creepy thought, just thinking about the language he used. Does the normal person say, "I sexually assaulted her, I killed her?" No, they don't.

Henry Lee continued with details of the case and told detectives there were other people with him during the killing. The people he said were with him were Ottis Toole's niece and nephew, Frieda and Frank Powell. He told detectives, "They were more or less running around the house in there, looking for stuff to steal" (*Interrogation Raw*, 2023, 11:34). Let's remember, the detectives knew that there wasn't a robbery or burglary because of the personal items of value still in the residence. So, was Henry Lee telling the truth or was he guessing?

The detective proceeded to ask Henry Lee about the telephone being taken apart and messed with. Henry Lee's reaction was interesting, he said, "Oh yeah" and turned the blame over to Ottis Toole's nephew, Frank. Are these details a coincidence? Detective Smith mentioned that Henry Lee would take his time with the photos given to him by the detectives. It's like he was studying them. The detectives believed they had their guy and wanted to provide the family with answers and justice for Kathleen.

According to Mark Oliver (2022), Henry Lee Lucas and Ottis Toole were "drawn together by shared childhood trauma, Henry Lee Lucas and Ottis Toole became lovers—then serial killers who terrorized America in the 1970s" (para. 1). Just wait, it gets better. Henry Lee Lucas and Ottis Toole not only had a rape and murderous adventure together, but they also even cannibalized some of their victims (Oliver, 2022). I doubt they killed hundreds of people, but no one knows, so they were known as the "Confession Killers" (Oliver, 2022).

To understand the history of Henry Lee Lucas and Ottis Toole, it was learned that they had both grown up in an abusive home. Their mothers not only made them dress like girls, but they were also sexually abused before they were ten years old (Oliver, 2022). Sexual trauma can play a huge role in a person's psychiatric awareness. Henry Lee had killed his mother when he was 23 years old in 1960. According to Oliver (2022), "All I remember was slapping her alongside the neck," Lucas would later tell the police. "When I went to pick her up, I realized she was dead. Then I noticed that I had my knife in my hand, and she had been cut" (para. 10).

If you think Henry Lee's life was terrible, Ottis Toole's was not any better. Ottis Toole was assaulted by just about everyone he knew and trusted (Oliver, 2022). According to Oliver (2022), "His mother dressed him up as a girl, his older sister raped him before he was ten years old, and his father prostituted him to a neighbor when he was only five" (para. 12). I can only imagine how Ottis Toole felt. He was only 14 years old when a salesman tried to use him for sexual favors, so he ran over the salesman with his car, killing him (Oliver, 2022).

If anyone could empathize with these two individuals, it would be hard. It is essential to recognize that having empathy for someone who commits murder does not mean condoning or justifying the actions they took. Empathy does not mean agreeing with someone's choices or validating their behavior. Instead, it is a way of understanding the factors that may have influenced their actions and exploring the complexities of human nature. We should recognize that empathy for a murderer does not absolve them of responsibility for their actions. In a moral and legal sense, individuals are still accountable for their actions and must face the consequences of their choices.

It was said that Henry Lee Lucas and Ottis Toole traveled to 26 states on their killing spree. The question is, how many people did they really kill? Oliver (2022) wrote that "Henry Lee Lucas later claimed that he coached Toole on how to get away with murder. 'He was doing his crimes all one way,' Lucas said. 'I started to correct him in his ways, in doing the crime where he would not leave information'" (para. 17). Lucas was finally arrested in Texas in 1983 after killing a woman and stuffing her into a drainage ditch.

Meanwhile, in 1984, Toole was living in custody in Florida for burning a 64-year-old man alive. What is even more interesting is that Henry Lee Lucas was arrested for weapon charges, not murder. Once in custody, Henry Lee spoke to police about their killing spree, which ultimately led Ottis Toole to talk to police.

By 1985, many of the confessions made by Henry Lee Lucas and Ottis Toole were brought into question by detectives working in homicide cases. Every time there is a possible lead in Kathleen's case it dissipates. Ottis Toole also confessed to the murder of Adam Walsh, John Walsh's son, who went missing on July 27, 1981, in a Sears department store at the Hollywood Mall located in South Florida. Adam Walsh was found in a canal two weeks later with his head severed. The Walshes were responsible for launching the popular television show *America's Most Wanted*, where the nation's most notorious criminals were put on television and motivated police agencies to change how authorities search for missing children.

The detectives kept investigating and waited for more leads. In April of 1986, the Texas Attorney General issued the "Lucas Report," which examined the facts and circumstances of the murders Henry Lee Lucas and Ottis Toole confessed to. According to the Commonwealth of Virginia Stipulation of Evidence:

> In the "confession" by Lucas to the murder of Kathleen Doyle given to the Norfolk Police Department, Lucas recounts that Toole's niece and nephew were present with Toole and Lucas on a trip to Virginia. The Lucas Report confirmed that either Toole's niece and nephew were present in school in Florida on September 9, 10, or 11, 1980, and that on September 10, 1980, Henry Lee Lucas had sold 97 pounds of scrap metal in Jacksonville, Florida.

Quite interesting, huh, but for Kathleen's murder investigation and based upon objective facts that disproved Henry Lee Lucas and Ottis Toole, they were not the suspects in the case. Their physical ability to be in two places at the same time was obviously not able to happen, not to mention they confessed to hundreds of murders that they most likely did not do. It is unknown if the arrest warrants for Henry Lee Lucan and Ottis Toole were ever executed; however, the Norfolk Police Department referenced the nolle prosse of the warrants for rape and murder. Were they trying to go down in history? Well, they certainly did, as the Confession Killers.

Toole later recanted his two confessions of killing Adam Walsh, leading the Adam Walsh case to be unsolved for decades. According to NBC 6 (2022), "Hollywood Police detectives were unable to verify Toole's confessions because of a series of errors they made in the investigation, including losing the bloody carpet from Toole's car and even the car itself" (para. 6). Interesting enough, in 2008, the former Police Chief of Hollywood, Florida, Chief Chad Wagner, officially named Ottis Toole the killer and apologized for past mistakes (NBC 6, 2022). Ottis Toole later died in prison at the age of 49 from cirrhosis of the liver on September 15, 1996. What were the odds that Ottis Toole died on September 15th? As we remember, Kathleen was pronounced on September 11, 1980. Henry Lee Lucas died at the age of 64 in a prison in Huntsville, Texas, from natural causes.

Ensuring fairness was crucial in this murder investigation. The detectives must ensure they do not discriminate based on race, gender, religion, or other irrelevant factors. Treating suspects like Henry Lee Lucas and Ottis Toole with respect and providing equal opportunity to present their side of the story is vital to maintaining fairness, even though they gave a false confession. Detectives must also respect the privacy and confidentiality of all individuals involved. They must handle sensitive information carefully, ensuring that it is disclosed only to those who have a legitimate need to know. The detectives kept this in mind when the Doyle family kept asking for answers that the detectives did not have.

From the moment after Kathleen's rape and murder into the 1990s, Kathleen's family wanted answers. Her father, the retired Navy Captain, John O'Brien, continually requested the reinvestigation of his daughter's murder. He brought this case to the City of Norfolk authorities and police department. Finally, in 1995, the Norfolk Police Department and the Office of the Commonwealth's Attorney began a full investigation of Kathleen's rape and murder. Now with a fresh set of eyes, the case continued to be investigated, especially with new technology arising.

Those fresh eyes started with Detective Scott Halverson from the Norfolk Police Department. Knowing there was new forensic science technology with DNA analysis, Detective Halverson tried to locate all the witnesses, family contacts, military contacts, or any other persons of potential interest to Kathleen's rape and murder case. Several years had gone by and this was not an easy task. People move and change their phone numbers. If anyone close to her killed her, then that person may have thought they were in the clear and moved away. It would be a perfect synopsis because no one really knew about DNA and the new technology that had started to be used in criminal cases. Detective Halverson was ultimately able to eliminate Henry Lee Lucas and Ottis Toole from being the suspects by the Virginia Division of Forensic Science. The Virginia Division of Forensic Science's analysis concluded that the spermatozoa recovered from the autopsy did not have Henry Lee Lucas or Ottis Toole's DNA. So once again, Kathleen case got colder.

As the case continued to get colder, detectives kept faith in finding a suspect in Kathleen's murder. This case touched many people, not just the family, but the Navy family as well. More fresh eyes picked up the file in 2001 and that was Detective Donnie Norrell. Once again, the case was reviewed, and evidence glanced at. Detective Norrell found a piece of evidence that was never sent to the Virginia Division of Forensic Science. Surprisingly, this evidence was the green print bed spread that was found under Kathleen's lifeless body and a box of slides containing fibers and hairs. These two pieces of evidence sat in the Norfolk Police Department's Property and Evidence Unit waiting for forensic technology to improve DNA analysis. Finally, some questions were answered.

Detective Norrell submitted the green print bed spread to the Virginia Division of Forensic Science for DNA analysis. On July 13, 2001, the Virginia Division of Forensic Science provided a certificate of analysis for the spermatozoa and a DNA profile was identified from the bed spread. Now the detectives knew for sure that Ottis Toole and Henry Lee Lucas were not involved. The neighbor and fellow pilot were also eliminated as suspects. Now that there was a profile, the detectives needed to get samples from individuals that encountered Kathleen. Detectives had found out that as of July of 2002, Vivienne Mahoney had passed away and was no longer available to answer any further questions from detectives. Kathleen's widower had now remarried and was stationed on the west coast. The detectives just knew the killer had been or was in the military, but once again, there were no more leads and the case remained cold.

In 2007, Cold Case Detective, Jon Smith, was assigned to the Norfolk Police Department's Homicide Squad. Detective Smith stated that he had a supervisor that came into the office with an accordion file and had placed it on his desk. Of course, Detective Smith inquired what type of file it was and wanted to know what his supervisor was working on. The file was the Kathleen Doyle case. Little did Detective Smith realize that this case would soon follow him.

Jumping to August of 2018, another set of eyes took hold of this cold case, Detective Jonathan Smith. Kathleen O'Brien Doyle's unsolved murder case was his first assignment. I worked with Jon for most of my career. We were in the police academy together in 2004, Class 72. After graduation, we did go into separate precincts, but it didn't take long for Jon to end up in the homicide squad. There were great homicide detectives in the squad at that time and it's no wonder why he's so great at his job. I finally got transferred into the Forensics Field Unit and I finally had a chance to work with him again. After a couple years went by, he ended up working with me in the Forensic Unit and then was transferred to the Cold Case Unit, where he once again worked with a great homicide detective, Victor Powell. Jon, learning the forensic aspect of crime scenes had allowed him to have the extra knowledge he needed to solve cold cases.

Remember, this wasn't the first time Detective Smith saw Kathleen's case. When he was in Homicide, another homicide detective took the reins on the case and did his best to look it over forensically with the new technology that arose throughout the years. Unfortunately, it remained cold. When Detective Smith was officially handed Kathleen's case, one of the first things he did was look at the breakthrough of DNA technology, specifically genetic genealogy. The thought about using genetic genealogy with the semen that was found on the bed spread made sense and was worth a try.

I asked Jon when he first opened the Kathleen Doyle case, what was the first thing he wanted to do involving the case? Here is his response:

> When I first opened the Kathleen Doyle case, my immediate priority was to establish a comprehensive understanding of the case details and gather all available information. I initiated a thorough review of the case file, starting from the initial call to the crime scene, then working my way outward, and organizing the information in a systematic fashion.

This approach allowed me to identify key events and potential investigative leads effectively.

Upon taking over the case, I was faced with the significant task of managing the substantial volume of information. There were about 3 banker boxes worth of material that needed careful scrutiny. I systematically went through each piece of evidence, witness statements, and reports, ensuring that no detail was overlooked. This meticulous review was crucial in identifying patterns, inconsistencies, and potential leads within the extensive material.

As I delved into the case, it became evident that Investigative Genetic Genealogy (IGG) could be a powerful tool in unraveling the mystery. In April of that year, I became aware of the potential of IGG following the breakthrough in the Golden State Killer case. Recognizing its groundbreaking implications, I proactively sought to stay abreast of developments in this emerging field.

Given the promising outcomes in other cases, I decided to explore the feasibility of applying IGG to the Kathleen Doyle case. In August of 2018, just months after the Golden State Killer case breakthrough, I joined the Cold Case Squad. This timing was crucial, as it allowed me to capitalize on the momentum generated by the success of IGG in other investigations.

Understanding the significance of genetic evidence in this case, I worked diligently to ensure that all necessary steps were taken to submit the relevant samples to a private lab specializing in genetic genealogy. By combining meticulous organization of case details with the strategic application of

Investigative Genetic Genealogy, I aimed to enhance the overall effectiveness of the investigation and bring us closer to resolving the Kathleen Doyle case.

Genetic genealogy relates to DNA and family history. More and more agencies are using genetic genealogy to solve cold cases and missing persons cases. According to the Library of Congress, Steen et al (2021) wrote, "Modern genealogy combines DNA analysis with traditional documents in order to provide reasonably exhaustive research and more reliable conclusions. This research guide provides tools to unite science with history as you grow your family tree" (para. 1). Steen et al (2021) described genetic genealogy in more detail by stating, "Genetic genealogy creates family history profiles (biological relationships between or among individuals) by using DNA test results in combination with traditional genealogical methods" (para. 2). This means that "by using genealogical DNA testing, genetic genealogy can determine the levels and types of biological relationships between or among individuals" (Steen et al, 2021, para. 2).

On November 4, 2019, the bed spread was sent to the forensic lab for modern DNA testing to run the DNA profile through the familial DNA databases. Was this going to be the breakthrough the detectives needed to finally solve this case? Perhaps, yes it does. The report provided 31 matches of close relatives. Now it's time to figure out where these individuals were during the murder on September 11, 1980. The 31 kin references could be cousins and such, but it was still a lead on finding the murder suspect.

Detective Smith started with typing in the names into a Google search, most names coming up with nothing, except one, Dennis Lee Bowman. When Bowman's name was searched, serious offenses started popping up throughout the State of Michigan. These crimes consisted of attempted murder, attempted rape, and abduction.

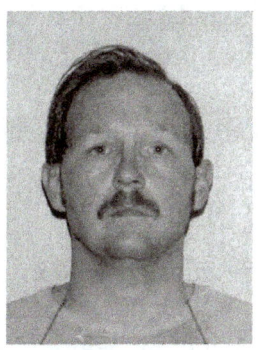

Finally, on November 11, 2019, almost 40 years later, Detective Smith had a lead for a possible suspect in the murder and rape of Kathleen Doyle. That lead was Dennis Lee Bowman, a 70-year-old man living in Michigan. Now the detective's job starts once again. Detective Smith needs to place Bowman in Norfolk during the time of the murder. How difficult can that be exactly? Well, let's see. Detective Smith started working with the Michigan State Police on finding out information needed for this case.

In the spring of 1980, Dennis Bowman attempted to assault a teenage girl by forcing her off the road while she was on her bicycle. The teenage girl was able to escape Bowman, and Bowman was later arrested. The hearing for Bowman was in September of 1980; however, his lawyer advised the court that Bowman could not attend due to his two weeks of military training in Norfolk, Virginia. The U.S. Navy confirmed with detectives that Bowman was in fact in Norfolk, Virginia during the time Kathleen Doyle was killed. Here's the link, now Detective Smith had to confirm for his investigation by looking into Bowman's criminal record and building a suspect profile.

Detective Smith later attended a national cold case conference from November 11-15, 2019, in Norfolk, Virginia with other police agencies. Detective Smith, amongst talking to other cold case detectives, ran into a Michigan State Police (MSP) detective sergeant. While conversing, the detective sergeant and Detective Smith quickly realized they had a suspect in common; that suspect was Dennis Lee Bowman.

Once again, I asked Jon what exactly happened at the conference and was he already in communication with MSP? Here was his response:

> During the conference, which commenced on Monday morning following the receipt of the Parabon Investigative Genetic Genealogy (IGG) report, I immediately delved into researching the names on the list. Dennis Lee Bowman, the second name from the bottom, caught my attention as I discovered articles on the Charley Project website detailing his adopted daughter Aundria's disappearance and his arrest in May 1980 for criminal sexual conduct in Michigan.
>
> Recognizing the potential significance of this information, I seized the opportunity provided by the presence of Michigan law enforcement at the conference. Instead of independently reaching out to various agencies, I decided to leverage the expertise and local connections of the Michigan State Police (MSP) officers in attendance.
>
> In a serendipitous turn of events that seemed straight out of a Hollywood script, I crossed paths with a Michigan State Police Detective Sergeant who was familiar with Bowman and his family. My gift of gab and networking skills set this unexpected meeting in motion. After a brief discussion, the Sergeant promptly assisted me, gathering documents related to Bowman's past and previous arrest/incarceration periods. Through this fortuitous collaboration, I learned that Bowman was not in custody during

the critical period from May 1980 to the September 1980 (Michigan offense.

Moreover, the MSP lab possessed a surreptitious DNA sample from Bowman. Upon their prompt response, I obtained the DNA profile, which I promptly sent to the DFS (Department of Forensic Sciences). The subsequent analysis revealed a match, solidifying Bowman as a suspect in the Kathleen Doyle case.

With the evidence aligning, I realized the next crucial step was to travel to Michigan to obtain a one-to-one DNA sample directly from Bowman. This entire process unfolded within a remarkable 72-hour timeframe from the start of the conference on that Monday morning. Following these swift developments, I found myself on a plane the next week armed with an arrest warrant, ready to locate and apprehend Dennis Lee Bowman.

It was already confirmed that Dennis Bowman was being looked at for a serious number of crimes. Attempted murder, attempted rape, abduction, and breaking and entering were all on the list. Sounds familiar, doesn't it? Bowman was known to also take items of women's clothing, like lingerie, during break-ins. Even one of the judges noted in the records that Bowman could be a future danger to women. What were the odds?

Wait, there's more! Detective Smith dug further into Bowman's life. One particular case came to the surface. The missing person's case of Aundria Bowman from 1989. Aundria was Bowman's 14-year-old adopted daughter. Aundria had gone to school officials and advised them that her father, Dennis Bowman, had been inappropriately making advances on her. Shortly after that, Aundria went missing under suspicious circumstances.

On November 21, 2019, Detective Jon Smith obtained an arrest warrant for Dennis Lee Bowman for the murder of Kathleen O'Brien Doyle. This time the ducks were in a row. The following day, Michigan State Police arrested Bowman at his residence and brought him in to be questioned. Michigan State Police advised Detective Smith that Bowman had a very alpha personality, always wanting to be in charge, running the conversation. Finally, Bowman was advised that he was being charged with the murder of a Naval Aviator's wife. Right then, Bowman requested a lawyer.

When a suspect requests a lawyer, the interview is done. There's no asking any questions related to the case. Many detectives hate this because some don't have enough information and must release the suspect. Good detectives already know most of the answers they're asking in an interview, so locking in any statements from the suspect always helps. It's always good when a suspect lies and the detective already knows what happened, especially because of CCTV and actual witnesses.

Dennis Lee Bowman's extradition to Norfolk, Virginia finally came on February 7, 2020. The arrest warrant for murder was elevated by the Commonwealth's Attorney to capital murder. Unfortunately, Bowman requested a lawyer so Detective Smith wouldn't be able to question him about the Doyle case. The only way that Detective Smith could question Bowman is if Bowman voluntarily requested him to talk about the case and legal rights would have to be completed once again. Also, if Bowman agreed to talk about other topics like rape or burglary, charges he didn't have at the time, Detective Smith would be able to talk to him.

Detective Smith had to create a rapport with Bowman. Although it was challenging, Detective Smith was able to learn about Bowman's life growing up and who he was as a person. This was very important in this case. During the interview with Bowman, Bowman made a point to say he had five older sisters and they never got struck. Bowman stated that his dad never punished his sisters and may have only yelled at them. The same for Bowman's baby brother; he never got hit or punished. Could this be when he began his hatred for women? Detective Smith just let him talk, gaining that rapport, so if Bowman finally wanted to talk about the case he would.

Three hours had gone by in the interview room where Bowman just talked about himself and his life growing up. Bowman was a man that hated his childhood. Once he turned sixteen, he felt he was forgotten about, no birthdays to celebrate, or any celebrations at that. Bowman, wearing an orange jumpsuit, looked at Detective Smith and said, "I never heard, ever, not one time in my life have I ever heard my mother say, 'I love you.' Not ever" (*Interrogation Raw*, 2023, 21:54). Bowman admitted that it had affected him later in his life. Bowman made another statement about his father this time, "The last thing my dad told me was, he said, 'Your mom's got a heart of gold. Hard and Cold" (*Interrogation Raw*, 2023, 22:19).

Dennis Bowman was now starting to become comfortable with Detective Smith. It's very important to treat everyone with respect, even if they did just kill someone. It's important to remain humble during these times. We, as detectives, don't know the person's past like they do through their eyes. Bowman saw Detective Smith as a person, a nonjudgemental person. Knowing Jon, he does care about the people in his cases. You kind of have to because you get to know the victim's family and potential suspects and witnesses.

Detective Smith got to the point where he told Bowman that he made arrangements for him at the Norfolk City Jail in case he wanted to talk over the weekend. Detective Smith explained to him that once he got his lawyer, he could no longer chat with him. The next morning, Detective Smith had two missed phone calls from his contact at the Norfolk City Jail and was advised that Bowman had been asking for him for about two hours. Bowman would have his lawyer in two days, so time was of the essence and Detective Smith knew it.

Now, Bowman was in the interview room once again, this time wearing Norfolk City Jail's black and white striped jumpsuit. Detective Smith told Bowman he was advised that he wanted to see him, and Bowman agreed; however, Bowman tried to run the conversation. Bowman was concerned with the capital charges because Virginia still had the death penalty at the time, and he had wanted to see if he could get them reduced. Obviously, the detective couldn't do that, that would be up to the prosecution. Bowman raised his hand while talking and suggested to Detective Smith, "I will forego the lawyer. I will tell you everything that I have remembered from that night. And I will go before the judge and plead guilty of my own volition" (*Interrogation Raw*, 2023, 24:55). Detective Smith advised him he couldn't do that unless both the prosecutor and defense attorneys were present. Detective Smith ran with it and from what Bowman wanted, he just wanted to have no lawyer and plead guilty to the judge.

Detective Smith had a strategy. He decided to repeat everything Bowman had told him and used it for the confession. Detective Smith told Bowman he understood that Bowman had a lot on his chest, and it was just building up. He also told Bowman that it probably fueled his aggression, and Bowman nodded his head in an up and down manner agreeing to what Detective Smith said. Detective Smith spoke to Bowman with a soft caring voice.

I was working at the same time Detective Smith was interviewing Dennis Bowman the second time. I happened to be in the office and hopped onto the interview while at my desk. I had heard about this case, and it intrigued me. Detective Smith was in the interview room with Bowman for over three hours talking the previous day, but not about the case. It was getting close though, you could just tell Bowman wanted to talk. Maybe he was having a mental fight with himself. He was a lot older now, was he ready to get things off his chest? The answer was YES!

Dennis Bowman had long been haunted by the shadows of his past, a past he recounted during a particularly unsettling encounter with the police. He vividly recalled a fateful spring day in 1980 when he found himself pulled over by officers alongside a quiet road. As the memory resurfaced, he described how the police positioned him next to a car and confronted him with a young girl who, to his chilling dismay, unequivocally identified him as her attacker. There was no ambiguity in her voice, she was certain it was him. Bowman remembered the harrowing incident with unsettling clarity: how he had attempted to forcibly divert the teenage girl from her path while she rode innocently on her bicycle. It was a moment that would linger in both their lives, casting a long shadow over the years that followed.

Bowman felt an urgent need to share most of every detail of the fateful day of the murder with Detective Smith. What makes Bowman particularly intriguing is that his memory of events from 1980 remains remarkably vivid. During that time, he found himself stationed in Norfolk, Virginia, for a two-week military assignment, a place where he knew no one and chose to embrace solitude. As his time away neared its end, the confinement began to weigh heavily on him, exacerbating a growing sense of cabin fever. Desperate for a break from the confines of the ship yet lacking the funds to venture far, Bowman resolved to explore his surroundings, driven by an instinctive need to break free from his isolation. Bowman stated the following:

> First of all, that was the period of which I go to the two weeks reserve. I'm 600 miles away from anybody I know. I'm wound up like an eight-day clock. I said, "Okay, I got to get off this ship." And I walked into a little bar. Well, I got stupid drunk, I mean, just crazy, stupid drunk. I sat there for about I'll bet three hours.

I didn't know how I was going to get back to base. I couldn't afford a, couldn't afford a cab or anything. It's night. And I'm walking down the street. And I walk past this house. And I said, "I wonder if they got some loose money laying around." And I went up to a window, got out a pocketknife. Got it open. Opened up the window. I almost fell in the house. I was drunk. I mean, I was just drunk. (*Interrogation Raw*, 2023, 26:49-27:52)

To provide some insight into Bowman's state of mind, it's important to note that he was not in a favorable mental space. Before departing from the bar, he tossed a tip onto the counter in a seemingly distracted gesture. Afterward, he meandered towards the Doyle residence. Notably, Bowman later conveyed to Detective Smith that as he passed by the Doyles' home, all the lights were extinguished, and the driveway was empty of any vehicles. This detail may carry significance in understanding his subsequent actions. He described in his police interview how he broke into the residence, stating, "I went to the back of the house and there was a pallet lying in the yard and I put it up against the house and I went up to a window, and the window had a hook and latch on it to lock it. So, I got out a pocketknife."

By this small bit so far, Bowman was just speaking softly about what he had done the night of the murder. Everything was finally coming to a close and starting to make sense of what the detectives saw on scene when the investigation began. Let's continue to see what else Bowman says about that night:

And I looked in the top drawers cause everybody's got a junk drawer. There was another door. I opened it up. And she was lying there. All right? She say (sic) up and started to scream. I still had that little pen knife in my hand. And when I went to push her back down, she grabbed that hand. I can vivid… I can see it right in my mind, that knife going right there (as Bowman points to his left side). I blanked out right there. And I said, "Lady, I'm leaving." And I walked out the front door. (*Interrogation Raw*, 2023, 27:52-28:28)

Remember what I said earlier about locking in a statement. This statement now becomes super important as Detective Smith interviews Bowman further. Detective Smith knows there's details about the case that Bowman is not talking about, like the rape and Kathleen being tied up. Detective Smith was smart and let Bowman talk and tell his version of what happened the night he broke into the Doyle residence. Bowman even made a point to tell Detective Smith that he went into the kitchen and looked inside the refrigerator for money. He even looked inside cookie jars. He appeared to be desperate. He noted small details like the living room had a little nightlight in the corner.

Where's the knife? This was the question from the beginning of this crime. There was nothing found on scene, so it was taken with the killer. Detective Smith asked Bowman where that knife went that he used to stab Kathleen. Bowman's response was disturbing, he said he lost the knife somewhere and that it wasn't a good knife. Then Bowman responded saying he couldn't take it on an airplane. Well, that's obvious, so did he get rid of it before he flew back home, or did he lose it because it was a crap knife? It's great to know the Navy helped a murderer escape, although they had no clue.

All of these small details would later play a big part in this investigation. Bowman continued to tell Detective Smith he couldn't remember everything that happened that night, but he did remember that Kathleen was still lying on the bed and was moving. He couldn't remember how long or even how he got back to the ship; however, he woke up with his mattress on the floor and still in his clothes. He also made a point to say that he didn't even know she was dead when he left or how long he was even there.

There was a break and Detective Smith went and got lunch for Bowman. I remember listening to this over my headsets. Detective Smith asked Bowman what he wanted to drink. Bowman responded with a "Squirt," and everyone was baffled because they didn't know what a Squirt soda was. Maybe it was a northern thing, but it's grapefruit soda, one of my favorites. They couldn't find a Squirt, so they ended up getting Bowman a Sprite. That moment kind of stuck with me because I thought it was hilarious.

Bowman was given a phone to use while he was in the interview room waiting. I remember listening to this conversation. He called his wife Brenda. I remember him talking to her and acting like nothing had happened, almost seeming like it was a misunderstanding. He mainly talked about how everything was going to be ok. Not once did he mention his adopted daughter, Aundria, who went missing years ago. He did not mention that he just confessed to killing a woman in 1980. Bowman hid everything from his wife. Always wanting to be in control. Although they had a lengthy conversation, it all came to an end when Detective Smith returned with food.

Finally, Detective Smith asked Bowman a question; one that turned Bowman upside down. He asked Bowman if he had ever had sex with the victim. Bowman said he was drunk as a skunk and didn't know how he would have had sex. Here's how the interview went:

Detective Smith: Do you remember having sex with her?

Bowman: No. In fact, I don't know how I ever had sex with her. I was drunk as a skunk.

Detective Smith: Do you remember if you tied her up at all?

Bowman: No. I don't know that either (Bowman shakes his head). (*Interrogation Raw*, 2023, 29:03-29:16)

Bowman was shaken by Detective Smith's questions. Detective Smith had to figure out if Bowman really did "blackout" or if he was just saying that to avoid telling what really happened. Blacking out genuinely doesn't get you off the hook for murder. Detective Smith had to try another technique with Bowman to see if he could remember some of the details about what happened.

This new tactic was to have Bowman draw a diagram of the house from what he could remember. Detective Smith was hoping to gather more information this way too. As Bowman draws the house, he describes what he's drawing to Detective Smith. Bowman pointed out on the diagram where everything happened. He seemed quite confident in his descriptions of the house. For once, this suspect had specific details and described things accurately, not like Henry Lee Lucas. This was all interesting until Bowman drew little figures and stated the following: "Here's Dennis (with heavy breathing). And the demon used to be right out here in front. All right? And had a little pointed beard. And horns. And claws" (*Interrogation Raw*, 2023, 30:35-31:01). The picture he drew was creepy. It was a stick figure with horns and claws. Bowman's voice was different and so was his demeaner according to Detective Smith. Bowman stated the demon is still there and tried to get out, but he won't let it. This was disturbing.

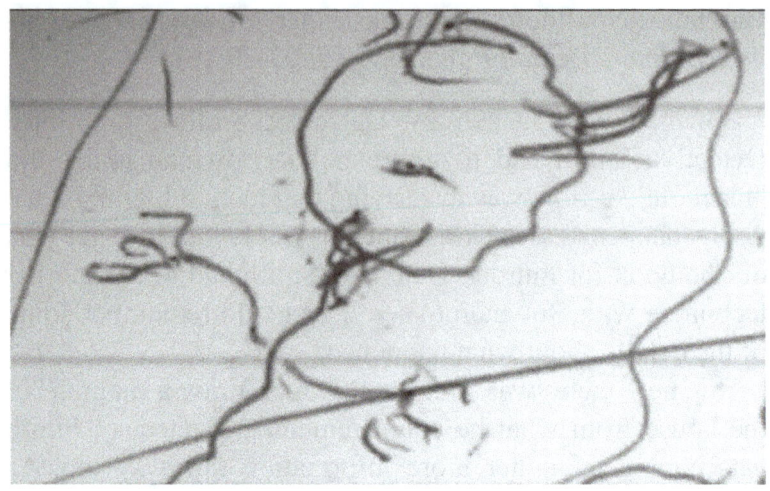

Bowman portrayed the demon as an electric current coursing through his veins, a vivid metaphor that illuminated the intense turmoil within him. As he spoke about the duality of his identity, referring to the two "Dennis-es," a poignant remark made by his sister to his wife, his emotions surfaced powerfully. This moment marked a significant awakening for Bowman, as he began to grasp the existence of conflicting aspects of himself that had previously gone unnoticed. He attributed the emergence of this inner demon to his inability to recall the details of the sexual assault on Kathleen; however, he did not dispute the fact of the assault itself. Instead, he remained trapped in a cycle of denial regarding his memory of the incident, leaving the complexities of his experience shrouded in ambiguity.

Detective Smith remained resolute in his pursuit of the truth surrounding the sexual assault. As Bowman animatedly gestured, running his hands through his hair in frustration, he stubbornly insisted that he had no recollection of the events. However, he was remarkably clear about one detail, he recalled distinctly walking out the front door after the murder. The contrast in his memory was striking; there were countless specifics he could recount from both before and after the crime, which only deepened Detective Smith's skepticism regarding Bowman's claim of amnesia. After an exhaustive five hours of relentless questioning about the murder, it became evident that a more confrontational strategy was needed. Yet despite the mounting pressure, Bowman continued to resist acknowledging any involvement in the sexual assault that night.

Detective Smith finally told Bowman they got his DNA from the sexual assault. Bowman looked down in the interview room and nodded his head in an up and down manner. Maybe he was shocked that the investigators found his DNA. Detective Smith may have had enough, enough of the lies and enough of a confession for prosecution, so he started calling Bowman out on his lies. Detective Smith knew he had their guy! Detective Smith told Bowman, "You beat the hell out of that girl, and you stabbed the hell out of that girl" (*Interrogation Raw*, 2023, 36:04). Bowman replied, "I did not!" (*Interrogation Raw*, 2023, 36:09). Bowman was still in denial, and he told Detective Smith that Kathleen was alive when he left the house. For the record, we know that's a false statement.

Even when Detective Smith left the interview room, Bowman still denied what he did. Something in him changed. The interview room started to become eerie once again. Bowman grabbed his sprite, clinking the cap on the interview table and repeating, "Done it again. I've done it again" (*Interrogation Raw*, 2023, 38.46). If those two sentences don't make you feel like something isn't right, guess again. Detective Smith came back, and Bowman stood up and began sobbing. Detective Smith took him back to the holding cell. I remember watching him walk down the hall, heading back to the cells. This old man, sobbing with his head held down. Was there more to say? Was Bowman really finished telling his secrets?

On February 4, 2020, during Bowman's time in custody, he had phone privileges and called his wife. He began talking about his adopted daughter, Aundria, that had disappeared 31 years prior. He said:

> Brenda, Aundria. Aundria is buried in our backyard. If you look towards the concrete, in the backyard? She's underneath the left-hand side of that in a cardboard bin. She's been with us all along. So now, here it is. Now you know where she is. At least you'll have her in a tin jar on a shelf. Now you know I'm a rotten, stinkin', son of a bitch. (*Interrogation Raw*, 2023, 40:47-41:19)

This whole time Bowman's poor wife was crying. This was certainly the best way to tell his wife, Brenda, he killed their daughter too and buried her in the backyard. Just when you think everything ended, it most certainly did not.

Since Bowman confessed and plead guilty to first-degree murder, rape, and burglary, the Commonwealth Attorney's took away the death penalty. On June 10, 2020, Bowman was given two life sentences for the murder and rape of Kathleen O'Brien Doyle and another 20 years for the burglary. The Kathleen Doyle case finally came to a close, but another case arose, the 1989 missing person case of 14-year-old, Aundria Bowman. How did Aundria's body end up approximately 30 yards from Bowman's back porch? This was a huge stir up in the Aundria Bowman case. Now that Dennis Bowman told his wife Brenda, the police finally had a new lead in the case and that lead had to be confirmed. Remember, after all, there were already false confessions in the Kathleen Doyle case.

The question is what exactly happened to Aundria Bowman? Bowman confessed he buried his adopted daughter, but the story gets worse. Aundria had told school officials about Bowman inappropriately making advances on her. Soon after that, Aundria was missing, and it was under suspicious circumstances. As a 14-year-old, she was brave and defiant and stood up for herself. Before her death, there was some sort of confrontation between her and Bowman. The confrontation was obviously about the inappropriate advances on her and her advising school officials.

Bowman and Aundria were near the stairs during this confrontation. Aundria may have said something to trigger Bowman. Knowing his anger, he slapped her across the face. Aundria fell down the stairs, her body lifeless. Did Bowman mean to slap her and her fall down the stairs? Maybe not. Bowman may have tended to her. Being his adopted daughter, he may have been in shock. To him, it was an accident; to everyone else, it was murder. I'm sure he was scared or knew he'd be in trouble. So, what happened to Aundria's body?

Bowman took Aundria's lifeless body and placed it in a barrel. She stayed in that barrel for a while until Bowman's wife decided to move after Aundria went missing on March 11, 1989. When the Bowmans moved, so did Aundria's deceased body. At their new house, Bowman buried Aundria approximately 30 yards from the back porch. Bowman laid a concrete slab over Aundria's burial site, covering her for what he thought was going to be forever.

Police authorities had gone to Dennis Bowman's residence in Allegan County, in Michigan to investigate further based on the confession he told his wife Brenda. The backyard became a cemetery for Aundria Bowman; a cemetery no one knew about except Dennis Bowman. On February 4, 2020, skeletal remains were finally located and a DNA profile was completed. It was finally confirmed that the skeletal remains were in fact the missing child, Aundria Bowman. Her cause of death was ruled homicide by unspecified means. If that wasn't enough to know, Aundria's body was also dismembered and her remains placed in several plastic bags according to Dr. Jered Cornelison, a forensic anthropologist that testified in court on February 22, 2021 (Muyskens, 2021). Apparently, Bowman buried Aundria with trash.

Consider the turmoil swirling within Bowman's mind. In a moment of tragedy, he had taken the life of his own daughter, Aundria—potentially in a horrific accident. Overcome with dread, he concealed her in a container within the confines of the barn, perhaps even dismembering her in a panic before hastily burying her. When the family relocated to a new home, Bowman seemed to act with chilling deliberation. Once the paperwork for their new residence was finalized, he unburied Aundria's remains and discreetly reinterred her in the backyard, laying her to rest beneath a layer of household refuse. To further obfuscate his actions, he poured concrete over the grave and erected a burn barrel nearby for disposing of trash. Each time he ignited the flames to incinerate waste, he must have been haunted by the grim reality of Aundria lying just beneath; a secret entwined with the very act of disposal.

According to Carolyn Muyskens (2021) from The Holland Sentinel:

> Detectives testified Bowman confessed to moving her body to a barn on the property and then calling police to report her missing. He told detectives he used a machete and later an axe to cut off Aundria's legs so that her body would fit in a container (para. 25).

Brenda Bowman took the stand to testify in court about her husband's confession to her on the phone about the murder of their daughter, Aundria. According to Carolyn Muyskens (2021), Brenda Bowman also said Aundria reported her father sexually abused her, but she didn't believe Aundria. "She told me one morning that Dad had molested her," Bowman said. "And I looked at her and told her, 'That's a lie, and you know it'" (Muyskens, 2021, para. 11).

The story Bowman told his wife was believable to her. Brenda was at work and Bowman should have been visiting family while their daughter was supposed to be doing homework at home (Muyskens, 2021). Bowman had returned home, and the rebellious daughter had taken money and ran away. Now, how believable is that? So, all these years, until 2019, Brenda Bowman thought Aundria had run away. Aundria's mother must have been heartbroken.

In December 2021, 75-year-old Bowman entered a no-contest plea regarding the second-degree murder of his adopted daughter, Aundria Bowman, in Michigan. A no-contest plea implies that the defendant does not formally admit guilt but accepts the charge as if it were a conviction, allowing the case to proceed to sentencing. Ultimately, Bowman received a sentence of 35 to 50 additional years in prison. During the proceedings, he not only confessed to the heinous murder and rape of Kathleen Doyle but also to the murder of Aundria Bowman. Additionally, he admitted to a sexual assault on a 27-year-old woman in Michigan in 1979, further intensifying the gravity of his crimes. At that time, the suspect's description was a white male between the ages of 25 and 30, with sandy hair and wire-rimmed glasses (Walker, 2021). This victim was also bound and gagged.

The unwavering dedication of the Norfolk Police Department, Kathleen Doyle's family, Brenda Bowman, the Michigan State Police, and all the detectives involved in these two cases played a pivotal role in bringing justice to light. Their relentless pursuit has led to crucial answers and the long-overdue conviction of Dennis Lee Bowman, sentencing him to spend the rest of his life behind bars. For the families affected, this revelation offers a sense of closure, allowing them to begin their journey of healing in the wake of profound loss. Yet, amidst this resolution, a haunting question lingers: Are there more victims whose stories remain untold?

BONUS: Q & A WITH DETECTIVE JON SMITH

Before I conclude this book, I wanted to provide you with a few questions I had for Jon to answer concerning this case. Jon is such a humble person and I'm glad I got to work with him in my career. Here is our mini question and answer session:

Did you have any doubts about the Doyle case once you opened the file?

Yes, I did have initial doubts about the Kathleen Doyle case when I first opened the file, and there were several reasons for my apprehension. Firstly, the age of the case presented a significant challenge. Cases that have remained unsolved for an extended period tend to accumulate a vast amount of information, making it daunting to sift through the details and identify crucial leads.

Additionally, the uncertainty about the availability of witnesses added to another layer of concern. The passage of time raised questions about whether key witnesses were still alive or accessible. This uncertainty added complexity to the investigation, as witness testimony often plays a pivotal role in reconstructing events and establishing timelines.

The aging process also took a toll on the health of former police personnel who had initially worked on the case. It was essential to gather insights and knowledge from those who were involved in the early stages of the investigation. The failing health of some individuals added a sense of urgency to extracting valuable information before it became inaccessible.

Moreover, the sheer magnitude of the case, involving about 3 bankers boxes worth of material, was a formidable challenge. Organizing and analyzing such a vast volume of information required a meticulous and systematic approach to ensure no crucial details were overlooked.

In addition to these challenges, I was also deeply concerned about evidence degradation, particularly regarding DNA items. Given the age of the case, the potential degradation of crucial forensic evidence was a constant worry. Preserving and extracting viable DNA samples became a top priority, and I took proactive measures to ensure that any available genetic material was handled with the utmost care to maximize the chances of obtaining valuable information.

Despite these initial doubts and challenges, my commitment to the case and determination to bring closure remained unwavering. I strategically navigated through the complexities, leveraging new investigative techniques like Investigative Genetic Genealogy, and coordinating with the Cold Case Squad. The 'Ah Ha' moment, when a viable suspect was identified 15 months later, validated the effectiveness of the approach and demonstrated that persistence and thoroughness can triumph over initial doubts in the pursuit of justice.

What was your "Ah Ha" moment?

My 'Ah Ha' moment in the Kathleen Doyle case occurred after 15 months of dedicated investigation. The journey involved meticulous review of extensive case materials, exploration of new investigative avenues such as Investigative Genetic Genealogy (IGG), and collaboration with the Cold Case Squad.

As I delved deeper into the case, analyzing evidence, witness statements, and the results of the IGG process, a pivotal realization struck me. It was the moment when I recognized that I had finally identified a viable suspect. This revelation was the culmination of relentless efforts, strategic thinking, and the application of cutting-edge investigative techniques.

The feeling of the 'Ah Ha' moment was both exhilarating and validating. It signified a breakthrough in the case, affirming that the persistence and thoroughness of the investigative process had paid off. With a viable suspect in sight, the focus shifted towards further substantiating the evidence and building a strong case for bringing resolution to the Kathleen Doyle case.

Did you talk to the Doyle family once you were able to find a suspect?

Upon identifying a suspect in the Kathleen Doyle case, I recognized the importance of reaching out to her family to keep them informed and provide any updates on the investigation. However, I faced significant challenges in this regard. Kathleen's father was already deceased, and her mother was failing in health, making direct communication with the family difficult. Regrettably, I was unable to speak with Kathleen's parents due to these circumstances. Despite my earnest efforts to connect with them, the challenges posed by their health and circumstances prevented direct communication.

In the absence of communication with Kathleen's parents, I did manage to establish contact with her former husband, Stephen, who was married to her at the time of her death. Throughout this process, my approach remained empathetic and considerate, understanding the sensitivity of the situation and the emotions involved. While I regretted being unable to directly communicate with Kathleen's parents, I remained committed to ensuring that all available avenues were explored to bring resolution to the Kathleen Doyle case.

How did you find out Aundria was killed by Dennis? Via the video chat with wife or did he tell you?

After Dennis's arrest, he began making statements that hinted at his involvement in Aundria's disappearance and potential role in causing her death. However, consistent with the behavior of many serial killers, he engaged in various cat-and-mouse games, providing elusive and cryptic information.

The breakthrough in the case and Dennis's ultimate confession occurred during my follow-up investigation in Michigan. Earlier that day, in collaboration with Michigan State Police Detectives, I had a crucial meeting with Dennis's wife, Brenda. During our meeting, we encouraged Brenda to engage in a conversation with Dennis over the phone, attempting to extract any information about Aundria's whereabouts.

Later that night, over a jail phone call, Dennis confessed to Brenda, providing details about where he had buried Aundria's body. This confession was a pivotal moment in the investigation, as it not only confirmed his involvement but also revealed crucial information about the location of Aundria's remains.

Furthermore, Dennis ultimately confessed to me and Michigan authorities. Although he never admitted to killing her, he did admit to dismembering her body and burying her in two separate locations. This admission, while not providing a direct acknowledgment of the act of killing, provided valuable insights into the grim circumstances surrounding Aundria's death and the disposal of her remains.

The strategic collaboration with law enforcement, the use of investigative techniques, and Dennis's confessions played a crucial role in obtaining the critical information needed to advance the case. It was a methodical and coordinated effort that ultimately led to the resolution of Aundria's case."

How did the notification go in regard to communicating about the remains in Michigan? Where did the notification come from, the wife or you?

Bowman told his wife, Brenda, over a recorded jail call where her remains were located.

"And the prayer of faith will save the one who is sick, and the Lord will raise him up. And if he has committed sins, he will be forgiven." ~ James 5:15

CHAPTER 14

REMEMBERING THE FORGOTTEN

As we conclude this exploration into the haunting stories of the forgotten girls, those women whose lives were cut short, whose voices were silenced, and whose cases remain shrouded in mystery, it becomes clear that our journey is more than just an examination of cold cases; it is a call to action and a reminder of the humanity behind each statistic.

Throughout these chapters, we have delved into the complexities of cold cases, understanding that each unsolved mystery is not merely a puzzle for detectives and researchers to solve, but a deep wound in the lives of families and communities left to grapple with loss, uncertainty, and grief. By bringing to light these stories, we shine a necessary spotlight not only on the victims but also on the systemic issues that have allowed these cases to go unanswered for so long, issues such as societal neglect, biases in law enforcement, and the stigmatization of women who have been marginalized in life and in death.

The stories of the Forgotten Girls urge us to confront difficult truths. They compel us to question the narratives that society clings to about justice and value and challenge us to advocate for those who cannot advocate for themselves.

It is here, in our collective responsibility, that we uncover the deeper significance of our exploration. Each time we remember a victim, each time we tell their story, we breathe life back into their narratives, affirming that they were more than just a case number, they were daughters, sisters, friends, and individuals with hopes and dreams.

While many of these cases remain unsolved, they do not have to be forgotten. As we step away from these pages, let us carry forward the momentum of our curiosity and compassion. Consider ways in which you can contribute to raising awareness, whether it be through sharing this book, supporting organizations that seek justice for the victims, or simply starting conversations in your communities about the importance of identifying and solving cold cases.

In closing, let us honor the forgotten girls not through the lens of tragedy alone but as symbols of resilience, reminding us that every life has value and deserves to be remembered. With renewed vigilance and compassion, we can help ensure that these stories are told, and that they matter. In doing so, we become the voices for the voiceless, dedicated to bringing light to the shadows and justice to the unjust.

Thank you for embarking on this journey. May we never forget.

REFERENCES

Baker, K. (2016). Father of teen missing since 2009 whom FBI has declared was held captive and murdered: "I'm begging anyone to help us bring her home." *People*. https://people.com/crime/murdered-teen-brittanee-drexels-father-come-forward-if-you-have-information/

Baker, K. (2021). Who killed teen lifeguard Molly Bish? 21 years after she was lured away, killer is possibly I'd. *People*. https://people.com/crime/molly-bish-teen-lifeguard-killed-2000-possible-killer-identified/

Becker, K. & Madeja, M. (2022). DNA in Molly Bish case isn't a match, sister says: 'it's disappointing.' *NBC10 Boston*. https://www.nbcboston.com/news/local/dna-in-molly-bish-case-isnt-a-match-sister-says-its-disappointing/2775879/

Benson, J. (1996). Jodi's disappearance: 1st year timeline. *FindJodi.com,Inc.* *https://findjodi.com/jodis-disappearance-1st-year-timeline/#google_vignette*

Binder, M. (2023). "Hell is other people:" Sartre's famous quote explained. *The Collector*. https://www.thecollector.com/jean-paul-sartre-hell-is-other-people/

Bruchey, B. (PIO) (2023). [Photograph of Teresa Lee Scalf]. Polk County Sheriff's Office solves 1986 homicide. *News & Investigations*. https://www.polksheriff.org/news-investigations/2023/10/16/polk-county-sheriff-s-office-solves-1986-homicide

Bruchey, B. (PIO) (2023). Polk County Sheriff's Office solves 1986 homicide. *News & Investigations.* https://www.polksheriff.org/news-investigations/2023/10/16/polk-county-sheriff-s-office-solves-1986-homicide

Carlson, A. (2023). [Photograph of a male and female tied up with duct tape provided by the Valencia County Sheriff's Office]. Tara Calico mystery: The true story behind notorious polaroid showing a girl and boy bound in a van. *People.* https://people.com/crime/tara-calico-polaroid-photo-true-story/

Castillo, M. (2024). Family of Mikelle Biggs works on documentary about 1999 disappearance. *Arizona News.* https://www.azfamily.com/2024/07/23/family-mikelle-biggs-works-documentary-about-1999-disappearance/

Cavallier, A. (2021). Loved ones still fighting for justice 31 years after St. Patrick's Day murder of Rachel Hurley. *NBC News.* https://www.nbcnews.com/dateline/loved-ones-still-fighting-justice-31-years-after-st-patrick-n1261667

Chan, E. (2025). Molly Bish's sister opens up about the day her skull was found after she went missing from her lifeguard job. *ChipChick.* https://www.chipchick.com/2025/08/molly-bishs-sister-opens-up-about-the-day-her-skull-was-found-after-she-went-missing-from-her-lifeguard-job

Chasan, A. (2023). Girl's killer identified more than 50 years after she was abducted in Georgia. *CBS News.* https://www.cbsnews.com/news/cold-case-killer-debbie-lynn-randall-georgia-identified-dna/

Collins, J. (2023). Sex offender gets life for killing teen during 2009 vacation. *Court TV.* https://www.courttv.com/news/sex-offender-gets-life-for-killing-teen-during-2009-vacation/

Croteau, S. (2016). 24 pieces of evidence in Molly Bish murder case to receive enhanced DNA testing. MassLive. https://www.masslive.com/news/worcester/2016/06/24_pieces_of_evidence_in_molly.html

Desmond, D. (2024). Tip leads police to Winsted construction site in case of long-missing TV anchor. *Bring Me the News*. https://bringmethenews.com/minnesota-news/tip-leads-police-to-winsted-construction-site-in-case-of-long-missing-tv-anchor

Dowler, L. (2018). Female firefighters defy old ideas of who can be an American hero. *The Conversation*. https://theconversation.com/female-firefighters-defy-old-ideas-of-who-can-be-an-american-hero-95342

Floren, T. (2002). History of women in firefighting. *Women & Firefighting*. https://wfsi.org/women_and_firefighting/history.php

Find a Grave, database and images, memorial page for Aundria Michelle Miranda "Alexis" Badger Bowman (23 Jun 1974–11 Mar 1989), Find a Grave Memorial ID 205546928; Cremated; Maintained by Roselvr (contributor 48049775). https://www.findagrave.com/memorial/205546928/aundria_michelle_miranda-bowman

Find a Grave, database and images, memorial page for Kathleen Mary O'Brien Doyle (8 Apr 1955–9 Sep 1980), Find a Grave Memorial ID 192521299, citing Forest Lawn Cemetery, Norfolk, Norfolk City, Virginia, USA; Maintained by Dottie (contributor 47226067) https://www.findagrave.com/memorial/192521299/kathleen_mary-doyle

FindJodi. (2004). The Huisentruit File: Episode 2, Last few days. *YouTube*. https://www.youtube.com/watch?v=uXgDyqo--gU

FindJodi. (2004). The Huisentruit File: Episode 9, The sister. *YouTube*. https://www.youtube.com/watch?v=kzenjdmBlfk&t=2s

Fuller, S. (2023). Statement from Jodi Huisentruit's family on the 28th anniversary of her disappearance. *FindJodi, Inc*. https://findjodi.com/statement-from-jodi-huisentruits-family-on-the-28th-anniversary-of-her-disappearance/

Grace, N. (Host) (2006, January 02). 16-year-old girl's murder remains unsolved. *Transcripts*. https://transcripts.cnn.com/show/ng/date/2006-01-02/segment/01

Grace, N. (Host). (2023, September 22). Louisiana's Caitlyn Rose disappears, nav system goes dead with dad on phone. [Audio podcast episode]. *Crime Stories with Nancy Grace*. Omny Studio. https://omny.fm/shows/crime-stories-with-nancy-grace/louisiana-s-caitlyn-rose-disappears-nav-system-goe

Harris, D. (2023). Advanced DNA technology, exhumed body help authorities solve cold case of 9-year-old girl raped, murdered. *Law & Crime*. https://lawandcrime.com/crime/advanced-dna-technology-exhumed-body-help-authorities-solve-cold-case-of-9-year-old-girl-raped-murdered/

Helmenstine, A. (2024). How many bones are in the human body? Science Notes and Projects. https://sciencenotes.org/how-many-bones-are-in-the-human-body/

Hori, L. & Tyrrell, D. (Producers). (2023). Interrogation Raw [TV series]. A+E Networks. Category 6 Media. https://play.aetv.com/shows/interrogation-raw/season-1/episode-19

Idle, J. (2019). 29 years later, search continues for who killed Jupiter teen Rachel Hurley. *5 WPTV*. Scripps Local Media. https://www.wptv.com/news/region-n-palm-beach-county/jupiter/29-years-later-search-continues-for-who-killed-jupiter-teen-rachel-hurley

Kopsky, A. (2017). [Photograph of Jodi Huisentruit, disappeared 1995]. 18 unsolved missing persons cases that'll shake you to your core. *Buzzfeed*. https://www.buzzfeed.com/annakopsky/unsolved-missing-persons-cases

Knarr, J. (2006). Filmmaker delves into murder mystery. *The Trentonian*.

Krupa, C. (2021). [Photograph of Left: a sketch, made available by the Bish family, shows the alleged abductor of Warren, Mass. Right: Molly Bish's potential killer Frank Sumner released by the district attorney's office]. *Fox News*. https://www.foxnews.com/us/molly-bish-family-shown-person-of-interest-photo-resemblance-sketches

Kumar, P. (2024). Netflix's Unsolved Mysteries: What happened to Sigrid Stevenson? Explained. *Sportskeeda*. https://www.sportskeeda.com/us/shows/netflix-s-unsolved-mysteries-what-happened-sigrid-stevenson-explained

Luperon, A. (2023). Cold case 'sexual rejection' murder of nurse solved by linking killer's DNA to distant out-of-wedlock cousin: Deputies. *Law & Crime*. LawNewz. https://lawandcrime.com/crime/cold-case-sexual-rejection-murder-of-nurse-solved-by-linking-killers-dna-to-distant-out-of-wedlock-cousin-deputies/

Mahaffey, L. (2020). Mapping Oklahoma's response to human trafficking: data and partnerships (63431) [MRes thesis, University of Nottingham]. *Nottingham ePrints*. http://eprints.nottingham.ac.uk/id/eprint/63431

McCandless, C. (2022). [Photogragh of a surveillance photo of Caitlyn Case taken on August 5]. *Nexstar Media*. https://

www.nwahomepage.com/news/around-the-region/osbi-looking-for-missing-louisiana-woman/

McCollum, S. (Host). (2023, December, 13). Zone 7 Legends: Detective Morris Nix and the Solved Cold Case of Debbie Lynn Randall. [Season 7 Episode 8]. *Zone 7*. Omny Studio. https://www.iheart.com/podcast/1119-zone-7-with-sheryl-mccoll-106023288/episode/zone-7-legends-detective-morris-nix-135134026/

McCollum, S. (Host). (2025, February, 5). Secret Recordings: How Steph Watts orchestrated a confession in the Brittanee Drexel case. [Season 76 Episode 1]. *Zone 7*. Omny Studio. https://omny.fm/shows/zone-7-with-sheryl-mccollum/stephen-watts-edited-mixdown#description

Monahan, L. (2023). Remains found in Choctaw County identified as missing woman, Caitlyn case. *News 9*. Griffin Media. https://www.news9.com/story/6570f938fc05cc23601f1789/remains-found-in-choctaw-county-identified-as-missing-woman-caitlyn-case

Monahan, L. (2023). 'Someone Did This To Her:' Family Anxiously Awaits Medical Examiner's Ruling. *News 9*. Griffin Media.

Muyskens, C. (2021). Wife: Hamilton man killed their daughter in 1989, dismembered and buried body. *The Holland Sentinel*. *https://www.hollandsentinel.com/story/news/2021/02/22/wife-testifies-cold-case-murder-aundria-bowman/4538293001/*

NamUs. (2021). Missing person / NamUs # MP402. *U.S. Department of Justice*. https://namus.nij.ojp.gov/case/MP402

NamUs. (2021). Missing person / NamUs #MP11115. *U.S. Department of Justice.* https://namus.nij.ojp.gov/case/MP11115

NamUs. (2021). Frequently asked questions. *U.S. Department of Justice.* https://namus.nij.ojp.gov/frequently-asked-questions#22-0

National Human Trafficking Hotline. (2021) Oklahoma. *Polaris.* https://humantraffickinghotline.org/en/statistics/oklahoma

NBC News. (2008). Police: 1981 killing of Adam Walsh solved. *NBC Universal.* https://www.nbcnews.com/id/wbna28257294

NBC 6. (2022). 40 years later, Adam Walsh's abduction and murder not forgotten in South Florida. *NBCUniversal Media, LLC.* https://www.nbcmiami.com/news/local/40-years-later-adam-walshs-abduction-and-murder-not-forgotten-in-south-florida/2508053/

NENA The 911 Association. (n.d). 9-1-1 origin & history. *NENA The 911 Association.* https://www.nena.org/general/custom.asp?page=911overviewfacts

Newland, E. (2014). Waiting for Brittanee Drexel: mother thinks missing daughter was trafficked. *MyHorryNews.Com.* https://www.myhorrynews.com/news/crime/waiting-for-brittanee-drexel-mother-thinks-missing-daughter-was-trafficked/article_1fcd7134-0055-11e4-b157-0017a43b2370.html

Oliver, K. (2010) [Photograph of Brittanee Drexel smiling]. Brittanee Drexel missing: authorities identify "persons of interest" in teen's Myrtle Beach disappearance. *CNS News.* https://www.cbsnews.com/news/brittanee-drexel-missing-authorities-identify-persons-of-interest-in-teens-myrtle-beach-disappearance/

Oliver, M. (2021). Henry Lee Lucas: The depraved serial killer who confessed to hundreds of murders. AllThatsInteresting.com. https://allthatsinteresting.com/henry-lee-lucas-ottis-toole

Pardue, D. & Smith, G. (2016). FBI agent: Missing teen Brittanee Drexel was kidnapped, shot and dumped in alligator pit. *The Post and Courier*. https://web.archive.org/web/20161015184506/https://www.postandcourier.com/20160826/160829517/fbi-agent-missing-teen-brittanee-drexel-was-kidnapped-shot-and-dumped-in-alligator-pit/

Paredez, A. (2024). 25 years later, detectives believe they can solve the Mikelle Biggs disappearance case. *Scripps Local Media, Inc.* https://www.abc15.com/news/crime/25-years-later-detectives-believe-they-can-solve-the-mikelle-biggs-disappearance-case#google_vignette

Patterson, K. (2020). Murder suspect in 1980 Norfolk cold case wants to plead guilty to killing Navy wife. *Nexstar Media Inc*. https://www.wavy.com/news/national/1980-cold-case-murder-suspect-expected-in-norfolk-court-monday/

Pombo, J. (2003). Molly Bish's remains identified: Bones, teeth used to make identification. *Hearst Stations Inc.* https://web.archive.org/web/20110927114026/http://www.thebostonchannel.com/news/2258530/detail.html

Ponushis, A. (2014). Who killed Rachel? *Florida Weekly Palm Beach Edition*. https://palmbeach.floridaweekly.com/articles/who-killed-rachel/

Raven, R. (n.d.). After 37 years, the cold case murder of Florida nurse Teresa Lee Scalf is finally solved. *Warner Bros. Discovery, Inc.* https://www.investigationdiscovery.com/crimefeed/murder/after-37-years-the-cold-case-murder-of-florida-nurse-teresa-lee-scalf-is-finally-solved

Reese, B. (2019). Police: 39-year-old Norfolk cold case solved, murder suspect arrested in Michigan. *Nexstar Media Inc.* https://www.wavy.com/news/local-news/police-39-year-old-norfolk-cold-case-solved-murder-suspect-arrested-in-michigan/

Ring, K. (2011). Possible break in unsolved Holly Piirainen and Molly Bish cases. *Boston.com.* https://www.boston.com/uncategorized/noprimarytagmatch/2011/11/18/possible-break-in-unsolved-holly-piirainen-and-molly-bish-cases/

Ring, K. (2014). Man linked to Bish case dies; Ex-Ware resident convicted for rape. *The Free Library.* https://www.thefreelibrary.com/Man+linked+to+Bish+case+dies%3b+Ex-Ware+resident+convicted+for+rape.-a0389961673

Ring, K. (2021). 21 years after Molly Bish's slaying, deceased sex offender from Spencer ID'd as suspect. *Telegram & Gazette.* https://web.archive.org/web/20210604025039/https://www.telegram.com/story/news/2021/06/03/who-killed-moly-bish-worcester-district-attorney-names-suspect/7529280002/

Salzbank, L. (2022). Who killed Rachel Hurley? The Jupiter teen's death remains cold 32 years later. *CBS 12 News.* https://cbs12.com/news/local/jupiter-inlet-march-17-1990-carlin-park-who-killed-rachel-hurley-the-jupiter-teens-death-remains-cold-32-years-later-palm-beach-county-sheriffs-office

Sarkar, D. (2021). What happened to Mikelle Biggs? Was she ever found? Is she dead or alive? *The Cinemaholic.*

https://thecinemaholic.com/what-happened-to-mikelle-biggs-was-she-ever-found-is-she-dead-or-alive/

Sarkar, D. (2021). [Photograph of Mikelle Biggs]. What happened to Mikelle Biggs? Was she ever found? Is she dead or alive? *The Cinemaholic*. https://thecinemaholic.com/what-happened-to-mikelle-biggs-was-she-ever-found-is-she-dead-or-alive/

Sarkar, D. (2021). Where are Mikelle Biggs' parents now? Where is Mikelle Biggs' sister today? *The Cinemaholic*. https://thecinemaholic.com/where-are-mikelle-biggs-parents-now-where-is-mikelle-biggs-sister-today/

Sarkar, D. (2021). Molly Bish's murder: How did she die? Who killed her? *The Cinemaholic*. https://thecinemaholic.com/molly-bishs-murder-how-did-she-die-who-killed-her/

Sherman, C. & Cox, E. (2005). Ex-Osceola, Florida fire chief arrested in pot-growing bust. *Firehouse.com*. https://www.firehouse.com/home/news/10509728/ex-osceola-florida-fire-chief-arrested-in-pot-growing-bust

Sisco, L. (2015). You're lying! Secrets from an expert military interrogator to spot the lies and get to the truth. *The Career Press, Inc*. p. 136.

Smith, T. (2016). Brittanee Drexel: FBI believes she's dead, offers $25K reward. *Democrat & Chronicle*. https://www.democratandchronicle.com/story/news/2016/06/08/brittanee-drexel-news-conference-south-carolina-missing-teen/85590106/

Stabile, L. (2011). Worcester private investigator Daniel Malley discusses possible suspect in Molly Bish, Holly Piirainen murders. *The Republican*. https://www.masslive.com/news/2011/11/worcester_private_investigator.html

Staff Writer. (2011). Molly Anne Bish timeline. *Telegram & Gazette*. https://www.telegram.com/story/news/2011/11/18/molly-anne-bish-timeline/49830451007/

Steen, T., Buchanan, C., & Budge, Sheree. (2021). Genetic genealogy: DNA and family history. *Springshare*. https://guides.loc.gov/genetic-genealogy

Sudborough, S. (2023). Here's where the Molly Bish case stands 20 years after her body was found. *Boston.com*. https://www.boston.com/news/crime/2023/06/07/molly-bish-case-frank-sumner-worcester-county-district-attorney-joseph-early-update/

Tisdale, J. (2024) [Photograph of Sigrid Stevenson on gurney being wheeled out]. The brutal murder of Sigrid Stevenson lead to a ghost story that haunts a college campus. *Distractify*. https://www.distractify.com/p/what-happened-to-sigrid-stevenson

The Associated Press. (2022). Virginia inmate sentenced in Michigan for daughter's killing. *NTD*. https://www.ntd.com/virginia-inmate-sentenced-in-michigan-for-daughters-killing_737536.html

The Charley Project (2006). Jodi Sue Huisentruit. *The Charley Project*. https://charleyproject.org/case/jodi-sue-huisentruit

The Charley Project. (2013). Mikelle Diane Biggs. *The Charley Project*. https://charleyproject.org/case/mikelle-diane-biggs

The Charley Project. (2020). Tara Leigh Calico. *The Charley Project*. https://charleyproject.org/case/tara-leigh-calico

The Deck. (2025). [Photograph of Rachel Hurley]. Rachel Hurley – 9 of Hearts, Florida. *Audiochuck, LLC*. https://thedeckpodcast.com/rachel-hurley/

Thompson, M. et al. (2025). Girlfriend of Brittanee Drexel's killer sentenced to prison for lying to FBI. *MSN* https://www.live5news.com/2025/02/13/angel-vause-sentenced-18-years-2009-brittanee-drexel-murder-case/

Torres, J. (Host). (2018, March 14). Bull creek (No. 2) [Audio podcast episode]. *Murder on the space coast.* Omny Studio. https://omny.fm/shows/murder-on-the-space-coast/season-3-episode-2-bull-creek?in_playlist=murder-on-the-space-coast-wheres-brandy-hall

Torres, J. (Host). (2018, March 19). Drug bust (No. 3) [Audio podcast episode]. *Murder on the space coast.* Omny Studio. https://omny.fm/shows/murder-on-the-space-coast/season-3-episode-3-drug-bust?in_playlist=murder-on-the-space-coast-wheres-brandy-hall

Torres, J. (Host). (2018, March 21). Last night (No. 4) [Audio podcast episode]. *Murder on the space coast.* Omny Studio. https://omny.fm/shows/murder-on-the-space-coast/season-3-episode-4-last-night

Torres, J. (Host). (2018, March 26). The truck (No. 5) [Audio podcast episode]. *Murder on the space coast.* Omny Studio. https://omny.fm/shows/murder-on-the-space-coast/season-3-episode-5-the-truck

Torres, J. (Host). (2018, March 28). Sex, lies, and silence (No. 6) [Audio podcast episode]. *Murder on the space coast.* Omny Studio. https://omny.fm/shows/murder-on-the-space-coast/season-3-episode-6-sex-lies-and-silence

Torres, J. (Host). (2018, April 2). Theories and suspects (No. 7) [Audio podcast episode]. *Murder on the space coast.* Omny Studio. https://omny.fm/shows/murder-on-the-space-coast/season-3-episode-7-theories-and-suspects

Torres, J. (Host). (2018, April 4). Alibi (No. 8) [Audio podcast episode]. *Murder on the space coast.* Omny Studio. https://omny.fm/shows/murder-on-the-space-coast/season-3-episode-8-alibi

Torres, J. (Host). (2018, April 9). The lost tip (No. 9) [Audio podcast episode]. *Murder on the space coast.* Omny Studio. https://omny.fm/shows/murder-on-the-space-coast/season-3-episode-9-the-lost-tip

Torres, J. (Host). (2018, April 11). Motive (No. 10) [Audio podcast episode]. *Murder on the space coast.* Omny Studio. https://omny.fm/shows/murder-on-the-space-coast/season-3-episode-10-motive

Torres, J. (Host). (2018, April 16). A new lead? (No. 10B) [Audio podcast episode]. *Murder on the space coast.* Omny Studio. https://omny.fm/shows/murder-on-the-space-coast/season-3-episode-10b-a-new-lead#description

Torres, J. (Host). (2018, April 18). A break in the case (No. 11) [Audio podcast episode]. *Murder on the space coast.* Omny Studio. https://omny.fm/shows/murder-on-the-space-coast/season-3-episode-11-break-in-the-case

Torres, J. (Host). (2018, October 22). Nebulous and murky (No. 13) [Audio podcast episode]. *Murder on the space coast.* Omny Studio. https://omny.fm/shows/murder-on-the-space-coast/season-3-update-episode-2-nebulous-and-murky

Torres, J. (Host). (2018, October 29). Brandy's final 26 minutes (No. 14) [Audio podcast episode]. *Murder on the space coast.* Omny Studio. https://omny.fm/shows/murder-on-the-space-coast/season-3-update-episode-3-brandys-final-26-minutes

Torres, J. (Host). (2019, November 5). The skid steer (No. 15) [Audio podcast episode]. *Murder on the space coast.* Omny Studio. https://omny.fm/shows/murder-on-the-space-coast/season-3-update-episode-4-the-skid-steer

Torres, J. (2018). [Photograph of the truck recovered from a pond belonging to a missing volunteer firefighter]. *Florida Today.* https://www.floridatoday.com/story/series/brandy-hall-missing/2018/03/26/episode-five-truck/381246002/

True Crime Diva. (2023). The 1990 unsolved murder of Rachel Hurley. *True Crime Diva.* https://truecrimediva.com/the-1990-unsolved-murder-of-rachel-hurley/

Walker, H. (2020). Michigan woman believes cold case suspect abducted her in 1989. *Nexstar Media Inc.* https://www.fox21news.com/news/national/michigan-woman-believes-cold-case-suspect-abducted-her-in-1989/

Walker, H. (2021). Convicted killer confesses to 1979 cold case crime. *Nexstar Media Inc.* https://www.woodtv.com/news/allegan-county/convicted-killer-confesses-to-1979-cold-case-crime/

Wildmoon, KC. (2023). Remains of missing Louisiana woman found across river from her vehicle, a year after she disappeared. *CrimeOnline.* https://www.crimeonline.com/2023/12/07/remains-of-missing-louisiana-woman-found-across-river-from-her-vehicle-a-year-after-she-disappeared/#google_vignette

Worcester Telegram & Gazette. (2016). Francis Sumner obituary. *Legacy.com.* https://www.legacy.com/us/obituaries/telegram/name/francis-sumner-obituary?id=9825017

WOODTV.com staff. (2021). Wife testifies that Michigan man also convicted in Norfolk murder previously admitted fault in daughter's 1989 death. *Nexstar Media Inc.* https://

www.wavy.com/news/local-news/norfolk/wife-testifies-that-michigan-man-also-convicted-in-norfolk-murder-previously-admitted-fault-in-daughters-1989-death/

Wright, I. (2023). Affair in 1949 leads to accused killer of nurse found dead in 1986, Florida cops say. *The Herald.* https://www.heraldonline.com/news/nation-world/national/article280603869.html

For More News About Alyce Clark,
Signup For Our Newsletter:

http://wbp.bz/newsletter

Word-of-mouth is critical to an author's long-term success. If you appreciated this book please leave a review on the Amazon sales page:

https://wbp.bz/forgottengirlsr

OBSESSED by DAVID McGRATH

http://wbp.bz/obsessed

Since the 1800s, the majority of Biblical scholars have interpreted the books of Leviticus and Numbers as a later addition to the original laws of Moses found in Exodus. The most obvious amendment to Moses' laws, is replacing the sacrifice of the firstborn with the establishment of the Levitical Priesthood. Exodus Chapter 13 includes a requirement that the firstborn Israelites must be slaughtered as a sacrifice to the Lord, however, allowed an animal to be substituted.

The book of Numbers also added the story of Korah, who God killed. Strangely, even though Korah and everyone who followed him were eaten by Adama, the Elbaite and Hurrian earth-goddess, his sons survived, and founded the Korahites, who Solomon appointed to oversee the temple in Jerusalem. Clearly, this story was not in the Torah until the time of Hezekiah, yet the name Adama in the Leningrad Codex version of the story is clearly anachronistic to the culture of iron age Israel, suggesting the book of Numbers was from the same era as Exodus.

ISBN 978-1-998636-54-9
90000

9 781998 636549